CATHOLIC ESSENTIALS

An Overview of the Faith

Michael Amodei

The Ad Hoc Committee to Oversee the Use of the Catechism, United States Conference of Catholic Bishops, has found this catechetical text, copyright 2009, to be in conformity with the *Catechism of the Catholic Church*.

Imprimatur: The Reverend Michael Heintz
Censor Liborum

Nihil Obstat: Most Reverend John M. D'Arcy
Bishop of Fort Wayne-South Bend
Given at Fort Wayne, Indiana on 3 March 2008.

The *Nihil Obstat* and *Imprimatur* are official declarations that a book or pamphlet is free of doctrinal or moral error. No implication is contained therein that those who have granted the Nihil Obstat or Imprimatur agree with its contents, opinions, or statements expressed.

Other references cited as Notes on page 353.

---

www.avemariapress.com

Founded in 1865, Ave Maria Press is a ministry of the Indiana Province of Holy Cross.

ISBN-10 1-59471-145-3 ISBN-13 978-1-59471-145-9

Project Editor: Catherine M. Odell.

Cover and text design by Andy Wagoner.

Photography acknowledgments on p. 378.

Cover photograph © Jupiter Images Unlimited.

Printed and bound in the United States of America.

Contents

Engaging Minds, Hearts, and Hands for Faith

An education that is complete is the one in which the hands and heart are engaged as much as the mind. We want to let our students try their learning in the world and so make prayers of their education.

Fr. Basil Moreau
Founder of the Congregation of Holy Cross

To know, love, and serve Jesus Christ is what is ESSENTIAL for your life!

This book is written to help you to integrate the dimensions of mind, heart, and hands in order to know, love, and serve Jesus through the Church in the following ways:

By mastering the language of faith through the study of key vocabulary items. By studying the doctrines of faith as outlined in the *Catechism of the Catholic Church*, including Creed, Liturgy and Sacraments, Morality, and Prayer.

By prayerful reflection on key lessons through the reading of Scripture and the teachings of the saints and Church Fathers.

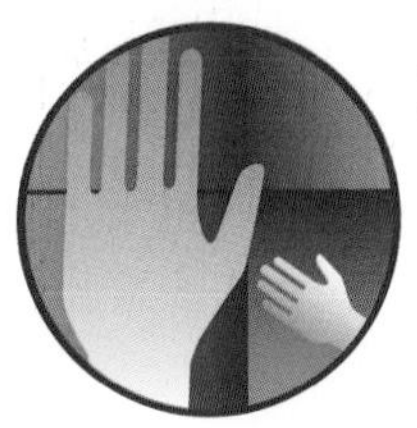

By acting on Jesus' mandate to "pick up your cross and follow me." The text suggests several real-life opportunities to put your faith into practice.

Introduction

WHY WE NEED JESUS

We can only imagine what it will be like to die. Pain may be involved. We could easily be scared. But what will the actual transition from this world to the next be like?

Again, we can only use our imaginations. For example, think about being knocked under a large ocean wave only to emerge to a large gasp of breath.

Go further: The surf, at first calm, begins to pick up. The waves that were the source of body or board surfing quickly add an increasingly powerful riptide to the mix.

A huge set of waves suddenly appears. Way too big to attempt to ride.

Imagine your heart beating faster as the crest of water rises high above you. What will you do? Before the wave crashes on you, you dive under. Unfortunately, you just miss diving under the wave's break. Thousands, millions of gallons of water take you toward the ocean floor. The sound, even below the surface, is deafening. You are not just being tossed and turned. You are being slammed to the sand.

Darkness abounds, and your only instinct is to try to rise to the surface.

Impossible.

The mass of the salt water and your depth below the gigantic wave prohibit this.

Then, just as suddenly as this situation came upon you, it ends. The wave bounds to the beach. The depth returns to manageable conditions. And you pop through to a fresh breath.

Could it be that our moments preceding death and our actual death will be something like this: impending doom, loss of control, fear, and finally new life?

Comparing this metaphor with death, as Christians we believe that our new life comes in Jesus Christ, the Son of God the Father. When we leave this world for the next, Jesus welcomes us into an everlasting Kingdom, where, as mystic Blessed Julian of Norwich described:

> I saw our Lord like a lord in his own house who has called all his valued servants and friends to a solemn feast . . . and Jesus filled the house with joy and mirth. He himself endlessly gladdened and solaced his valued friends . . . with marvelous melody of endless love in his own fair, blessed face.

At death, Jesus himself will transform our lives from this world to the next, our earthly bodies to glorious ones, our hope for eternal life to contentment, our faith in him to deeper friendship, and our love to a bliss that will last forever.

Why open this book with a story about death? Hopefully such a topic will grab your attention and let you know the necessity and the urgency of keeping the name "Jesus" on your lips and close to your heart. St. Paul wrote in his Letter to the Romans:

> If you confess with your mouth that Jesus is Lord and believe in your heart that God raised him from the dead, you will be saved. For one believes with the heart and so is justified, and one confesses with the mouth and so is saved. For the scripture says, "No one who believes in him will be put to shame." . . . For "everyone who calls on the name of the Lord will be saved." (Rom 10:9–13)

It is important for you to be saved from a life in eternity apart from God, your family, and your friends. It is important for you to be assured of being able to defeat death and to live forever. This is accomplished only through Jesus Christ.

St. Paul went on to ask,

> But how can they call on him in whom they have not believed? And how can they believe in him of whom they have not heard? And how can they hear without someone to preach? And how can people preach unless they are sent? (Rom 10:14–15)

The subject of this book is Jesus Christ and how to know him better so you can rise with him to a new and wonderful life. This is a goal worth your time and effort.

You will discover that when you grow in your knowledge of Jesus, your life will be transformed well before your death. Think of how this is true. You may know peers, parents, grandparents, or friends who have changed their focus in life, come to a new peace or satisfaction, and become more loving because they have "put on the Lord Jesus Christ," as St. Paul described (Rom 13:14). When you put on Christ, it will give you new perspective to face challenges of career and vocational goals, get along with others, and live a life of peace.

Knowing Jesus is not a journey you take on your own, though reflection through solitary prayer is certainly part of it. Discovering more about Christ and the Good News he preached takes place in the life of the Church, where Jesus remains present to this day. The Church is Christ's Body on earth. He is the head of the Body; we are its members. It is in the Church that we can know him, especially in the sacraments, where we are assured he is always with us. When we

know Jesus, we want to introduce him to others. This sharing of the Gospel takes place through the moral and upright way we live.

This book is intended to help you grow in knowledge of Jesus while providing you with questions, answers, and inspiration to take your part in Christ's Church and share the Gospel with others.

WAYS TO USE THIS BOOK

This book may be used in several settings and in several ways.

It may be used as a resource to accompany a full study of Jesus Christ and his teaching through several courses you may take while in high school, wherever and however this take place: in a Catholic high school, in a parish religious education program or youth ministry, or as part of religious instruction at home.

The organization of the book provides many ways to know Jesus better and more deeply.

Chapter 1, The Revelation of Jesus Christ in Scripture, traces our hunger for God and his Revelation to us through a survey of the Bible.

Chapter 2, Who Is Jesus? examines the gift of the Incarnation and Jesus' Revelation of the Mystery of the Holy Trinity, including his special relationship with his Father.

Chapter 3, Paschal Mystery: The Mission of Jesus Christ, views the entrance of sin into the world through the lens of God's immediate promise of a Redeemer.

Chapter 4, The Church: Christ's Mission Continues in the World Today, shares the means for communion with Jesus today and the marks that define Christ and his disciples.

Chapter 5, The Sacraments of Christ, reminds us of sacred and visible signs of Christ and his loving grace active in the world.

Chapter 6, Our Life in Christ, teaches that being a disciple of Jesus means putting him before all else while combating sin through the help of the grace of the Blessed Trinity.

Several features within each chapter help provide breadth and depth to your knowledge of Jesus:

Review questions help you summarize each main section.

Write or Discuss prompts offer ways to reflect on the material and apply it to what is going on in your life.

Vocabulary terms, boldfaced in the text, are defined in the *Glossary of Selected Terms.*

Jesus: Friend and Savior is a section at the end of each chapter with practical applications for furthering your study including activities, apologetics questions and answers, and a prayer.

The Appendix is filled with information that will serve you well as you deepen your study of Jesus and the Catholic faith. Additional topics covered include Scripture study, Catholic Social Teaching, Christian vocation, and ecumenical and interfaith study. A collection of Catholic creeds, devotions, novenas, and prayers is also part of the Appendix.

May You Come to Know Jesus Christ

"For us and for our salvation," Jesus, God, the Second Person of the Holy Trinity, came down from Heaven. Jesus became human to save us by reconciling us with God. He became flesh so we might know God's love. He became flesh so we can also model his holiness. Jesus Christ came to earth so we can share God's divine nature—so we may be all that God intends for us. May you come to know

> Christ Jesus,
> Who, though he was in the form of God,
> did not regard equality with God
> something to be grasped.
> Rather, he emptied himself,
> taking the form of a slave,
> coming in human likeness;
> and found human in appearance,
> he humbled himself,
> becoming obedient to death,
> even death on a cross.
> Because of this, God greatly exalted him
> and bestowed on him the name
> that is above every name,
> that at the name of Jesus
> every knee should bend, of those in heaven

> and on earth and under the earth, and every tongue confess that Jesus Christ is Lord, to the glory of God the Father.
>
> —Philippians 2:6–11

1 The Revelation of Jesus Christ in Scripture

OUR DESIRE FOR GOD

The Gospel reading for the Second Sunday of Easter each year is always taken from the Gospel of John. It tells the story of the Risen Jesus appearing to the disciples behind locked doors. Jesus greeted his friends with "Peace be with you" and showed them his hands and side. He breathed on them and gave them the gift of the Holy Spirit. He told them, "Receive the Holy Spirit. Whose sins you forgive are forgiven them, and whose sins you retain are retained" (Jn 20:22–23).

What you probably remember most about hearing the Gospel at Mass that day is that one of the Apostles happened to be absent when Jesus appeared. Do you remember his name? Yes, the Gospel goes on to say that "Thomas, called Didymus . . . was not with them when Jesus came" (Jn 20:24).

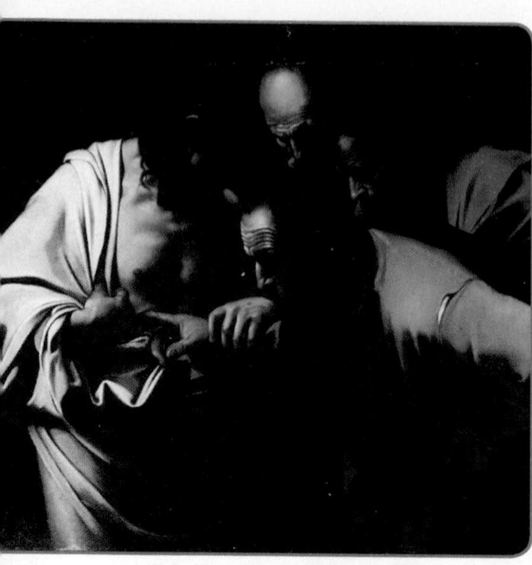

"My Lord and My God!"

You can probably recall the rest of the reading, too. Thomas told the others, "Unless I see the mark of the nails in his hands and put my finger into the nailmarks and put my hand into his side, I will not believe."

The next week Jesus came to the Apostles again. This time Thomas was there. Jesus let Thomas do as he wished—put his finger in the wounds of Jesus' hands and his hand in the wounds of Jesus' side. Jesus told Thomas to "not be unbelieving, but believe."

Thomas answered and said to Jesus, "My Lord and my God!" Once an unbeliever, Thomas was the first person recorded in the Gospels to identify Jesus as God. Presumably the peace Jesus had offered the others was received by Thomas, for he had found God face to face.

Human beings are created with a desire or longing for God that can't be satisfied until we come to know, **praise**, and love him. God likewise has a desire to draw each person to himself. Imagine the seven days between Jesus' appearances to the disciples without Thomas present to the day when Jesus and Thomas met face to face. Thomas did not abandon the group of believers in the meantime. He stayed with the hope he would experience what they had experienced. And Jesus returned specifically to reach out to Thomas.

Christ is the eternal Word that became flesh. The Son of God assumed a human nature in order for us to be saved. Thomas, like the others disciples, was given an opportunity unique to human history: to meet and know God *incarnate*, in

Church
The Body of Christ; that is, the community of God's People who profess faith in the Risen Lord Jesus and love and serve others under the guidance of the Holy Spirit. The Pope and his bishops guide the Roman Catholic Church.

the flesh. Putting his finger and hand into Jesus' wounds, Thomas was reminded that Jesus was a human being with real flesh and blood. The testimony of the other disciples about Jesus' **Resurrection**—and now this special Resurrection appearance—convinced Thomas that Jesus was also God. The belief in the **Incarnation**—that God assumed human nature—is a distinctive sign of Christian faith.

Today, our search for God might be easier if we could speak to Jesus face to face. The Gospel for the Second Sunday of Easter acknowledges this. Jesus said to Thomas, "Have you come to believe because you have seen me? Blessed are those who have not seen and have believed." But Jesus has "blessed" our search for him and offered us many ways to know him. These ways to know Jesus—revealed in the **Church**—are the subject of this book.

The natural human search for God requires that we make every effort with our mind and heart while knowing that even if we forget God or reject him, he will never stop calling us to himself. In this search, we can find lasting happiness and the meaning of life. St. Augustine wrote about this search for God and what it brings:

> Despite everything, man, though but a small part of your creation, wants to praise you. You yourself encourage him to delight in your praise, for you have made us for yourself, and our heart is restless until it rests in you.[1]

REVIEW

1. According to the Gospels, what did Thomas do before anyone else?
2. Why did Jesus assume a human nature?
3. Define *Incarnation*.

WRITE OR DISCUSS

- How has your journey to know Jesus been blessed?

WHO IS GOD?

"I believe in God" is the first statement of the **Catholic** creeds. This profession of faith begins with God because God is the beginning and the end of everything. Most people—whether or not they practice a **religion**—do believe in or acknowledge a supreme being. A belief in God further affects their lives, leading to an obedience or a worship of a power or a being larger than they are.

However, there are many different understandings of God. All the major religions believe in some invisible, higher reality, though it may be named differently in the other religions. For example, Hindus name this deity "Brahma." Buddhism does not name a personal God but does acknowledge an Ultimate Reality of the universe. Muslims call God "Allah." Judaism has such great respect for the name of God that the most important name given to God—represented by four Hebrew letters for **YHWH**—cannot be pronounced. Judaism also has many other names for God,

Covenant
The open-ended contract of love between God and human beings. Jesus' Death and Resurrection sealed God's New Covenant of love for all time. Testament translates to covenant.

Adonai, or "My Lord," being the first name used in Scripture. The Catholic creeds continue by naming our central beliefs about God:

- There is one God.
- God is Creator, not created.
- God is almighty.
- God is Trinitarian.

The belief in one God is different from what people once believed. This belief seems natural to us now, but it wasn't always so. Prior to God's self-revelation and his **covenant** with the Israelites from the Old Testament, ***monotheism***—the belief in only one supreme God—was not developed. For example, Hinduism, though it proclaims one supreme God, also permits and worships lesser gods. Zoroastrianism believes in the triumph of a good god but also acknowledges an equally powerful evil force. This makes its beliefs essentially dualistic. Buddhism, in some forms, considers Siddhartha Gautama as the supreme god, but he is also considered essentially a man who achieved enlightenment.

Monotheism contradicts not only ***atheism*** (the belief in no God), but also ***polytheism*** (belief in many gods) and ***pantheism*** (belief that God and nature are the same). Of the major religions, only Judaism, Christianity, and Islam are monotheistic.

Apologetics: CATHOLIC FAQs

Use this chapter and other sources to formulate your own answers to these questions. Then check your answers at "Catholic FAQs" at **www.avemariapress.com: Religious Education.**

- ☞ How is God the author of the Sacred Scripture?
- ☞ Who wrote the Bible?
- ☞ Why should Christians bother reading the Old Testament?

One of the central beliefs about God that most religions have in common is that "God is good." If this wasn't so, theologians (those who study God) and faithful people in general would likely not spend time trying to figure out much more about God's identity. If people believed God to be evil and vindictive, they would likely look for ways to appease this power or simply run for cover and hide!

We know from our personal experience, from the words of the Scriptures, and from other Divine Revelation passed on to us in the Church that God is indeed good. Not only that, but he loves each person even more than the person loves himself or herself. God's love for Israel is compared to a father's love for his son. His love for his people is stronger than a mother's for her children. And in the course of history, "God so loved the world that he gave his only Son" (Jn 3:16). Also, God is capable of receiving love in return and hopes we will offer our love to him freely.

The monotheistic religions believe in a God who is not only good, but also almighty—above all others. They see God as the Creator of all that exists. These major characteristics of God help fill in more of the details of God's nature.

Attributes of God

St. Thomas Aquinas (1225–1274), one of the most important theologians in Church history, named nine attributes that tell us about God's nature. They are as follows:

1. *God is eternal.* He has no beginning and no end. Or, to put it another way, God always was, always is, and always will be.
2. *God is unique.* God is the fullness of being and perfection. God is the designer of a one-and-only world. Even the people he creates are one of a kind.

3. *God is infinite and omnipotent.* There are no limits to God. ***Omnipotence*** is a word that refers to God's supreme power and authority over all of creation.

4. *God is omnipresent.* This reminds us of a lesson we learned early in life: God sees everything. God has no space limitations. He is everywhere. You can never be away from God.

5. *God contains all things.* All of creation is under God's care and jurisdiction.

6. *God is immutable.* God does not evolve. God does not change. God is the same God now as he always has been and always will be.

7. *God is pure spirit.* Though God has been described with human attributes (e.g., a wise old man with a long beard), God is not a material creation. God's image cannot be made. God is a pure spirit who cannot be divided into parts. God is simple but complex.

8. *God is alive.* We believe in a living God, a God who acts in the lives of people. Most concretely, he came to this world in the incarnate form of Jesus Christ.

9. *God is holy.* God is pure goodness. God is pure love.

Of all the attributes of God, only his omnipotence is named in the creeds. Our belief in an almighty God affects how we live our lives. We believe that God not only *rules* everything, but he can *do* everything and anything. When we read that an angel visited Mary and told her she would give birth to a son without conceiving it with a man, this is believable to us because of God's almighty power. The angel reinforced this by saying, "Nothing will be impossible for God" (Lk 1:37).

God's almighty power does not coerce us into obedience. In fact, his power is loving. God is a loving Father who takes care of our needs. He says, "I will be a father to you, and you shall be sons and daughters to me" (2 Cor 6:18). Jesus teaches that our heavenly Father "knows all that we need" (see Luke 12:30) and will grant us these things when we accept him first.

Finally, God's almighty power sustains even the "evidence" of weakness when we witness evil and suffering in our world. This is part of another of God's attributes—his **mystery**. Still, though we might not fully understand why there is evil, suffering, and death, we do witness how the Almighty God is even able to conquer these, too—through the Resurrection of his Son, Jesus, and through that the ultimate end of all sin and death.

God Is Creator

In our Catholic creeds, we confess that God the Father is "Creator of heaven and earth," of "all that is, seen and unseen." The first words of the Scriptures say that "In the beginning . . . God created the heavens and the earth" (Gn 1:1).

Through our examination of creation, we learn several other things about God.

First, we know that God created from nothing. God did not use any preexistent thing, nor did he need any help to create. As St. Theophilus of Antioch put it:

> If God had drawn the world from pre-existent matter, what would be so extraordinary in that? A human artisan makes from a given material whatever he wants, while God shows his power by starting from nothing to make all he wants.

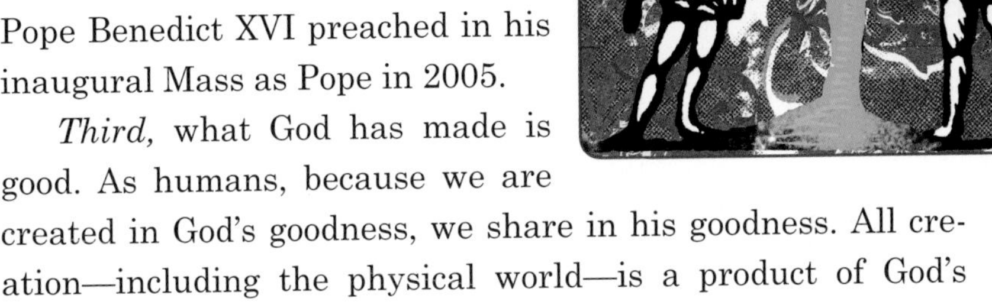

Second, God creates what he wants. Creation is not left to blind fate or chance. God made his creatures because he wanted to share his being, goodness, and wisdom. "Each of us is the result of a thought of God. Each of us is willed, each of us is loved, each of us is necessary," Pope Benedict XVI preached in his inaugural Mass as Pope in 2005.

Third, what God has made is good. As humans, because we are created in God's goodness, we share in his goodness. All creation—including the physical world—is a product of God's goodness.

Fourth, God is greater than his works of creation. God is outside of his creation, yet at the same time, he is present to it. As the Acts of the Apostles puts it, "In [God] we live and move and have our being" (Acts 17:28).

Fifth, God supports his creation. For example, we are not created and then abandoned by God. Rather, God's **providence** leads and guides us to our final end: **salvation** and union with God.

God's act of creation was the first witness to his love and wisdom. In creation, we get the first glimpse of God's saving plan of love, one that culminates in Jesus Christ. This plan of God's is one in which we, his creations, take an active involvement. God intended for people to share not only in the saving work of the world, but also in creation itself. That is why humans are made as male and female. God created man and woman to be

salvation
The extension of God's forgiveness, grace, and healing to the world through Jesus Christ in the Holy Spirit.

procreators, to share in the divine activity of bringing life in his image to the world.

Creation itself is the work of the **Holy Trinity**—Father, Son, and Holy Spirit. Traditionally, God the Father has been given the role of Creator. It was said that he made everything by himself—by the Son and the Spirit who are, according to St. Irenaeus, "his hands."

Ultimately, the work of creation is the common work of the Holy Trinity.

Jesus Christ: God Incarnate

And the Word became flesh
and made his dwelling among us,
and we saw his glory,
the glory as of the Father's only Son,
full of grace and truth. (Jn 1:14)

Belief in the true Incarnation—the taking on of human nature and human flesh by the Son of God—is the distinctive element of Christianity. What a challenging belief, that the God with attributes such as eternal, infinite, omnipotent, omnipresent, immutable, pure of spirit, and holy would empty himself to become a human being! God, in fact, entered human history by becoming one of his creatures while all the time remaining the Creator of the universe.

It would be wise to digest the previous paragraph (including the passage from the Gospel of John) before moving on. The purpose of this book in total is to help you understand and believe more deeply that Jesus is the Christ, the chosen Messiah who has come to earth to offer you the promise of Redemption and life in his eternal Kingdom. The purpose of each of these chapters is to show you ways that you can know Jesus, God incarnate, and how he can lead you to know the eternal God. These tasks are built around the life and the teachings of the Church.

God in Three Persons

Christians are monotheistic; we believe in one God. Yet through the teachings of Jesus and through experiencing him, it was gradually revealed to the early Christians that there is one God who acts in Three Persons—Father, Son, and Holy Spirit.

Actually, there was one experience at the beginning of Jesus' ministry when the Trinitarian nature of God was clearly revealed. It was at Jesus' baptism by John in the River Jordan.

Jesus, God incarnate, was there. John the Baptist recognized that Jesus was the chosen one of the Scriptures. "I need to be baptized by you, and yet you are coming to me?" John wondered aloud (Mt 3:14).

After Jesus was baptized, God the Holy Spirit was visible in the form of a dove. "He came up from the water and behold, the heavens were opened, and he saw the Spirit of God descending like a dove, coming upon him" (Mt 3:16).

Finally, the voice of God the Father was heard from Heaven: "This is my beloved Son, with whom I am well pleased" (Mt 3:17).

From this Revelation and others connected with Jesus and his teaching, the Church's understanding of Three Persons in one God originated and grew. More ways to understand and explain the mystery of the Holy Trinity will be covered in Chapter 2.

REVIEW

1. What are the central beliefs about God according to the Catholic creeds?
2. How do we know that God is good?
3. Which attribute of God is named in the Catholic creeds?
4. What is God's power like?
5. What do we learn about God from his creation?

THE REVELATION OF GOD THROUGH HISTORY

Beyond what we can know about God through our own experience, God has freely and fully revealed himself. Why does God want himself known by his creatures? God has revealed himself to draw us nearer to him and to make us more like him. God gradually shared more and more of himself through history. Eventually, his **Revelation** culminated in the person and the mission of the Incarnate Word, Jesus Christ. This Revelation takes place in the course of human history.

God's plan of gradually sharing knowledge of himself is easy to understand from our human experience. Think of your own growth and development. You may now be adept in a fairly sophisticated level of mathematics. But you were hardly ready to learn calculus before algebra, or for that matter before multiplication and division, when you first started school. Or think of a husband and wife, married for more than fifty years. Over time this man

Revelation
The way God communicates knowledge of himself to humankind, a self-communication realized by his actions and words over time, most fully by his sending us his divine Son, Jesus Christ.

and woman have come to know each other more and more. And their love for each other has deepened over the years.

In a similar way, God offered his Revelation to human beings in stages. He made himself known to our first parents, Adam and Eve, from the time of creation, offering his intimate communion with them and clothing them "with resplendent grace and justice" (*CCC*, 54). Even after Adam and Eve sinned, God did not abandon them. In the Book of Genesis, the Lord addresses the serpent, the source of evil:

> I will put enmity between you and the woman, and between your offspring and hers; He will strike at your head, while you strike at his heel. (Gn 3:15)

This passage is called the ***Protoevangelium*** (first gospel). It is the first announcement that God will send a Messiah and Redeemer, who is a descendant of Eve.

The Stages of God's Revelation

Immediately when Adam and Eve sinned, "God at once sought to save humanity part by part" (*CCC*, 56). God made a covenant with Noah after the flood: "I will establish my covenant with you, that never again shall all bodily creatures be destroyed by the waters of a flood; there shall not be another flood to devastate the earth" (Gn 9:11).

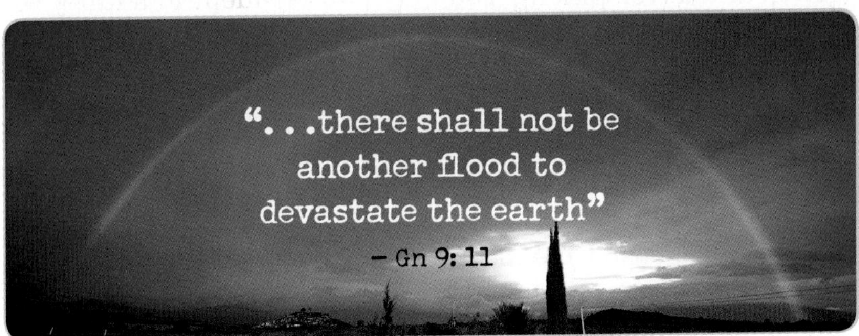
". . .there shall not be
another flood to
devastate the earth"
– Gn 9: 11

God then chose Abraham, a farmer from Chaldea, to leave his own people to become "the father of a host of nations" (Gn 17:5). The covenant with Abraham helped prepare the way for the coming of Christ. The people descended from Abraham would be God's **Chosen People**, the Israelites, who would be stewards of the promises God made to Abraham and from whom Christ would be born. When Christ came, the **Gentiles** who came to believe in him were grafted like a branch to the Chosen People.

God formed the Chosen People in preparation for the coming of the promised Messiah, who would save the human race from its sinfulness. Through Moses, God gave them his Law so they would be able to recognize him and serve him as the one and true God as they anticipated the Savior. The prophets of the Old Testament preached about a new and everlasting covenant that would supersede all others. This was to be a covenant written on the hearts of all believers. It is a covenant that promises Redemption of God's People, purification from all infidelities, and salvation for all.

Chosen People
The descendants of Israel (also called Jacob). God chose the Israelites to be his People. In this covenant, the Israelites also promised to worship YHWH.

Jesus is God's final Revelation. There are no other "stages" beyond Jesus. As the Letter to the Hebrews begins, "In times past, God spoke in partial and various ways to our ancestors through the prophets; in these last days, he spoke to us through a son, whom he made heir of all things and through whom he created the universe" (Heb 1:2). In Jesus, God has revealed everything the world needs to know to be made holy and to be saved.

Yet that doesn't mean that our generation has nothing to do in order to grow in knowledge of God and to live according to the New Covenant. It remains for individuals and the Church collectively to continue to search out and understand the meaning of God's full Revelation in Christ as it applies to our own lives and times.

How God's Revelation Is Communicated

Before gasoline prices skyrocketed in recent years, a common fundraising activity for high-school students was to hold a "car rally." For an entry fee, drivers and their team of navigators would be given a series of clues that would take them from place to place around the immediate area. Only if they solved one clue would they be given another. The team that made it through all of the clues to the finish line first would win a prize.

Car rallies were fun, but no life or death was at stake. The losers lost only their entrance fee. Can you imagine if pursuing salvation were more like a car rally, a mystery in which the ultimate "secret" of salvation were not revealed until the very end—and then to only one or a limited number of winners?

The Good News of salvation is not given to us piecemeal like clues in a car rally! Since God wants *everyone* to be saved, he wants his way, truth, and life to be made known to all nations and all people in every generation.

Apologetics:
CATHOLIC FAQs
☞ Is it true that Catholics do not use or read the Bible?
☞ Isn't the Bible just another piece of literature?
☞ Is the Bible always literally true?

Jesus Christ is "the way and the truth and the life." Jesus shared the Good News of God's mercy and love that was revealed in his own Life,

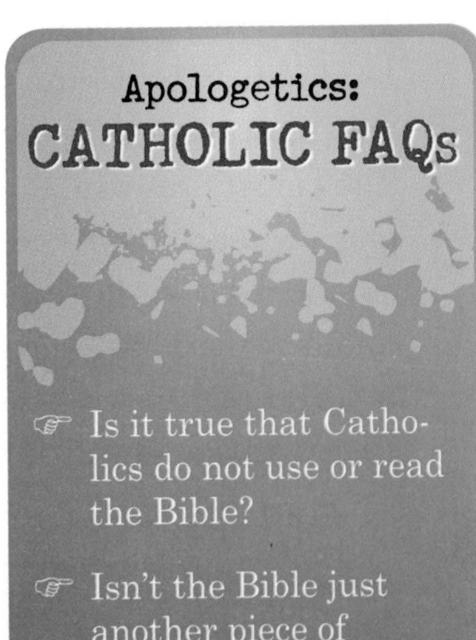

Death, and Resurrection. It is this **Gospel** that Christ entrusted to the **Apostles**. "The Gospel was to be the source of all saving truth and moral discipline" (*CCC*, 75). The Apostles were to share the Gospel with all people. The Apostles handed on the Gospel in two ways. First, it was transmitted orally using what they heard and witnessed directly from Christ or what they learned from the inspiration of the Holy Spirit. Second, it was given to us in writing. Written Gospels came from those Apostles (or men associated with them), who were inspired by the Spirit to put the salvation message into written form.

The Gospel was not intended to die out or stop being preached after the death of the Apostles. Rather, it was to be preserved until the end of time. Obviously, one way the Gospel has been preserved is in the Bible, the **Sacred Scripture**. In the second and third centuries, following the instructions of the Apostles, the Church determined which writings to include in the Bible. The complete list is called the **canon** of Scripture. While these books contain the fullness of God's Revelation, the teaching of the Church continues to guide the successors of the Apostles—the Pope and the bishops—in every generation. They must preserve, expound on, and spread God's Word. This ongoing teaching is known as the Church's Tradition.

Sacred Scripture and **Sacred Tradition** complement one another. Both have the same source—God. Together they form a single reality with the same goal—to make the mystery of Christ alive and fruitful until the end of time.

REVIEW

1. How was the Gospel first shared?
2. Briefly trace the stages of Revelation.

WRITE OR DISCUSS

- What do you find challenging about the fact that God became human?
- How does the fact that God became human help you face the challenges of life?

JESUS AND SACRED SCRIPTURE

Unlike St. Thomas and the other Apostles, we don't have the opportunity to interact with Jesus face to face. But we can hear his words and know his presence in other ways given especially by God. Jesus is present in the Eucharist when he makes himself sacramentally present to us in the forms of the bread and wine. Jesus is also truly present in Sacred Scripture, the Bible. In fact, in the words of Sacred Scripture, God "speaks only one single Word, his one Utterance in whom he expresses himself completely" (*CCC*, 102). That word is *Christ*, who permeates the entire Scripture, Old Testament and New Testament. Jesus is the Word of God who became human in all things but sin. Scripture is the wisdom of God revealed to us in words and language we can understand.

Reading and praying with the Bible and hearing the words of Scripture in liturgy help us know Jesus. God is the author of Scripture. What does this mean? Did God magically pen the Sacred Scripture and then rain it down from the sky so it suddenly appeared in places of worship and bookstores besides? Hardly. Rather, the Holy Spirit inspired the human authors of the sacred books. But be careful how you envision the inspiration's occurring.

Very few biblical scholars would hold that God spoke each word of the Bible into the ears of human authors and they simply transcribed what they were told, word for word, punctuation and all.

More accurately, as the Second Vatican Council explained, God "chose certain men who, all the while he employed them in this task, made full use of their own faculties and powers so that, though he acted in them and by them, it was as true authors that they consigned to writing whatever he wanted written, and no more" (*Dei Verbum*, 11). This is a good summary of the Catholic understanding of how the Holy Spirit inspired the Sacred Scriptures.

While the Sacred Scriptures faithfully teach the truth, it is important to understand that the Christian faith is not a "religion of the book." Instead, the Bible is the "book of the Church," meaning that the words of Scripture must be incarnate and living—not locked into the century in which they were written. Christ himself, the eternal Word of the living God, must open our minds to understand the Scriptures as he once did for the disciples traveling on the road to Emmaus (see Luke 24:13–35).

Jesus interpreted the Scriptures for the disciples.

How to Interpret Scripture

We must be attentive to the Scriptures in two ways if we are to interpret the words correctly. We have to understand what the human authors were attempting to say *and* what God wanted to reveal by their words.

To understand the authors' intentions, the reader must take into account the historical and cultural context of the writing. The authors wrote for the people of their own time and place. They used the language and the literary styles of their audience. Biblical scholars help today's readers sort through these issues. For example, *The New American Bible* is annotated to help the reader understand the background and context of the Scriptures.

This detailed study or explanation of a biblical book or passage is known as ***exegesis***. This is a Greek word that means "to lead." The goal of exegesis is to lead or bring out the biblical author's intentions, purpose, and meaning related to the writings. Biblical exegesis takes into account the original language in which the book was written. (The Old Testament was written mostly in Hebrew, the New Testament in Greek.) Exegesis also considers the cultural and social background of the author and the audience. Other factors looked at are the geographical setting of the text, Church doctrines related to the Bible and biblical studies, the quality of the translations of the biblical texts, and the literary styles or forms of writing used.

However, since the Sacred Scripture is inspired, there is another way to interpret it. As the Second Vatican Council taught: "Sacred Scripture must be read and interpreted in light of the same Spirit by whom it was written" (*Dei Verbum*, 3). How is this done? In reading the Bible, special attention must be given to three modes of study:

1. Pay attention to the Bible as a whole, not just individual passages or even books. The entire Scripture is a unity of God's plan, and Christ is at the center of it.
2. Read the Bible in light of the living Tradition of the Church. The Scripture is written and remains alive because it is interpreted by the Holy Spirit through the

Church. Scripture must be read from the perspective of the Church rather than individualistically—that is, you must consider what the Church says about its meaning.

3. Be attentive to the analogy of Faith. There exists an entire hierarchy of truths of Faith—of which Scripture is a part—that must be placed in the context of the whole of God's Revelation. The Scriptures must be understood within the whole plan of God's Revelation.

Finally, there is an additional point to consider for understanding Scripture. It is Jesus Christ, the Incarnate Word of God, who is present throughout the Bible. The Old Testament sets the stage, if you will, for Christ's coming. The New Testament completes the story and tells how Jesus brought salvation to all who believed in him. Jesus, the Word of God, is the one unique Word of Sacred Scripture. As St. Augustine explained:

> You recall that one and the same Word of God extends throughout the Scripture, that it is one and the same Utterance that resounds in the mouths of all the sacred writers, since he who was in the beginning God with God has no need for separate syllables; for he is not subject to time.

Senses of Scripture

There are two main senses of Scripture—the literal and the spiritual. These two ways for looking at and interpreting Scripture shape the way the Bible is to be understood.

The literal sense of Scripture refers to the literal meaning conveyed by the words and discovered by exegesis. This sense is twofold. The precise literal sense refers to what the written words mean as they are written. For example, a literal approach to a Passion narrative would tell us that what happened to Jesus through his trials, suffering, and Death occurred exactly as it was reported in that Gospel. A figurative application of the literal approach to Scripture emerges in the interpretation of metaphors. For example, Jesus described himself as the "true vine, and my Father is the vine grower" (Jn 15:1). A figurative understanding of this reference that uses the literal approach suggests that Jesus saw himself drawing his life from his Father.

The spiritual way of interpreting Scripture looks not just at the words themselves, but also at what the words signify. For example, the spiritual interpretation can be:

- *Allegorical.* Recognizing the significance of Christ in scriptural events offers more understanding of their meaning. For example, the crossing of the Red Sea is a sign of Christ's victory and also of Christian Baptism.
- *Moral.* The Scripture teaches us how to live and act. For example, Abraham is a model of faith for all generations.
- *Anagogical.* The anagogical (from a Greek word for "to lead") meaning of Scripture reminds us that the sacred words are leading us onward to eternal life.

Unifying these two major ways of interpreting Scripture brings richness and life to the Bible. They keep the Bible from becoming a "dead" book.

Truth in the Bible

You may have wondered at different times and in various ways, "Is the Bible true?" For example, can you really believe that Moses lived to be 120 years old?

Answering the question about whether the Bible is true demands expanding our understanding of truth. A dictionary defines truth as "conformity to fact or actuality." This definition works well when speaking of mathematical or scientific truth, two kinds of truth we are used to today. Mathematical truth is well defined through calculation and the laws of arithmetic, and it is verifiable through the use of calculators or computers. Scientific truth operates in much the same way. A hypothesis is drawn, it is proved by experiments and observations, and it is verified by others through many other occasions of testing.

The Bible is hardly true in those ways. There is little mathematical truth in the Bible, though weights, measurements, and currencies are occasionally mentioned. The same could be said of its scientific "truth." The Bible reflects the scientific understanding of its day, which by our standards is very primitive.

Nonetheless, there are other kinds of truth besides mathematical truth and scientific truth. These other categories of truth statements expand our understanding of truth.

For example, consider the statement "My mom loves me." Wouldn't most people consider that to be true? This type of truth—call it *relational truth*—cannot be verified by any experiment or calculation. Rather, you *know* it is true from your experience and from the testimony of others.

Or consider this frequently heard comment on the weather: "It's raining cats and dogs!" How is this true? Certainly we know that animals are not falling from the sky. We also know that the statement probably describes a torrential downpour. This type of truth may be described as *symbolic truth.*

The Bible has many examples of both relational truths and symbolic truths. People described in the Bible are relational in all the ways we are familiar with. They are sons and daughters, husbands and wives, friends and enemies. Within all of these different relationships are the normal give-and-take dynamics that are part of human life. Symbolic truths are also common in the Bible. Think of one of the ways Jesus taught. The Gospels recount that many times Jesus taught through the use of ***parables***. A parable is a story that uses easily understood symbols and ends with a surprising moral lesson.

Two other major areas of truth must be mentioned here. The first is *moral truth.* The Bible contains many moral truths that are given as laws and standards for living. The most obvious example in this category is the **Ten Commandments**. The other type of truth is *religious truth.* This type of truth describes God's relationship with humankind, both in the Old Covenant between YHWH and the Jews and in the New Covenant established by Jesus between all who come to believe in him and the Father who sent him.

REVIEW

1. What is the "one Word" of Scripture?
2. How does God inspire Scripture?
3. What are two ways to correctly interpret Scripture?
4. What does Scripture exegesis take into account?
5. Explain the two senses of Scripture: literal and spiritual.
6. How is the Bible true?

WRITE OR DISCUSS

- On the road to Emmaus, how did Jesus break open Scripture? How have your eyes been open to God's Word?

OVERVIEW OF THE BIBLE

The Sacred Scripture—both the Old Testament and the New Testament—were written under the inspiration of the Holy Spirit. The Church, relying on the faith of the Apostles, "accepts as sacred and canonical the books of the Old and New Testaments, whole and entire, with all their parts, on the grounds that, written under the inspiration of the Holy Spirit, they have God as their author, and have been handed on to the Church herself" (*Dei Verbum*, 11).

As you might know, the word *Bible* is from the Greek word *biblion*, which means "book." You also might know that the Bible is different from other, typical books you are used to. The most easily recognized difference is that the Bible is not actually one book at all, but made up of seventy-three books divided into the Old Testament and the New Testament.

There are other anomalies about the Bible as compared with compendiums of modern writings. For example, the books in the Bible are not organized in the order they were written. Genesis comes first because it deals with topics of creation and beginnings, not because it was the first book written. In the same way, Revelation is placed at the very end of the New Testament because it deals with the end times and the **Last (Final) Judgment**. It was likely *not* the last book of the Bible that was composed.

Also, interestingly, very few biblical books were written by a single author. The writings developed from years of oral sharing and when finally written down were considered more a production of a community than of a single author. In fact, it was a commonly accepted practice to put the name of a famous member of the community or a famous ancestor of faith on the book rather than the actual author or authors.

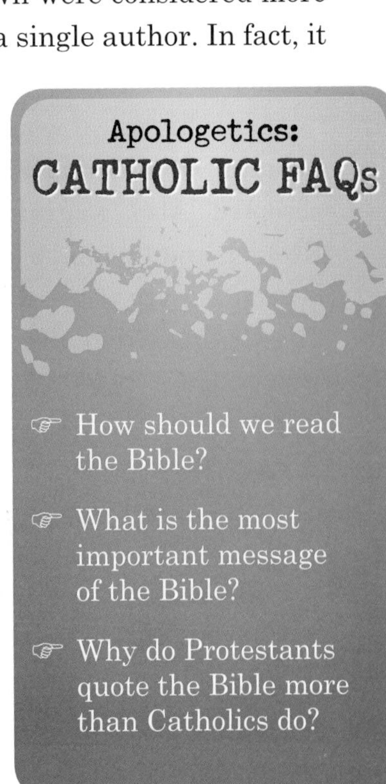

Apologetics:
CATHOLIC FAQs
How should we read the Bible?
What is the most important message of the Bible?
Why do Protestants quote the Bible more than Catholics do?

The biblical writers also had a different way of recording history than we have today. The biblical writers began with a central theme or teaching—salvation offered by God through his covenant with humankind—and worked backward to illustrate this theme with historical evidence. For example, Mark's Gospel begins by announcing to the reader that Jesus is the Son of God. The author then arranges events in

Jesus' life and ministry that help reveal this mystery to his disciples and explain it to the reader.

The "canon" of the Scriptures comes from the Greek word *kanon*, which means "measuring rod" or "rule." The canon refers to the twenty-seven New Testament books and forty-six Old Testament books that the Church accepts as inspired books.

The Old Testament

The Old Testament canon took many years to develop. The Law found in the Book of Deuteronomy was discovered in 621 BC and attributed to Moses. Over the next two hundred years, other writings of the Law and the stories about creation were also credited to Moses. Eventually these first five books of the Bible became known as the Pentateuch (Greek for "five books") or the Torah.

Later historical works, such as the accounts of Joshua, the Judges, Samuel, and Kings, were recorded, widely read, and accepted. Also, writings of prophets (e.g., Isaiah, Jeremiah, Ezekiel, and the minor prophets) were being circulated. These became a part of the Jewish Bible known as the "Prophets." The writings from after the Jews returned from exile became known as the "Writings," a category that basically covered anything not part of the Torah or the Prophets. There were some disputes over the authenticity of some of these later books. The results of these disputes are still present today.

The Torah

In the third century BC, the Hebrew Scriptures were translated into Greek. This translation is called the *Septuagint*, Latin for "seventy." According to a traditional story, the Library of Alexandria did not include the great writings of the Jews, so the Ptolemy rulers commissioned seventy-two Hebrew elders (six from each tribe of Israel) to come to Egypt and translate the Bible into Greek. The translators divided into teams, and when they were finished, a miracle had occurred: Each of their translations was exactly the same! Though an interesting story, the only verifiable truth to the tale is that the Septuagint was produced in Egypt in the time of the Ptolemaic rule over Palestine.

The Greek version of the Scriptures also included new material. The Book of Esther, for example, grew to almost twice the size as the original book. Daniel picked up a few new chapters. Whole books such as 1 and 2 Maccabees, Judith, Tobit, Baruch, Sirach, and Wisdom were made part of this collection. This expanded collection became for Christians the Old Testament.

A group of Jewish rabbis met around AD 90 and decided to consolidate the Scriptures and include only those found in Hebrew. Catholic Bibles include the seven additional books from the Greek translation but refer to them as *deuterocanonical*—"second canon"—to show that these are not accepted in the Jewish canon. In the sixteenth century, Martin Luther and other Protestants decided to include only those books approved by the Jewish rabbis. Most Protestant Bibles do print a separate section in the back with these books, referring to them as *apocrypha*, which means "hidden."

The Church has always held that the Old Testament is the true Word of God and rejected any claim that the New Testament has voided the Old. Rather, the Old Testament is oriented and bears witness to the coming of Christ. All its books are inspired by God and contain a great store of teaching about God, wisdom on human life, a treasury of prayers, and a glimpse at the mystery of salvation.

As an old saying, quoted by St. Augustine, puts it, "The New Testament lies hidden in the Old, and the Old Testament is unveiled in the New."

The New Testament

The accepted books of the New Testament canon came relatively quickly by comparison to the Old Testament. By the second century AD, several Church leaders—including St. Clement of Rome, St. Ignatius of Antioch, and Tertullian—were using the term *New Testament.* This term referred to the accepted books for teaching and praying the faith. By the year 367, St. Athanasius fixed the canon at twenty-seven books. Finally, the Council of Trent in the sixteenth century confirmed that the canon was the inspired Word of God, using the following criteria: 1) each book had origins with the Apostles; 2) it was widely circulated and accepted by more than one local Christian community; and 3) the doctrine it taught was essential to the Christian faith.

The books of the New Testament are divided into three categories: the Gospels, letters written to local Christian communities or individuals, and letters intended for the entire Church. Many of the letters, or *epistles*, are either attributed to or were actually written by St. Paul. The heart of the New Testament, and in fact all of the Scriptures, are the Gospels, a word that means "good news." They are the principal source of the life and teachings of Jesus Christ.

The Gospels were formed in three stages. The first stage was the life and teachings of Jesus Christ. While he lived,

Jesus preached and taught like all of the rabbis of his time, with the spoken word. In the years after his Resurrection, his followers did the same thing. They spread the Good News in the oral tradition of their ancestors. This was the second stage of Gospel formation. The only difference was that the understanding of Jesus and his message was even fuller in his disciples than it had been before. They had received and were inspired by the promised Holy Spirit. These first disciples had no need to write down the Gospel as long as they were alive to share it and clarify it. Besides, they expected Jesus' return to be imminent.

Finally, in the third stage, the Gospels were written, beginning with Mark's Gospel (in about AD 65 to 70) and concluding with the writing of the Gospel of John near the end of the first century. Why the need to *write* about the life and the teachings of Jesus after so many years of the oral tradition? There were several reasons:

- The Apostles were dying. As the years went on and the eyewitnesses to Jesus realized he may not soon return, it became imperative to record the Gospel.
- There were weaknesses in the oral tradition. The stories needed a consistency in their telling and transitions between one story and the next. The stories themselves needed to be arranged in chronological order.
- A catechetical manual and worship aid was needed. So many new Christians were being instructed that a written document was necessary because the Apostles could not be everywhere at once. Christians needed worship aids for the same reason. The written Gospels would help bring unity to the liturgy.

It's important to remember that the four Gospels were written for different Christian communities. The Gospels of Mark, Matthew, and Luke are very alike, so much so that they are known as the *Synoptic Gospels*. *Synoptic* is Greek for "one-eye." The Gospel of John is different from the Synoptic Gospels and reflects a fuller understanding of Jesus' divinity.

The Acts of the Apostles is really in a special category all its own. It was written by the author of Luke's Gospel, almost as a sequel to that Gospel in order to fill in the details following Jesus' Resurrection through the early days of the Church. Acts details how the Gospel message spread through the Roman Empire, with much of the credit going to the missionary efforts of St. Paul, a Jewish convert whom Acts details as initially persecuting Christians before his conversion.

Paul wrote many of the letters of the New Testament. Some of the letters ascribed to him may actually have been written by other members of local churches. Paul may have written

St. Paul authored several of the New Testament epistles.

only the introductory or concluding remarks and signed the letter. Paul's letters are addressed both to whole communities —for example, those in Corinth, Philippi, or Rome—and to individual people such as Titus, Philemon, and Timothy.

Letters that don't have a specific audience are called *catholic* or *universal* letters. They were credited to various Apostles such as John, Peter, and Jude.

The Book of Revelation is written in a particular style of writing known as *apocalyptic literature*. The Book of Revelation centers on visions of events that are to come and uses veiled language that is difficult to decipher. This book speaks primarily of the persecutions faced by the early Christians and their faith in the saving power of Christ.

REVIEW

1. How are the books of the Bible arranged?
2. What is the canon of Scripture?
3. What is the difference between the Catholic Bible and the Bible accepted by most Protestants?
4. What are the three categories of the New Testament books?
5. What are the Synoptic Gospels?

WRITE OR DISCUSS

- As a Catholic, what do you believe about the Bible? How do your beliefs differ from those of a friend or a peer?

WAYS WE CAN KNOW GOD

Hopes and Dreams

We are built to look outward to a positive future. Think about how you look forward to the end of a term, summer vacation, graduation, and life after school. Our dreams are positive ones as we imagine a better future for our family and ourselves than we have now. Ultimately, these hopes and dreams lead us to strive for a presence before God where what we hope and dream for, and more besides, will come true.

Beauty and Awe

No matter what region you live in, or if you live in the country or city, God's beauty as expressed in the world cannot be dismissed. How can the seasonal color and both the immenseness and simplicity not lead you to God?

Love

In the end, we best know God because of love. Love is the greatest reality of all. We marvel at the unconditional dimension of love (e.g., how a parent can still love a child who has been convicted of murder). We rack our brains to understand where love came from and where it will take us. That there is no concrete answer leads us to name a God who is Love.

Church Councils have pointed out "proofs" of God's existence and the ability of humans to know of God. Think about these ways that you can come to know of God through your own personal experience:

Death and Rebirth

Life is fragile and ever-changing. Think about some of these changes. You have a broken relationship with a friend only to reconcile or begin a friendship with someone new. You fail a test one week, get a better grade the following week. And we experience the transitions of generations in our own families. The death of a loved one is followed shortly by the birth of a new grandchild, cousin, brother, or sister.

Justice and Compassion

How often have you thought "life isn't fair"? Cheaters get away with their crimes. Bullies and mean people seem to get the best dates and keep their place in the pyramid of popularity. Worse, the world is filled with poverty. Innocent children get sick and die. But the "life isn't fair" lament doesn't hold up when we give or receive compassion. Also we seem to know instinctively that those who suffer in this life will be rewarded in the next.

SCRIPTURE IN THE LIFE OF THE CHURCH

Scripture now has a much more accessible role in the life of the Church than it did just a hundred years ago. At that time, Scripture read at Mass was all read in Latin. It was rare for a course specifically devoted to the study of the Scriptures to be offered in either Catholic high schools or colleges. When the Scriptures were covered, students usually read only summaries of the stories and did not read directly from the Bible. Catholic biblical scholarship—for example, studying the literary forms of the Scriptures—was also relatively limited prior to the 1900s.

The Second Vatican Council of the 1960s contributed greatly to the Church's renewed interest in the Scriptures. Prior to the Council, only a few selections of Old Testament and New Testament passages were read at Mass. Now the Church has a three-year cycle of Sunday readings and a two-year cycle of weekday readings. As a result, Catholics are able to hear a good selection of the Old Testament and samples from virtually all of the books of the New Testament at Mass over a three-year period. And now, all readings are read in the vernacular, the common language of the people.

Besides hearing the Scriptures read at Mass, the Church also encourages Catholics to study and pray with the Bible as part of a lifelong effort, always keeping in mind that the Sacred Scriptures along with Sacred Tradition form together the Word of God. As the Second Vatican Council's *Constitution on Divine Revelation* reminds us:

> Easy access to Sacred Scripture should be provided for all the Christian faithful. . . .

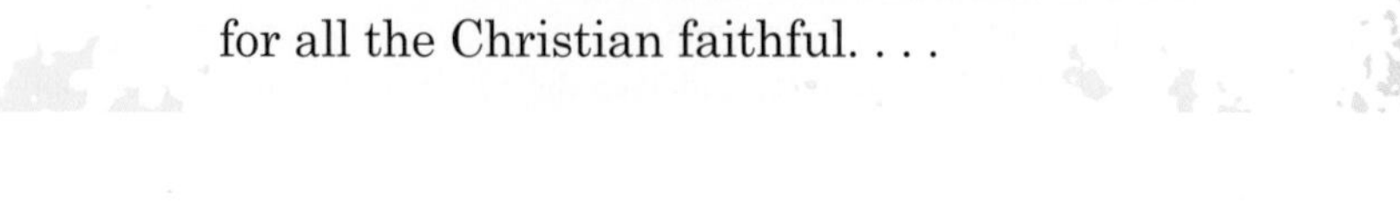

> This sacred Synod earnestly and specifically urges all the Christian faithful, especially religious, to learn by frequent reading of the divine Scriptures the "excelling knowledge of Jesus Christ." (Phil 3:8) "For ignorance of the Scriptures is ignorance of Christ." (St. Jerome)

In addition, the Bible is a great bridge for unity with other Christians who are separated from the Church. The healing words of Scripture can help heal the wounds of disunity.

The Bible in Liturgy

For most Catholics, Mass is their greatest exposure to the Scriptures. At each Mass there are two or three readings from the Scriptures—always one Gospel reading—as well as a Psalm response, a Gospel acclamation, a Communion antiphon, and several songs that are based on Scripture. The Scriptures are a vital part of the liturgy, for just as Christ is truly present in the person of the priest and especially in the consecrated species of bread and wine that are his Body and Blood, he is also present in the Scriptures. As the Second Vatican Council taught: "He is present in his word, since it is he himself who speaks when the holy Scriptures are read in Church" (*Constitution on the Sacred Liturgy*, 7).

Scripture readings for Mass are gathered in the Lectionary ("book of readings"). The Lectionary is organized around the cycle of the Church Year, which unfolds the whole mystery of Christ beginning with the Incarnation and the Nativity, with the primary focus being the **Paschal Mystery**—the Passion, Death, Resurrection, and **Ascension** of Jesus.

Paschal Mystery
The saving love of God most fully revealed in the life and especially the Passion, Death, Resurrection, and glorious Ascension of his Son, Jesus Christ.

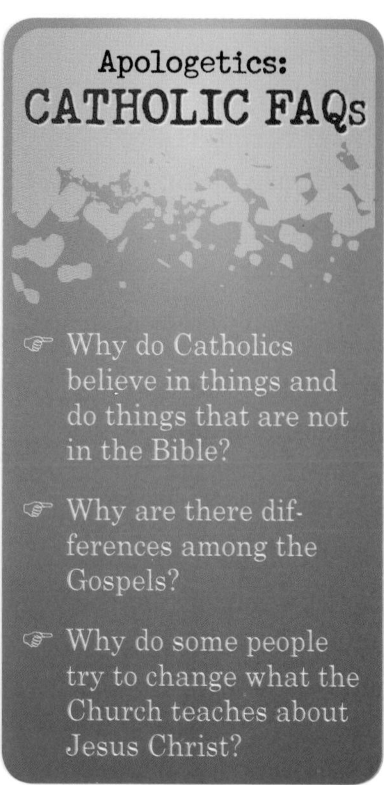

The texts of the readings are limited in length so people can listen attentively more easily. Gospel readings are sometimes longer because they contain parables and stories of Jesus that are more capable of holding a person's attention. One of the three Synoptic Gospels—Matthew (Year A), Mark (Year B), or Luke (Year C)—is read throughout a particular liturgical year. The Gospel of John is read during Lent, the Easter season, and in five Sundays of Year B to make up for the shortness of Mark's Gospel.

Prior to the Gospel, a first reading is read from the Old Testament. It is selected especially to relate to the theme of the day's Gospel and often foreshadows something that will occur in the Gospel. For example, for Year B, the Ninth Sunday of the Year, the first reading from Deuteronomy 5:12–15 is the Lord's command to keep the Sabbath day holy. The Gospel for that day, from Mark 2:23–28, details the Pharisees' question to Jesus about why his disciples disregarded some of the Sabbath laws. (Jesus explained, "The Sabbath was made for man, not man for the Sabbath.")

A Psalm response follows the first reading. On Sundays and holy days, a selection from one of the New Testament letters is read. This reading does not usually have a thematic connection to the first reading or the Gospel. During the homily, the bishop, the priest, or the deacon explains the meaning of the Scripture readings. His primary focus is on the main theme from the first reading and the Gospel and how it applies to our lives. He may also touch briefly on the teaching found in the second reading.

Studying the Bible

The Church exhorts all Christians to study the Bible faithfully. Again, since the Second Vatican Council, there are many more organized efforts to help Catholics do that. For example, for Catholics your age, Catholic high schools typically offer courses in Scripture. Second, even though your study may be personalized, you join your study with the teachings of the universal Church, especially through the teaching authority of the **Magisterium**. This can be done by consulting with many sanctioned biblical handbooks or study editions of the Bible as you read a specific book or passage.

As to the question of what biblical passage to begin with, there are really no "right" answers. Some people have attempted to read the Bible from cover to cover—usually without much success. Others who delve more deeply into the readings may study both the Old Testament and the New Testament in separate one-semester courses. Likewise, youth ministry and parish religious education programs offer Bible study for teens and adults alike.

> **Magisterium**
> The official teaching office of the Church. The Lord bestowed the right and the power to teach in his name to Peter and the other Apostles and their successors. The Magisterium is the bishops in communion with the successor of Peter, the Bishop of Rome (Pope).

You are also encouraged to do individual Bible study. This can be a daunting assignment because of the size of the Bible, the number of books, and the perceived difficulty in deciphering material that is thousands of years old. You may have considered studying the Bible on your own only to be turned back by not being able to answer the question, "Where do I begin?"

Here are two hints for getting started: First, remember that the Bible is different from any other book in the world. It is the inspired Word of God. You may choose to read specific Bible readings for a particular Sunday liturgy. Or you may begin by focusing on one part of the Bible, for example, the Gospels. You may wish to use the following strategy:

1. *Choose a passage.* Let's say you've chosen the parable of the Good Samaritan from Luke 10:29–37.
2. *Read the passage all the way through, paying special attention to the people and the setting.* In the parable of the Good Samaritan, the setting is a steep road, and the characters are the man victimized by robbers and those who pass his way, including the Samaritan.
3. *Read the passage again, this time writing down any questions you have about the passage or anything else that drew your attention.* Example: "Who are priests and Levites?" or "Why is it so surprising that the Samaritan helped the man?"
4. *Seek answers to your questions as well as more background on the passage from biblical commentaries either within or separate from your Bible.* Example: Priests and Levites are representatives of Jewish leadership and would have been expected to come to the aid of the man. Samaritans and Jews were enemies going back to the time of the Babylonian Exile. (This step helps you keep your study connected to the larger teaching Tradition of the universal Church.)

5. *Pray over the passage.* Listen for a special message God is giving you regarding this passage.

Step Five reminds us of the most important way to use the Bible—as a book of prayer.

Praying with the Bible

You can't treat the Bible like your favorite novel or simply as a school textbook. The Bible is primarily a book of prayer. As St. Ambrose put it, "We speak to God when we pray; we hear God when we read the divine sayings." The Bible's central importance in the liturgy and the sacraments reinforces its place as a book of prayer. But Catholics must also use the Bible for personal prayer. As God truly speaks through the words of Scripture, reading and praying these words allows us a very intimate way of communicating with God.

You can pray with the Bible on your own in many ways. One common form of prayer is called by its Latin name, ***lectio divina***, which literally means "divine reading." You can also think of *lectio divina* as "prayerful reading." To pray this way with the Bible, choose a passage. Your choice may be from the Gospel reading of the day or a nearby Sunday, another familiar passage, or chosen through a random paging through the Scriptures. (St. Augustine once randomly opened the pages of the Bible to a passage from Romans 13:12, where he read it was time to "throw off the works of darkness and put on the armor of light." This was the catapult for Augustine to reform his own life and seek Baptism.)

Call on the Holy Spirit to be with you when you pray with the Bible. Read through the passage slowly. Don't rush through in an effort to see what comes next. Let each verse speak to you. If you do hear God speaking in your heart, pause and listen to the message. Take more time to mull over what the Scriptures and the message may mean for you. Use the reading as a springboard for further prayer.

Other tips for praying with the Scriptures:

- Choose a quiet place for prayer. This may simply mean throwing a soft pillow in the corner of your room or finding a peaceful place under a backyard tree.
- Reserve a regular time each day (or week) to pray with the Bible. Try to keep to your schedule.
- Don't always expect to feel inspired or that God has directly spoken to you. Occasions of spiritual dryness are to be expected, learned from, and eventually cherished along with the "high" moments.
- Always conclude with a prayer in your own words, sharing with God your gratefulness for your time spent together.

REVIEW

1. How did the Second Vatican Council contribute to the Church's renewed interest in the Scriptures?
2. How are the Scriptures a vital part of the Church's liturgy?
3. What is the Lectionary? How is it organized?
4. Define *lectio divina.*

WRITE OR DISCUSS

- Choose a passage from the Bible for personal reading. Follow the strategy outlined on page 52. When you have completed the assignment, share one insight you gleaned from the passage.

IMAGES OF CHRIST

Icons have been described as "windows into Heaven" where God can reach out and touch us on earth. In Greek, *icon* means "image." Praying before an icon puts us in the presence of the holy person and helps us enter the mystery that is being portrayed.

Look at these icons and images of Christ. Also, do an Internet search for "icons of Christ." Reflect on a favorite icon in more detail. Write a prayer to Jesus based on your reflection.

Use any form of art media to create your own "icon" or image for Christ. Plan to keep your icon for future reflection.

Christ the Pantocrator

Christ the Good Shepherd

Christ of the Oppressed

Jesus of the People

GETTING TO KNOW JESUS

What was Jesus really like? Read these Gospel passages to find out more about Jesus. Write your answers to these questions:

- Did Jesus have a best friend? (See Matthew 17:1–2.)
- Did Jesus have women friends? (See Luke 8:1–3.)
- Did Jesus ever get in trouble? (See John 2:13–17.)
- Did Jesus have any fun? (See John 2:1–2.)
- Was Jesus ever confused or depressed? (See Mark 14:32–35.)
- Did Jesus ever get bothered by his friends? (See Mark 10:13–14.)
- Did Jesus ever have disagreements with his parents? (See John 2:15.)
- Did Jesus hang out with the "in" crowd? (See Matthew 9:9–13.)
- Did Jesus get along with everybody? (See Matthew 22:15–22.)
- Did Jesus ever get stressed out? (See Mark 3:7–12.)

What did you find most surprising about Jesus from this exercise?

PRAYER

Thank you, Lord Jesus Christ,
For all the benefits and blessings which you have given me,
For all the pains and insults you have borne for me.
Merciful Friend, Brother and Redeemer,
May I know you more clearly,
Love you more dearly,
And follow you more nearly,
Day by day.

—St. Richard of Chichester

2
Who Is Jesus?

ALL BECAUSE OF JESUS

> I believe in Jesus Christ, his only Son, our Lord.
> He was conceived by the power of the Holy Spirit
> and born of the Virgin Mary.

If you are Catholic, you have probably pledged your belief in Jesus Christ countless times using the words above from the Apostles' Creed. Jesus himself told his disciples: "Do not let your hearts be troubled. You have faith in God; have faith also in me" (Jn 14:1). As pointed out in Chapter 1, most people maintain a belief in God. Christians believe in Jesus Christ because he is himself God.

Interestingly, if you surveyed a group of Christians and asked, "Who is Jesus?" you might not find out for certain what country Jesus was born in, the exact age at which he died, or the number of sermons he preached. But you could hear from believers how Jesus has changed their lives. You might hear from an alcoholic who no longer drinks or a person who was once promiscuous but now is committed to remaining pure. People plagued by fits of anger or saddled with depression might now proclaim themselves free from these ailments. All because of Jesus.

In this book you will learn a lot of information about Jesus—including where he was born and raised. You will also encounter his teachings and miracles and his Death and Resurrection. You will study what the Church believes about Jesus, the sacraments he left us, and the ways he expects us to live. Knowledge about Jesus is essential for formation of an informed and deep faith in him.

Yet knowledge about Jesus is never enough. A transforming relationship with Jesus is one of friendship and love. This type of experience is initiated by Jesus himself through his grace and fulfilled by you through discipleship. This chapter will look at what

Catholics believe about Jesus. It will also address some of what we are called to when we say, "I believe in Jesus Christ."

WRITE OR DISCUSS

- How is learning *about* Jesus different from really knowing Jesus?

"I BELIEVE IN JESUS CHRIST, HIS ONLY SON, OUR LORD"

The Good News was shared early in the morning on the first Christmas. An angel of the Lord preached the Gospel to shepherds camping in the fields near Bethlehem, a small village just south of Jerusalem. The message was essentially this:

> A baby was born nearby to a Jewish mother.
> This baby came from God.
> He descended from Heaven.
> He is the eternal Son of God made man.
> His name is Jesus.

The birth of Jesus was the wonderful end to the Old Testament. His birth fulfilled the prophecy made to Abraham and his descendants. As the Letter of Paul to the Galatians recounted:

> But when the fullness of time had come, God sent his Son, born of a woman, born under the law, to ransom those under the law, so that we might receive adoption. (Gal 4:4)

Jesus is the absolute, final, and fullest Revelation of God. The invisible God, from the fullness of his love, became a human being and invites us to know him, love him, and befriend him. These were the angel's words: "For today in the city of David a savior has been born for you who is Messiah and Lord" (Lk 2:11). How you respond to that angelic announcement defines your faith. While we can believe in this Good News only through the help of God's grace, having faith remains an authentically human act. When we come to believe in Christ, we cooperate with the grace of the Holy Spirit, who reveals to us who Jesus is.

The titles and names for Jesus confessed in the Apostles' Creed provide answers to his identity and help us answer the questions of who he is and why we should believe.

Titles of Jesus

In Hebrew, the name *Jesus* means "God saves." Jesus' name is also his mission. Jesus saves all of humanity from sin. This task was expressed even before his birth. The angel Gabriel told Joseph that Mary "will bear a son and you are to name him Jesus, because he will save his people from their sins" (Mt 1:21).

The **Redemption** of the entire human race—for all times and all places—was the work of Jesus. Only God can save people from sins. The name *Jesus* shows that God's name is present in his Son. The Acts of the Apostles reports of the name *Jesus*, "There is no salvation through anyone else, nor is there any other name under heaven given to the human race by which we are to be saved" (Acts 4:12).

Christ is not Jesus' family name. The word *Christ* is the Greek translation of the Hebrew *Messiah*, which means "anointed." Jesus could be called "the Christ" only because he perfectly accomplished what he had come for.

And what was it he came for?

Peter, Jesus' chosen disciple, correctly understood that Jesus was the Messiah (see, for example, Mark 8:29). But Peter's understanding of what the Messiah stood for and accomplished was different from Jesus' understanding. Perhaps Peter felt that God's anointed one would be a powerful earthly king who would remove the Romans from power and restore Israel as the ruling people of the time. Jesus told Peter and the others who were gathered that it wasn't to be like that. Instead, the Messiah would suffer, be rejected, be killed, and then rise after three days. As Jesus put it, "For the Son of Man did not come to be served but to serve and to give his life as a ransom for many" (Mk 10:45).

Redemption
A word that literally means "ransom." Jesus' Death is ransom that defeated the powers of evil.

Jesus is also called the "Son of God." Depending on how this title was used, those who said it did not necessarily mean that Jesus was more than human. In the Old Testament, "son of God" was used as a title for angels, kings, and others among the Israelites who had a particularly intimate relationship with God. However, the title takes on new meaning at certain times in the New Testament. For example, there are two times—at Jesus' baptism and his **Transfiguration**—when a voice from Heaven is heard to say, "This is my beloved Son" (see Matthew

The Transfiguration

3:17; 17:5). In Matthew's Gospel, when Peter confesses Jesus' identity, he says to Jesus: "You are the Messiah, the Son of the living God" (Mt 16:16). Jesus calls Peter blessed because "flesh and blood has not revealed this to you, but my heavenly Father" (Mt 16:17). Through his teachings and his actions, Jesus revealed himself to be the only Son of God.

The title *Lord*—used often to address Jesus—also has various meanings. For example, a king or a ruler could be addressed as "Lord." However, as with "Son of God," the title *Lord* means something more regarding Jesus. In the Greek translation of the Old Testament, the Hebrew name for God, YHWH, is translated as *Kyrios*, "Lord." From that point on, the use of *Lord* indicates divinity. From the time of the early Church on, to address Jesus as "Lord" implies that all power, honor, and glory due God are also due Jesus.

REVIEW

1. Why is having faith essentially a human act?
2. Explain the meaning of the names and the titles for Jesus: Christ, Son of God, Lord, and Jesus.

WRITE OR DISCUSS

- Which of the titles of Jesus connects you most to him in a personal relationship? Explain.

FAITH IN JESUS CHRIST

Faith is the human response to God's Revelation, that is, God's free gift of self-communication. A gift of the Holy Spirit, faith enables us to commit ourselves to God totally, both our intellects and our wills.

The gift of **faith** makes it possible to recognize and accept Jesus Christ as the Son of God, the Messiah, and our Lord. Because of faith we can believe in God's Revelation, the fullness of which is found in Jesus.

Having faith is not primarily an individual act. Rather, the faith of the Church comes before the faith of the individual. The faith of the Church results in religion (from a Latin word meaning "to tie fast"). Religion ties us into a relationship with God. The Catholic religion extends God's invitation to believe in, accept, and dedicate our lives to Christ. At Baptism, Catholics become members of the Church, which is a community of the faithful who believe that Jesus is Lord.

faith
One of the theological virtues. Faith is an acknowledgment of and an allegiance to God.

The faith of the Church gives life to, supports, and nourishes the faith of the individual Christian. When we cooperate with faith, we are on the path to eternal life through Jesus Christ. If we ignore faith, we are subject to God's disapproval: "Whoever believes in the Son has eternal life, but whoever disobeys the Son will not see life, but the wrath of God remains upon him" (Jn 3:36).

True God and True Man

One of the most significant questions of faith the early Church had to answer about Jesus' identity was this: Is Jesus Christ God? In answering the question, the Church also needed to explain that Jesus was also human. The question is still one of the first and most pressing today as people come to know and believe in Jesus.

The New Testament authors only moderately addressed the question. The Gospel of John—the final Gospel written—most clearly addresses the divinity of Jesus. John's Gospel focuses on seven "signs" of Jesus, beginning with the changing of water into wine at the wedding in Cana. *Sign* is an important choice of words for John. These events are viewed as more than miracles or displays of power, but evidence that Jesus is the Great Sign of God the Father. John's Gospel puts more emphasis on Jesus' divinity by showing him always in command of the various situations he faced. This focus on Jesus' divinity is present from the very opening of the Gospel:

> In the beginning was the Word,
>   and the Word was with God,
>   and the Word was God.
> He was in the beginning with God.
> All things came to be through him,
>   and without him nothing came to be.
> (Jn 1:1–3)

This passage refers to Jesus as the ever-present Word of God (*Logos* in Greek) who was always one with the Father before the beginning of time.

After the apostolic era, the Church looked more deeply at the question "Is Jesus Christ God?" along with the accompanying question "Is Jesus true man?"

The answers to these questions developed mainly in response to several *heresies*, that is, false beliefs about Jesus' identity. The earliest heresies denied that Jesus was human.

They said that Jesus only took the *appearance* of a man. The Christian faith has always insisted on the true Incarnation of Jesus—that God took on human flesh.

An early bishop in the Church, Arius, taught that Jesus was *not* truly God. He said Jesus "came to be from things that were not" and was "from another substance" than God the Father.

The Church answered these false teachings in several early gatherings or councils of bishops and Church leaders. After the first of these councils, at Nicaea in 325, a Creed was composed called the Nicene Creed. This is the Creed we recite at Sunday Mass. Many of the teachings about Jesus' divinity and humanity are answered in the statements of the Nicene Creed:

Jesus is eternally begotten of the Father. The Council of Nicaea confessed that Jesus is "begotten, not made, of the same substance as the Father." The meaning of the word *begotten* is different from the meaning of the word *created.* The Son always existed in relationship to the Father. God the Father did not make or create the Son in the same way human fathers help create their children.

Jesus is God from God, Light from Light, true God from true God. Jesus is truly God. Just as the light that comes from a source is the same light that it produces, Jesus is truly God as he comes from the Father and is "one in Being with the Father."

Through Jesus all things were made. Since the Son was present from the Father from the beginning, he shared in the Father's creative action.

There were likewise many debates about the humanity of Jesus. How could the all-powerful God take human form? But that is exactly what needed to happen so God could save the world from sin. Years and years of sacrifice by the Jewish People—including prayer, fasting, and Temple sacrifice of animals—were not enough to bring salvation. As the Letter to the Hebrews points out, "It is impossible that the blood of bulls and goats take away sins" (Heb 10:4). Continuing, Hebrews quotes Jesus praying the words of the Psalms:

> Sacrifice and offering you did not desire,
> but a body you prepared for me;
> holocausts and sin offerings you took no delight in.
> (Heb 10:5–6)

By becoming fully human, God united himself to us. Unlike the early heresies that supposed that Jesus only "appeared" to be human, the Church believes that Jesus is truly human—in body, mind, and soul.

A Jewish sin offering could not bring salvation.

As both true God and true man, Christ had two intellects and wills, divine and human, which cooperated with one another. As a human, Jesus was like us in all things but sin. In his humanity, Jesus modeled what it is to be a person. While the human will and intellect of Jesus developed in completely human ways, they never lost touch with his divine will and the mission the Son of God came to accomplish.

REVIEW

1. Define *faith*.
2. How does faith result in religion?
3. How did John's Gospel emphasize Jesus' divinity?
4. How does the Nicene Creed answer questions about Jesus' humanity and divinity?

WRITE OR DISCUSS

- Which do you have a more difficult time believing and accepting: Jesus' humanity or Jesus' divinity? Explain.

Growth of the Kingdom

"The kingdom of heaven is like yeast that a woman took and mixed with three measure of wheat flour until the whole batch was leavened" (Mt 13:33).

Three measures of flour is a tremendous amount, making enough bread to feed a hundred people. The dough rises mysteriously when baked. Similarly, God is at work miraculously bringing invisible growth to the Kingdom.

Besides the parable of the mustard seed (Mt 13:31–32; Lk 13:18–19), which Jesus told to explain the growth of the Kingdom of God (or Kingdom of Heaven), he used other parables to explain what the Kingdom would be like.

The utmost precious

"The kingdom of heaven is like a merchant searching for fine pearls. When he finds a pearl of great price, he goes and sells all he has and buys it" (Mt 13: 45–46).

God's Kingdom is of such supreme value that we must give up whatever it takes to obtain it.

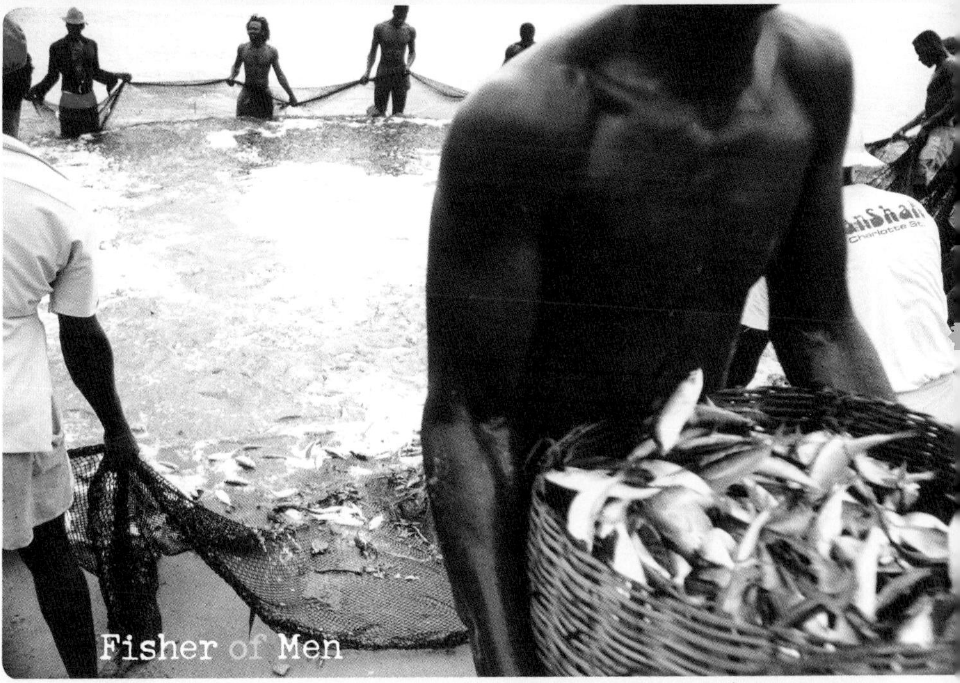

Fisher of Men

"Again the kingdom of heaven is like a net thrown into the sea, which collects fish of every kind. When it is full they haul it ashore and sit down to put what is good into buckets. What is bad they throw away" (Mt 13:47–48).

It is not clear in this world who has chosen membership in God's Kingdom. However, at the end of time, God will separate the wicked from the righteous.

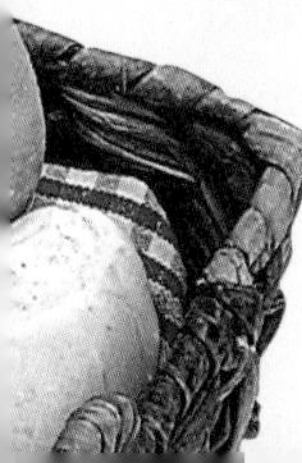

LIFE OF CHRIST

The entire Bible is a testimony to the life and the meaning of Jesus. The ***Catechism of the Catholic Church*** teaches that Christ is "the unique word of Sacred Scripture" because the Scriptures are the wisdom of God revealed to us in human words and language, and the Scriptures reveal the life of Christ, the Second Person of the Holy Trinity, who became man and like us in all things but sin.

The Gospels particularly take up Jesus' public ministry—his teaching, his miracles, and his Passion, Death, and Resurrection. The Gospels are expressions of faith, inspired by God and written by believers who accepted that Jesus Christ is Lord and Savior. Yet it is also important for all Christians and those who seek to deepen their faith in Christ to realize that impartial observers and even enemies of Christ recorded evidence of his existence. These records are useful to you whenever you confront nonbelievers or skeptics today who fuel their own doubts by questioning if Jesus even existed.

For example, four Roman authors and historians of Jesus' era—Josephus, Suetonius, Pliny the Younger, and Tacitus—wrote about Jesus and his followers.

Flavius Josephus was a Jew who was also a Roman citizen. In his *Antiquities of the Jews*, written in AD 93, Josephus mentions Jesus twice.

Suetonius was a biographer of the second century who compiled the life stories of twelve Roman

Apologetics:
CATHOLIC FAQs

- Why did God become man?
- Why is there suffering if God is good?
- Did Jesus have brothers and sisters?

emperors from Julius Caesar onward. In his *Life of Claudius*, he used the term *Chrestus,* determined by scholars to be a term for Christ, when discussing the expulsion of Jews from Rome under the emperor Claudius:

> As the Jews were making constant disturbances at the instigation of Chrestus, he expelled them from Rome.[2]

Pliny the Younger, the Roman governor of Pontus and Bithynia, wrote to the emperor Trajan in 112 with questions about how to deal with Christians who worshiped "Christus" but refused to worship the emperor. Pliny's letter mentioned that the "superstition" of Christianity had spread so rapidly that the pagan temples had fallen into disuse. Those who sold sacrificial animals to the temples were in danger of going broke. Pliny also wrote that he had freed Christians who rejected Christ and who agreed to worship pagan gods but had put to death any who persisted in their belief about Jesus. Pliny also reported on how Christians met regularly for Eucharist "on a fixed day before dawn and sing responsively a hymn to Christ as to a god."[3]

Pliny the Younger

Tacitus was a Roman historian who wrote in 116 that Christians had existed in an "immense multitude" in Rome at the time of the Great Fire of AD 64. He also substantiated that Christ had been put to death in Judea by the "procurator Pontius Pilate."

Another reference to Jesus is in the Babylonian Talmud, a commentary on Jewish Law written in the third century.

> **Kingdom of God**
> The reign of God proclaimed by Jesus and begun in his life, Death, and Resurrection. It refers to the process of God's reconciling and renewing all things through his Son; to the fact of his will being done on earth as it is in Heaven.

A passage mentions a certain "Yeshu" (Jesus), who practiced magic and led Israel away from true Jewish worship. It also reports that this man had disciples and was "hanged on the eve of Passover."

These references of non-Christian writers to Jesus, while not statements of faith, are evidence that Jesus of Nazareth did live in Palestine in the first century. Joined with the faith testimony of the New Testament, these non-Christian "witnesses" provide support for Christian belief. All of Christ's life on earth—both the hidden years and the public years—are worthy of reflection and imitation.

Events in the Life of Jesus

Though the Creed speaks only of the beginning and the end of Jesus' earthly life, Pope John Paul II wrote that the "whole of Christ's life was a continual teaching." The Gospels tell more of Jesus' public ministry, from approximately the age of thirty to thirty-three. All the events of Jesus' life are part of the mystery of faith: his hidden life in his early years in Nazareth living with Mary and Joseph, as well as his public life, beginning with his baptism in the Jordan River and including his proclamation of the coming of the **Kingdom of God**. A summary of several of these important events follows.

The Incarnation

On the first Christmas, Jesus Christ was born of the Virgin Mary. *Incarnation* literally translates to "in the flesh." Only the Gospels of Matthew and Luke mention Jesus' birth. They both agree Jesus was born in Bethlehem, a village about six miles southwest of Jerusalem.

Bethlehem was the City of David, and the Jews believed that the Messiah would come from David's descendants and be born in Bethlehem. Jesse, David's father, made his home in Bethlehem. It was in Bethlehem that the prophet Samuel anointed David the king of Israel (see 1 Samuel 16:1–13).

Central to the Incarnation is Jesus' Mother, Mary. The announcement to Mary, or Annunciation, of the virginal conception of Jesus by the angel Gabriel is recorded in Luke's Gospel. The angel said to her: "Hail, favored one! The Lord is with you" (Lk 1:28). The **Virgin Birth** of Jesus adds to this profound statement of truth: Jesus is unlike any other person ever born. He is both divine and human.

To be "favored" by God and to be the Mother of the Savior! Mary was destined for that role from her very conception. The **dogma** of the **Immaculate Conception**, proclaimed by Pope Pius IX in 1854, is that Mary was "preserved immune from all stain of Original Sin" from the moment of her conception. In order for Mary to pronounce her complete assent to God's will to the announcement of her vocation to become the Mother of God, it was "necessary that she be wholly borne by God's grace" (*CCC*, 490).

dogma
A central truth of Revelation that Catholics are obliged to believe.

The birth of Jesus occurred in a miraculous way. The angel foretold to Mary that "the Holy Spirit will come upon you, and the power of the Most High will overshadow you" (Lk 1:35). At first, Joseph, who was engaged to Mary, was dismayed when he found out Mary was pregnant. Jewish Law would have allowed Joseph to legally separate from his engagement with Mary if she had sexual relations prior to marriage. Joseph decided to break the engagement and divorce Mary quietly. Before he could act, an angel appeared to Joseph in a dream and told him that Mary's Son "will save his people from their sins"

(Mt 1:21). When he awoke from his dream, Joseph was committed to take Mary as his wife, which he did.

Joseph's hometown was Nazareth. As the birth of Jesus approached, however, a Roman census was ordered throughout Judea. This required all Jews to return to their ancestral homes. The family of Joseph had to go to Bethlehem from Nazareth. And so it was that circumstances fell into place for the birth of Jesus in Bethlehem—the predicted birthplace of the promised Messiah.

Early Church Tradition held that Jesus was born in a cave and laid in a manger because there was no room for Mary and Joseph in the inn. Jesus' humble birth reminds us to also humble ourselves. The Incarnation reminds us we must make ourselves like little children and depend on God for all our needs.

Infancy of Jesus

Jesus was a common name in first-century Palestine. It was a late form of the Hebrew name Joshua (*Yehoshua*). This name was given to Jesus on the eighth day after his birth, the day of his circumcision. To distinguish Jesus in the Scriptures, he is referred to as:

- Jesus of Nazareth. People were sometimes identified by their hometowns.
- Jesus the Carpenter. People often took the name of their profession. The Gospel of Mark identifies Jesus as a carpenter before he began to preach (see Mark 6:3).
- Jesus, son of Joseph. In John 1:45, Philip said to Nathaniel, "We have found the one about whom Moses wrote in the law, and also the prophets, Jesus, son of Joseph, from Nazareth."

The Scriptures also tell of Jesus' circumcision on the eighth day after his birth. Jesus was Jewish. He was to be raised in a Jewish family. To be circumcised was to be incorporated into the Jewish faith. It was also a sign that he would submit himself to Jewish Law and worship the God of his ancestors. At the **Epiphany**, the foreign magi from the east came bearing gifts. The magi were probably astrologers from Persia, Babylon, or the Arabian deserts. They were Gentiles, or non-Jews. The inclusion of their visit in Matthew's Gospel foreshadowed the far-reaching benefits of the Incarnation: God's salvation was to be offered to people of all nations.

The Presentation of Jesus at the Temple

When he was forty days old, Jesus was presented in the Temple according to Jewish Law. These religious rituals concerned Mary's purification along with the presentation of Jesus. According to Jewish Law, a mother became ritually unclean for seven days after the birth of a son. She was to remain separated from all religious ceremonies for forty days. At the end of this period, she underwent a rite of purification.

This rite roughly coincided with the presentation of Jesus in the Temple, a ritual prescribed by the Jewish rite of redemption. According to the Law, every firstborn male was consecrated to God in thanksgiving for the sparing of the Israelites' firstborn children at the time of the Exodus. Mary and Joseph sacrificed a pair of turtledoves to praise God for his goodness in sending them a Son.

Also at the Temple, Simeon and Anna recognized Jesus not only as the long-awaited Messiah but also as one who would bring sorrow to his Mother. Simeon and Anna were the very first people to herald the significance of Jesus' birth, and they did so at the very center of Jewish worship—the Temple in Jerusalem.

It was at the time that King Herod ordered the execution of infant boys that Joseph fled with his family to Egypt. After Herod died, they returned to Judea. This event recalls the emergence of Moses in Egypt and the Exodus of the Israelites into the freedom of the Sinai desert.

The Hidden Life of Jesus

The majority of Jesus' life was spent without fanfare. From the time of Jesus' infancy until the beginning of his public ministry at about the age of thirty, little is known about Jesus. Rather, he lived a life of obedience to his parents, performed manual labor, and studied Jewish teaching and the Law. He "advanced in wisdom and age and favor before God and man" (Lk 2:52). The only event from those years mentioned in the Gospels is the finding of Jesus in the Temple by his parents. Jesus answered his worried parents by saying, "Did you not know that I must be in my Father's house?" (Lk 2:49).

What was Jesus' "hidden life" like? It was probably in many ways similar to that of other children being raised in his time and place. Families of Nazareth typically lived in one-room dwellings, perhaps partly a cave. Jesus would have slept on the floor on a mat, covering himself with a tunic or a cloak. His diet would have consisted of wheat or barley bread, fruits, milk, eggs, and, on special occasions, meat.

Jesus spoke Aramaic, the language that had been adopted during Persian rule centuries before. Aramaic words such as *Golgotha* and *mammon* and expressions such as ***Abba*** and

Talitha, koum ("Little girl, I say to you, arise!" Mk 5:41) appear in the Gospels.

Jesus undoubtedly helped Joseph with his occupation as a carpenter. Ordinary work would have included repairing yokes for plow animals as well as crafting tables, lampstands, and couches.

We know more about this "hidden life" because Jesus was part of a devoutly religious Jewish family. First, Jesus would have obeyed his Mother and foster father because obedience to the Fourth Commandment would have fulfilled his Father's will for him in his early years. Besides instruction in his Jewish faith from his parents, Jesus also studied in the local synagogue, a place of worship and assembly. Synagogues also served as local schools, and Jesus would have learned Hebrew and studied the Scriptures at a synagogue near his home.

The finding of Jesus in the Temple breaks the silence of the hidden years of Jesus' life. Jesus was obviously an excellent student of the Scriptures to be in a discussion with the learned and older Jewish teachers. "Did you not know that I must be in my Father's house?" indicates Jesus' total dedication to his heavenly mission. Mary "kept all these things in her heart" (Lk 2:51) regarding the hidden years. Like the vast majority of people who have ever lived, Jesus spent these years doing ordinary things with his family—without a hint of his greatness.

Apologetics:
CATHOLIC FAQs

- Does God want us to be happy?
- How do we know that what the Catholic Church teaches came from God?
- Why is Mary the Mother of God?

The Baptism of Jesus

The public ministry of Jesus began with his being baptized by John in the Jordan River. John, a relative of Jesus, wore a garment of camel's hair and a leather belt. John ate grasshoppers and wild honey. This dress and behavior are reminiscent of Old Testament prophets, especially Elijah. John the Baptist served as the bridge between the Old Covenant and the New.

The Jordan River

John offered a baptism of repentance. Those who were baptized by him gave a public statement of their willingness to repent and change their lives and to live more like their ancient ancestors. A crowd of tax collectors and soldiers, Pharisees and Sadducees came to be baptized by John. When Jesus appeared and asked to be baptized, John hesitated, stating, "I need to be baptized by you, and yet you are coming to me?" (Mt 3:14). Jesus insisted and was baptized. Then the Holy Spirit, in the form of a dove, appeared and proclaimed from Heaven, "This is my beloved Son" (Mt 3:17).

Jesus did not need to be baptized. He had no sins to be forgiven. He did not need to repent and convert his life. But his baptism revealed who Jesus was and what his mission would be. It punctuated the fact that Jesus' life and ministry were to be to accomplish his Father's work of salvation, a work that would be empowered by the Holy Spirit.

From the beginning of his ministry, Jesus associated with sinners and was the "Lamb of God who takes away the sins of the world" (Jn 1:29). His baptism was a sign for us to do the same. To be baptized in Christ is to share not only his Passion and Death, but also his Resurrection. We, too, enter the water of the Sacrament of Baptism with Jesus in order to rise with him, to be reborn in water and Spirit, and to "live in newness of life" (Rom 6:4).

Temptations of Jesus

The Gospels tell us that Jesus spent a time of solitude in the desert immediately after his baptism. Jesus remained in the desert for forty days without eating. He lived among wild beasts, and the angels ministered to him. He was also tempted by Satan three times. Unlike Adam, who had given in to the attacks of Satan, Jesus rebuffed them. The faithfulness of Jesus over forty days also contrasts with the complaints and the infidelity to God shown by the Israelites during their forty years of wandering in the desert after the Exodus.

The temptations of Jesus helped him identify with humanity. Though he was tempted like us in every way, he never sinned. Temptations force us to respond, showing what we will do in a particular situation. Nevertheless, it is not wise to seek out temptation. In fact, in the Lord's Prayer, Jesus taught us to pray that we not be led to "the test" or "temptation." During his Agony in the Garden the night before he died, Jesus admonished Peter and the other disciples for not being able to stay awake. He told them: "Watch and pray that you may not undergo the test. The spirit is willing but the flesh is weak" (Mk 14:38).

The temptations Jesus faced in the desert helped define his mission. His test set the course for his mission of salvation. He was not taking the easy way out. The victory Jesus won over Satan in the desert anticipated his ultimate victory at the Passion, his supreme act of obedience to God the Father.

Ushering in the Kingdom of God

"Kingdom of God" is a term with origins in the Old Testament. Jesus began his public ministry with these words: "This is the time of fulfillment. The kingdom of God is at hand. Repent, and believe in the gospel" (Mk 1:15). The "Kingdom of God" means the rule of God over all people. In the understanding of the Kingdom ushered in by Christ, it is established in stages, beginning with Jesus' public ministry and ending, finally, at the end of time when he comes again. Through powerful signs (miracles) worked by Jesus and his teachings, we know that:

- The Kingdom of God is for everyone.
- The Kingdom of God belongs to the poor and the lowly.
- Sinners are welcome in the Kingdom.
- Jesus' invitation to enter the Kingdom comes in the form of parables.
- The coming of God's Kingdom means the defeat of Satan.
- Certain authority—keys of the Kingdom—was given by Jesus to St. Peter, whom he made the visible foundation of the Church.

Jesus used parables to explain what the Kingdom of God is like. Parables are short stories with a moral lesson that feature commonly understood people and things. The moral lesson is usually told around a surprising ending. In one parable Jesus compared the Kingdom of God to the smallest of seeds: "It is like a mustard seed that a person took and planted in the garden. When it was fully grown, it became a large bush and 'the birds of the sky dwelt in its branches'" (Lk 13:19). The parable is meant to describe the future enormity of God's Kingdom, which begins deceptively small in the preaching and healing ministries of Jesus.

Matthew's Gospel contrasts the ease of children entering God's Kingdom with the difficulty of rich people who have many possessions (see Matthew 19:13–15, 23–24). In fact, Jesus said, "It is easier for a camel to pass through the eye of a needle than for one who is rich to enter the kingdom of God" (Mt 19:24). Another point Jesus made was that achievement of salvation is beyond human capabilities. Salvation and entrance into God's Kingdom depend solely on his grace.

The Miracles of Jesus

The Gospel accounts share that within Jesus' public ministry he performed many signs or wonders such as healings or controls of nature—actions that could be attributed only to God. These are called *miracles*. They are signs of God's Kingdom present in Jesus and his mission.

Four major types of miracles are in the Gospels:

- *Healing miracles.* For example, the healing of the blind (Mt 20:29–34; Mk 10:46–52; Lk 18:35–43) and the healing of the leper in Capernaum (Mt 8:2–4; Mk 1:40–45; Lk 5:12–14).
- *Nature miracles.* For example, the multiplication of loaves and fishes (Mt 14:13–21; Mk 6:30–44; Lk 9:10–17; Jn 6:1–13) and the calming of the storm (Mt 8:23–27; Mk 4:35–41; Lk 8:22–25).
- *Exorcisms.* For example, the cure of the demoniac (Mk 1:23–28; Lk 4:33–37) and the healing of the mute person (Mt 9:32–34; Lk 11:14–15).
- *Raisings from the dead.* For example, the raising of the widow's son (Lk 7:11–16) and the raising of Jairus's daughter (Mt 9:18–26; Mk 5:21–43; Lk 8:40–56).

Jesus healed the mother-in-law of Peter.

Miracle accounts recorded in the Gospels focus on something Jesus did. They follow a general pattern: There is a problem, Jesus solves the problem with a miraculous action, and the people react to the solution.

The miracles of Jesus revealed God's power. As the Creator of all, God is the ruler of nature. Jesus' miracles reveal his close relationship with the Father. His raisings from the dead show his power over physical death. The miracles also show Jesus' mastery over evil and Satan. Jesus combines his miraculous actions with the forgiveness of sins to show that, as God, he has the power to work miracles and forgive sins.

The miracles of Jesus are signs of the Kingdom of God. Sin, sickness, and death entered the world when Adam sinned. Jesus is the New Adam who inaugurates God's reign. When John the Baptist sent his followers to ask Jesus if he was indeed the promised Messiah, Jesus sent back the following answer:

> Go and tell John what you have seen and heard: the blind regain their sight, the lame walk, lepers are cleansed, the deaf hear, the dead are raised, the poor have the good news proclaimed to them. And blessed is the one who takes no offense at me. (Lk 7:22–23)

The Transfiguration of Jesus

The Transfiguration was a foretaste of the Kingdom and of Jesus' divine glory. It is also a contrast with the dire predictions about the horrible fate of Jesus—his arrest, suffering, and Death.

In Mark's Gospel, the first prediction of the Passion brings with it an argument between Jesus and Peter. Peter could not accept that Jesus must "suffer greatly and be rejected by the elders, the chief priests, and the scribes, and be killed" as well as "rise after three days" (Mk 8:31). Peter took Jesus aside and began to rebuke him. Then Jesus, looking at the other disciples, rebuked Peter and said, "Get behind me, Satan. You are thinking not as God does, but as human beings do" (Mk 8:33). Jesus then explained the true meaning of discipleship: It will be difficult and hard. A **disciple** must "deny himself, take up his cross" (Mk 8:34), and then follow Jesus.

While the prediction of the Passion and the instruction in discipleship were hard lessons to learn, the Transfiguration prefigured the Resurrection and the eternal Kingdom. The face and the clothing of Jesus appeared a dazzling white as he stood with Moses and Elijah from the Old Testament before witnesses Peter, James, and John. Peter was terrified at the sight; nevertheless he told Jesus, "Rabbi, it is good that we are here!" (Mk 9:5). Peter wanted to construct memorials to the event on the mountain where the Transfiguration took place. Instead, a cloud cast a shadow over them, and a voice said, "This is my beloved Son. Listen to him" (Mk 9:7). Suddenly the three disciples saw no one but Jesus with them.

The next series of events in the life of Jesus brought about our salvation—his Passion, Death, Resurrection, and Ascension to Heaven. This Paschal Mystery continues to be made present in the sacraments, especially the Eucharist. The events of our salvation will be covered in more depth in Chapter 3.

REVIEW

1. What is the purpose of the Gospels?
2. What other historical sources are evidence of Jesus' existence?
3. Define *Immaculate Conception.*
4. Why was Jesus born in Bethlehem?
5. Identify the magi, Simeon and Anna, and King Herod.
6. What event from Jesus' hidden life is covered in the Gospels?
7. Why did Jesus allow himself to be baptized?
8. Name the four types of miracle stories found in the Gospels.
9. What lesson about the meaning of messiahship did Jesus reveal at his Transfiguration?

WRITE OR DISCUSS

- Name a recent temptation you faced that tested your faith.
- Describe God's Kingdom in your own words.

JESUS REVEALS THE HOLY TRINITY

One of the most remarkable things about Jesus' life and public ministry is that he revealed to human beings more about the mystery of God than had ever been known before. Just prior to his arrest, Jesus prayed, "I revealed your name to those whom you gave me" (Jn 17:6).

The "name" referred to in this prayer is *Abba*, a common Aramaic word that means "daddy." That Jesus exclusively referred to God as "Daddy" or "Father" is significant. Many other words and titles from the Hebrew Scriptures could have been used (for example, Lord, Shepherd, Rock, etc.). As the word of this prayer communicates, Jesus came to earth to tell us about his Father. He came to tell us that the name of God is "Father." Church Father Tertullian reported it this way:

> The expression of God the Father had never been revealed to anyone. When Moses himself asked God who he was, he heard another name. The Father's name has been revealed to us in the Son, for the name "Son" implies the new name "Father."

What is God the Father like? Even in the Old Testament, where Yahweh is often depicted more in his power, the image of fatherhood to describe God is used several times; the compassion of Yahweh comes through. The Book of Hosea describes Yahweh's relationship with the people of Israel:

> I drew them with human cords,
> with bands of love;
> I fostered them like one
> who raises an infant to his cheeks. (Hos 11:4)

Yet Jesus not only names the intimate form of Father, "Abba," but also allows us to really know God as Father. Jesus said, "No one knows the Son except the Father, and no one knows the Father except the Son and anyone to whom the Son wishes to reveal him" (Mt 11:27). To help us know God in this way, Jesus spoke over and over of his Father. He called on his disciples to also address and know God as Abba. St. Paul wrote to the Romans:

> For those who are led by the Spirit of God are children of God. For you did not receive a spirit of slavery to fall back into fear, but you received a spirit of adoption, through which we cry, "Abba, Father!" (Rom 8:14–15)

What God the Father is like is perhaps best summed up by the parable Jesus told about the Prodigal Son (Lk 15:11–32). In this story, a father showed unconditional love for a son who had wasted his inheritance. Jesus told us that Abba's love for us is the same: He will never abandon us and will always rejoice in our returning to him.

Finally, Jesus told us to address God as Father in **prayer**. In doing so, we learn to depend on God's providence for us, that his will, not ours, would be done.

Jesus also revealed the third Divine Person, the Holy Spirit. Though he didn't reveal the Holy Spirit completely in his ministry, he alluded to the Spirit on several occasions. For example, he told the Samaritan woman at the well that "the hour is coming, and is now here, when true worshipers will worship the Father in Spirit and truth; and indeed the Father seeks such people to worship him. God is Spirit, and those who worship him must worship in Spirit" (Jn 4:23–24).

The Holy Trinity

It was not until the Last Supper that Jesus finally promised his disciples that he would send the Holy Spirit. "I will ask the Father, and he will give you another Advocate to be with you always, the Spirit of truth" (Jn 14:16–17). At Jesus' Death, he commended his Spirit into his Father's hands. After his Resurrection, he breathed on his disciples and said to them, "Receive the Holy Spirit. Whose sins you forgive are forgiven them, and whose sins you retain are retained" (Jn 20:22–23). From that time on, the mission of Jesus and the Holy Spirit became the mission of the Church.

Theology of the Holy Trinity

From these revelations and from others connected with Jesus and his teaching, the Church's understanding of three Persons in one God originated and grew. This central mystery of the Christian faith is known as the Holy Trinity.

The mystery of the Holy Trinity is difficult to understand and explain. Some of the Church's dogmas or beliefs about the Trinity can help. For example:

- *The Trinity is One.* The Trinity does not mean there are three Gods, but one God in three Persons. The three Persons do not share their divinity among themselves. Each one of them—Father, Son, and Holy Spirit—is God whole and entire. There are not three separate consciousnesses, intelligences, or wills in God. There is one God.
- *The three Persons are distinct from one another.* This means that the Father is not the Son, nor is the Son the Holy Spirit. Rather, the Father generates the Son, the Son is begotten of the Father, and the Holy Spirit proceeds from the Father and Son.
- *The divine Persons are intimately related to one another.* The three Persons are of one nature or substance. The Father is wholly in the Son and wholly in the Holy Spirit; the Son is wholly in the Father and wholly in the Holy Spirit; the Holy Spirit is wholly in the Father and wholly in the Son.

The theological Tradition also presents two basic ways of understanding the Trinity that are inseparable from one another.

The first explains the Trinity in terms of God alone and is based on how humans understand God's Revelation. This is known as the ***immanent Trinity***, that is, God's inner life considered in itself as the communion of Father, Son, and Holy Spirit.

This is a very difficult concept to grasp, suffice it to say that *Person* cannot be thought of in the way we imagine distinct human persons. There is only one God. When one Person of the Trinity acts, the other two Persons also act. Though the Persons—Father, Son, and Holy Spirit—are distinct, they do not act apart from each other.

In this understanding, the first Person of the Trinity is God the Source. In Greek, the name for source is *Arché*, which means "first." God is the first Source of all being, all knowledge, all love.

God the Source knows himself perfectly. When he speaks this perfect knowledge of himself, it is known as *Logos*, or the Divine Word. The Word of God is the second Person of the Trinity.

The first and second Persons of the Trinity communicate with one another in love. This love is "breathed out" between the two as a third Person, the Divine Spirit, or *Pneuma* in Greek. As our Creeds describe, the love *proceeds* from the Father and the Son.

These human attempts to understand how God understands himself are of course incomplete. Understanding God completely is an impossible task, except for what he reveals to us of himself. The Revelation of the immanent Trinity is known as the ***salvific Trinity*** or ***economic Trinity***. In this second understanding (which makes the first understanding possible), we focus on what God does, that is, how he acts in our lives and in the world. We begin with a knowledge of Jesus and our faith in him as the Son of God. He was sent by the Father to reveal the Father to us. Yet he and the Father are one. And after his earthly life was ended and he had returned to the Father, he fulfilled his promise by sending, in union with the Father, the Holy Spirit.

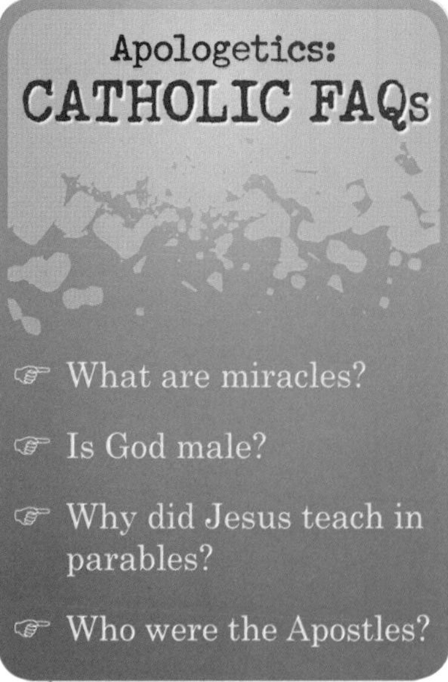

Apologetics:
CATHOLIC FAQs
☞ What are miracles?
☞ Is God male?
☞ Why did Jesus teach in parables?
☞ Who were the Apostles?

Thus it is that the work of our salvation reveals to us the Trinitarian nature of God. We know God by the way he has acted as Father, Son, and Holy Spirit. The ultimate work of the Trinity is to bring all of creation into unity with God in three Persons. As Jesus told his disciples, "Whoever loves me will keep my word, and my Father will love him, and we will come to him and make our dwelling with him" (Jn 14:23).

REVIEW

1. How was Jesus' name for God unique?
2. When did Jesus first promise to send the Holy Spirit?
3. Name and explain three Church beliefs about the Trinity.
4. Explain the difference between the immanent Trinity and the economic Trinity.

WRITE OR DISCUSS

- What does Jesus say can be our relationship with God the Father? How do you relate to God in this way?

RUN IT UP THE FLAGPOLE

"Let's stand for opening prayer."

If you attend a Catholic high school, these are among the first words you hear each day over four years. Or do you? Have you tuned out much of the instructions for morning prayer and the prayer itself? Have you made it a rote procedure, a mindless routine? Or do you use the time to pray for yourself, your friends, your family, and your school? Do you consciously take time to put yourself in the presence of the Lord when you pray with your classmates?

Do you pray *before* you arrive at school?

Ellen Franconelli, 15, of Los Osos, California, tells of praying with her dad every day in the car on the way to school. "We might not even be speaking to each other about anything else, but we do pray. He always says, 'Come, Lord Jesus. Be with us today. Keep us safe and help us to do our best.' We make the Sign of the Cross."

Jon Sobieski of Chicago rides the Red Line commuter train to school and plays downloaded music on his iPod. "Some of the songs I listen to remind me of very specific times I spent with my friends. Or the lyrics help me to connect how I am feeling. Sometimes I think about my whole life and God too on my ride."

It is illegal to pray in an organized way in public schools in the United States. However, in 1990 in Burleson, Texas, a local church youth group began a tradition of before-school prayer called "See You at the Pole." Since that time, this practice has caught on worldwide. Students from many faith traditions gather near their school's flagpole before the morning bell to pray. An annual day to kick off the tradition is now held on the fourth Wednesday of September. In a recent year, more than two million teens took part in See You at the Pole in the United States.

Dustin Law, a sixteen-year-old from Skyline High in Mesa, Arizona, participated in the event in 2006. "I put Christ as the center of my life," he said. "This is just another way to show the people at this school who Christ is."

Marissa Simmons, a seventeen-year-old senior at Mesa High School, said she is used to praying before meetings of her Catholic club. She participated in See You at the Pole, too. "I think it's appropriate that you live your religion in school too," she explained.

Students at Catholic high schools participate in the event, too, even though they can pray inside school. In Alton, Illinois, Marquette Catholic High School campus minister Paula Mattix-Wand said, "Even though we're a Catholic school, not all students are comfortable expressing their faith in public. It really does bring us together as a student body and faculty."

How do you begin your day—with prayer?

When and in what ways are you in touch with the Lord?

How comfortable are you to witness your faith in Christ with others?

For more information on See You at the Pole,
visit www.syatp.com.

GETTING TO KNOW JESUS

A reading from Luke 19:1–10:

> [Jesus] came to Jericho and intended to pass through the town. Now a man there named Zacchaeus, who was a chief tax collector and also a wealthy man, was seeking to see who Jesus was; but he could not see him because of the crowd, for he was short in stature. So he ran ahead and climbed a sycamore tree in order to see Jesus, who was about to pass that way. When he reached the place, Jesus looked up and said to him, "Zacchaeus, come down quickly, for today I must stay at your house." And he came down quickly and received him with joy. When they all saw this, they began to grumble, saying: "He has gone to stay at the house of a sinner." But Zacchaeus stood there and said to the Lord, "Behold, half of my possessions, Lord, I shall give to the poor, and if I have extorted anything from anyone I shall repay it four times over." And Jesus said to him, "Today salvation has come to this house because this man too is a descendant of Abraham. For the Son of Man has come to seek and to save what was lost."

Imagine that Jesus comes to your house, like he did to Zacchaeus's. He spends about a week with you, your family, and your friends. In your mind, walk through the events and the situations of a typical week. The presence of Jesus might cause you to see things about everyday places and people that you sometimes fail to see. Imagine what Jesus would be pleased to see happening in your family, among your friends, and at your school or workplace. Hear also what Jesus would say is displeasing to him.[4]

Jesus says: "I am pleased with . . ."	**Jesus says:** I am displeased with. . ."

YOUR FAMILY
because

YOUR FRIENDS
because

YOUR SCHOOL OR WORKPLACE
because

YOU
because

PRAYER

Memorare
Remember, O most gracious Virgin Mary, that never was it known that anyone who fled to your protection, implored your help, or sought your intercession was left unaided. Inspired by this confidence, I fly unto you, O Virgin of virgins, my Mother. To you I come, before you I stand, sinful and sorrowful. O Mother of the Word incarnate, despise not my petitions, but in your mercy hear and answer me. Amen.

3
Paschal Mystery: The Mission of Jesus Christ

LIVING GOSPEL

When Alexander Anthony of Indianapolis, Indiana, reached his thirteenth birthday, he registered for his first state identification card. He told his family he wished to have the sticker placed on the back of the card to further identify him as a willing organ donor.

Sadly, one early Monday evening in the fall of 2006, Alexander was shot in random gang fire as he walked up the street near his house. For the next few days, Alexander was kept on life support at a hospital. This was done to honor his wishes while doctors waited for someone who could benefit from his organs after he died.

His grandmother Mary said, "I loved that child. I would have died myself to save him."

Earlier in the same year, fifteen-year-old Sabrina Aguilar had died in a three-wheeler accident in Las Cruces, New Mexico. Her parents were devastated. Two months after Sabrina's death, her mother received a letter from a sixteen-year-old Texas girl, Lawerencia Keys. Lawerencia had received one of Sabrina's kidneys during a transplant. "I thank Sabrina. I got life through her," Lawerencia wrote.

Sabrina's father, Geraldo, said of her, "She touched so many lives when she was alive, and she's still doing it."

Despite their tragic deaths, Alexander and Sabrina each have legacies in the words of Pope John Paul II as "people of life and for life." The Pope addressed these words in his **encyclical** *The Gospel of Life.* He wrote:

> The *Gospel of life* is to be celebrated above all in *daily living,* which should be filled with self-giving love for others. . . .
>
> It is in this context, so humanly rich and filled with love, that *heroic actions* too are born. These are *the most solemn celebration of the Gospel of life,* for they proclaim it *by the total gift of self.* They are the radiant manifestation of the highest degree of love, which is to give one's life for the person loved (cf. Jn 15:13). They are a sharing in the mystery of the Cross, in which Jesus reveals the value of every person, and how life attains its fullness in the sincere gift of self. Over and above such outstanding moments, there is an everyday

> heroism, made up of gestures of sharing, big or small, which build up an authentic culture of life.
>
> A particularly praiseworthy example of such gestures is the donation of organs, performed in an ethically acceptable manner, with a view to offering a chance of health and even of life itself to the sick who sometimes have no other hope. (86)

In Hebrew, Jesus' name means "God saves." Like Alexander or Sabrina, Jesus literally saves the lives of those in great need. Through his Paschal Mystery—his Passion, Death, Resurrection, and Ascension to Heaven—Jesus saves us from our sins. He freely gave up his life that we might live. Similarly, working through people in every generation, Jesus continues to bring salvation. Jesus saves

> . . . the recovering alcoholic from ever having another drink.
>
> . . . the man with the violent temper from fits of rage directed at his family.
>
> . . . the teenage couple from giving in to sexual behavior outside of marriage.
>
> . . . the Internet addict from viewing pornography.
>
> . . . people engaged in every other sinful behavior imaginable.

"Jesus Saves" is a popular phrase written as graffiti under a bridge on the interstate or posted on a bright sign high above a downtown building. This chapter examines the fall of humankind and the consequences of sin while quickly tracing God's promise of salvation that was answered when the promise the angel made to Joseph regarding Mary came to be: "She will bear a son and you are to name him Jesus, because he will save his people from their sins" (Mt 1:21).

WRITE OR DISCUSS

- "Jesus Saves." What does this statement mean to you?

THE FALL AND THE CONSEQUENCES

You might have heard the lesson that "something good can come from something bad." Certainly, how we define *bad* can make a difference in how true this lesson is for us. For example, we often call weather "bad." Think of a thunderstorm that washes out a trip to the beach or a severe snowstorm that closes an interstate. However, what is "bad" for one may be "good" for another. That summer rain is good for the owner of an apple orchard; it helps sweeten the apples in time for early autumn. And that snow that closes the interstate is a blessing for a ski lodge needing snow. Skiers need snow, too! What is bad or unfortunate for some people may be both necessary and good for others.

If you were asked to think about the worst thing that ever occurred in human history, you might eventually settle on the fall of humankind through the first sin, or **Original Sin**. This event was certainly not what God had planned for our first parents, Adam and Eve. They were not only created good, but also enjoyed continual friendship with God. They lived in harmony with themselves and with creation around them. The Council of Trent described this as an original "state of holiness and justice."

Original Sin
The fallen state of human nature into which all generations of people are born. Christ Jesus came to save us from Original Sin.

The grace of **original holiness** was for human beings to share in God's life. Adam and Eve had been placed in paradise in friendship with God, with each other, and with the world around them. The gifts of **original justice** included immortality and the absence of suffering and pain.

Like Adam and Eve, we are created in God's image and in friendship with him. We can live in friendship with God only when we freely respond to him. This is God's plan for us. Our understanding of God's plan also helps us understand ***sin*** as "an abuse of the freedom" against God (*CCC*, 387). The reality and the consequences of Original Sin are an essential truth of our faith. Through this sin, the first human beings disobeyed God's command and chose to follow their own wills rather than God's will.

Through many centuries, God has revealed more and more of himself, a Revelation that culminated in the Death and Resurrection of Jesus Christ. Only in the light of Jesus can the meaning of Original Sin be fully understood. As the *Catechism* teaches, "We must know Christ as the source of grace in order to know Adam as the source of sin" (*CCC*, 388).

Behind the Original Sin lurks the temptation of a fallen angel called "Satan" or the "devil." The Church teaches that Satan and the other fallen angels were at first good angels, created by God. At one point, however, they rejected God "radically and irrevocably" (*CCC*, 392). The worst harm done by Satan was the deceptive seduction and temptation of Adam and Eve. Tempted by the devil, man "let his trust in his Creator die in his heart and, abusing his freedom, disobeyed God's command" (*CCC*, 397). In that sin, man preferred himself to God. St Maximus the Confessor wrote that man wanted to be "like God" but "without God, before God, and not in accordance with God."[5] The temptation and the resulting Original Sin are described in Genesis 3:1-11. The consequences of the sin were immediate. After Eve ate from the forbidden fruit and gave it to Adam to do the same,

> Then the eyes of both of them were opened, and they realized that they were naked; so they sewed fig leaves together and made loincloths for themselves. (Gn 3:7)

Adam and Eve then hid from God. When the Lord questioned Adam as to why he had eaten from the forbidden fruit, Adam blamed Eve. The woman, Adam said, "gave me fruit from the tree, so I ate it." God then asked Eve, "Why did you do such a thing?" She answered: "The serpent tricked me into it, so I ate it" (Gn 3:12–13).

The consequences of Original Sin affect us all. St. Paul wrote in the Letter to the Romans that "through one person sin entered the world, and through sin, death, and thus death came to all, inasmuch as all sinned" (Rom 5:12). How can one sin affect all of humanity? The Council of Trent explained that the whole human race is in Adam "as one body of one man." By this "unity of the human race" we all share in Adam's

Apologetics:

CATHOLIC FAQs

Use this chapter and other sources to formulate your own answers to these questions. Then check your answers at "Catholic FAQs" at www.avemariapress.com: Religious Education.

☞ How can Adam's sin affect me?

☞ Was Jesus Mary's Savior?

> **concupiscence**
> An inclination to commit sin. It can be found in human desires and appetites as a result of Original Sin.

sin, just as we all share in salvation through Christ. Because Adam's sin permanently wounded our human nature, it is transmitted to all generations—we are all born in this condition. Adam received original holiness and justice for himself and all of humanity. By his personal sin, all of human nature was then affected and took on a fallen state.

Like our first parents, we are subject to a certain domination by Satan. We are prone to ignorance, suffering, and death, and inclined to sin—a trait known as **concupiscence**. Life is complicated by and filled with the consequences of Original Sin and all of the personal sins of men and women. For all of us, there is a constant battle with Satan and evil. Thankfully, the sad reality of Original Sin is more than answered by the wonderful and glorious reality of Christ's Redemption.

"So Great a Redeemer!"

There has never been a better example of something good coming from something bad than what happened after the sin of Adam and Eve. From the worst catastrophe that has ever befallen humankind came the most glorious victory over sin and evil. And that good fortune can never be reversed. Even with the dire consequences of Original Sin—including the deprivation of original holiness and justice for all people—God did not abandon the human race. Rather, God immediately disclosed his plan for conquering evil and for restoring the goodness in all relationships, including relationships between human beings and God.

This first announcement of the Messiah and Redeemer is called the Protoevangelium. It describes a battle between the serpent and the woman, and the final victory of a descendant of hers. After speaking to Adam and Eve, God tells Satan what will happen next:

> I will put enmity between you and the woman,
> and between your offspring and hers;
> He will strike at your head,
> while you strike at his heel. (Gn 3:15)

The First Letter of John tells us, "The Son of God was revealed to destroy the works of the devil" (3:8). Thus the passage from Genesis 3:15 is understood as the first promise of a Redeemer for a fallen humankind. The woman is understood to be Mary, and her offspring is recognized as Jesus Christ.

The passage also helps us understand Jesus as the "New Adam" who was freely obedient to God even to his Death. The Death of Jesus on the cross won for us our Redemption; it was the needed atonement for our sins. Mary, the Mother of Jesus, was the first to benefit from his victory over sin. Mary was immaculately conceived without Original Sin and by God's special grace committed no sin of any kind while on earth.

You may have wondered many times why God simply did not prevent Adam from sinning. Wouldn't life for him and all of his descendants—including us—have been much easier? You need to recall that sometimes a greater good can come from a bad situation. This is the case here as well. As St. Thomas Aquinas offered:

> There is nothing to prevent human nature's being raised to something greater, even after sin; God permits evil in order to draw forth some greater good. Thus, St. Paul says: "Where sin increased, graced abounded all the more"; and the Exultet

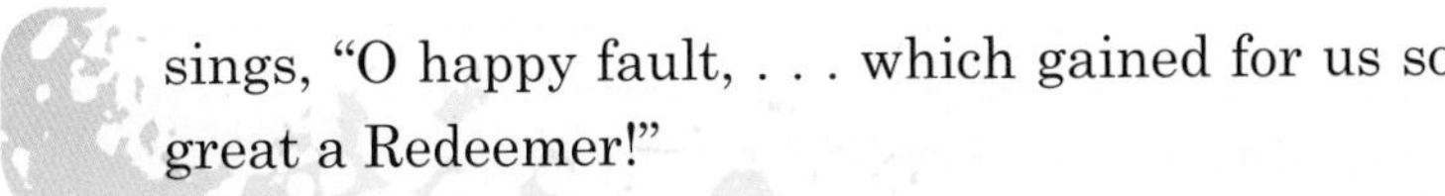

sings, "O happy fault, . . . which gained for us so great a Redeemer!"

Christ's sacrifice on the cross is the source of our salvation. As the Letter to the Romans describes, "For just as through the disobedience of one person the many were made sinners, so through the obedience of one the many will be made righteous" (5:19). In the Sacrament of Baptism, we die with Christ in order to live a new life.

While the Protoevangelium was immediate after the fall of man, its completion took place over several generations and included the formation of a holy nation, Israel, and covenant promises made to them and their leadership. This covenant made to our first parents eventually culminated in the birth of the Messiah.

REVIEW

1. What was the grace of original holiness?
2. What are the gifts of original justice?
3. Define *Original Sin.*
4. How can Original Sin be fully understood?
5. After the Original Sin, when did God promise to conquer evil and restore goodness?
6. How is Jesus the New Adam?

WRITE OR DISCUSS

- Name an occasion when you discovered good coming from bad.

Birthplace of Jesus

Bethlehem is the place where Jesus was born. It is located about six miles south of Jerusalem and has a population of 30,000 people. The photo is of the Church of the Nativity, built over the place believed to be the birthplace of Jesus.

The "Holy Land" refers to the historical and geographical region in modern Israel that has significant religious importance to three religions: Christianity, Judaism, and Islam.

For Christians the Holy Land is significant because this is where the birth, early life, ministry, Death, and Resurrection of Jesus occurred. Three important places are listed here.

Hometown of Jesus

Nazareth was the hometown of Jesus. It was where Mary grew up and the place of the Annunciation. It is located about fifteen miles from the Sea of Galilee.

Tomb of Jesus

Jerusalem was the setting of several of Jesus' important teachings, the Last Supper, his trial, Crucifixion, and Resurrection. The Church of the Holy Sepulchre is commemorated as the place that contains the tomb of Jesus.

TRACING SALVATION HISTORY

Perhaps the greatest disaster that ever befell the University of Notre Dame was the fire that destroyed its Main Building on April 23, 1879. The building contained classrooms, dormitories, offices, the library, and the dining hall. At the time, it was really the only building that made Notre Dame a college campus.

The fire devastated the students and faculty as well as the school's founder and first president, Father Edward Sorin, C.S.C. However, Father Sorin was a missionary from France who had traveled over two hundred miles through the Indiana wilderness to found the school in 1842. Fr. Sorin was not about to let the tragedy of the fire ruin the plans he had for Notre Dame.

In 1879, a fire destroyed the Main Building at Notre Dame.

When the fire was put out, Fr. Sorin called the students and the faculty to the church, where he stood on the altar steps and spoke to them: "I came here as a young man and dreamed of building a great university in honor of Our Lady," he said. "But I built it too small, and she had to burn it to the ground to make the point. So, tomorrow, as soon as the bricks cool, we will rebuild it, bigger and better than ever."

And that's what happened. Later that same day, Fr. Sorin, sixty-five years old at the time, grabbed a wheelbarrow full of bricks and moved to the site of the fire to start the rebuilding. When completed, the administration building included, for the first time, a statue of Mary placed high on a golden dome.

Fr. Sorin's resolve to immediately rebuild Notre Dame from the devastating effects of the fire reminds us of God's immediate promise to restore hope to the human race after the ruinous state of affairs produced by Original Sin. This was not an easy task because Original Sin is called "sin" only in an analogical sense: It is different from personal sin in that it passed on to us as part of a fallen human nature. Humans contract this sin without having personally offended God. But the effects of this evil had immediate and dire consequences on humankind. The Genesis story of Cain and Abel, the first descendants of Adam, shows how sin led to one brother's murdering the other (see Genesis 4:1–16). Out of jealousy, Cain killed Abel. As punishment, God banished him from the land and condemned him to a life of wandering. "The Lord put a mark on Cain, lest anyone should kill him at sight" (Gn 4:15). While the punishment was swift and just, the punishment did not mean abandonment by God. Rather, God desired to rebuild humanity part by part, step by step, and to do so immediately.

Genesis 6:5–9:29 tells of the Great Flood and God's desire to rid the world of human wickedness and depravity. After the Flood, God made a covenant with Noah that would stabilize nature. God blessed Noah and instructed him and his children to repopulate the earth. As in the

Apologetics:
CATHOLIC FAQs

- Who is responsible for the Death of Jesus?
- Why would God the Father allow his Son, Jesus, to suffer and die the way he did?
- Is believing in Jesus all I need to do to be saved?

creation of Adam, Noah was instructed to be fertile, multiply, be master of the animals, and subdue the earth. The Lord's part of the agreement was a promise to never destroy the earth again. A rainbow symbolized this agreement:

> I set my bow in the clouds to serve as a sign of the covenant between me and the earth. When I bring clouds over the earth, and the bow appears in the clouds, I will recall the covenant I have made between me and you and all living beings, so that the waters shall never again become a flood to destroy all mortal beings. (Gn 9:13–15)

This covenant prepared the world for the covenant with Abraham, which remained a living covenant until the coming of Christ.

God Calls Abraham

Abraham is known as the "father of faith," for not only Christianity and Judaism but also for Islam. Abram, as he was originally known, was not a powerful ruler or a soldier. Rather, he was a herdsman and a wanderer who was born in Ur in Mesopotamia (now Iraq). God called him to go with his family from his homeland "to a land that I will show you" (Gn 12:1). Abram traveled with his family through much of the known world to keep his part of the agreement. His journeys foreshadowed those of the Hebrew people, who would travel from Egypt to Canaan. They also were similar to the missionary trips of St. Paul, a spiritual descendant of Abraham, who would travel throughout the Roman Empire to share the Good News of Jesus Christ.

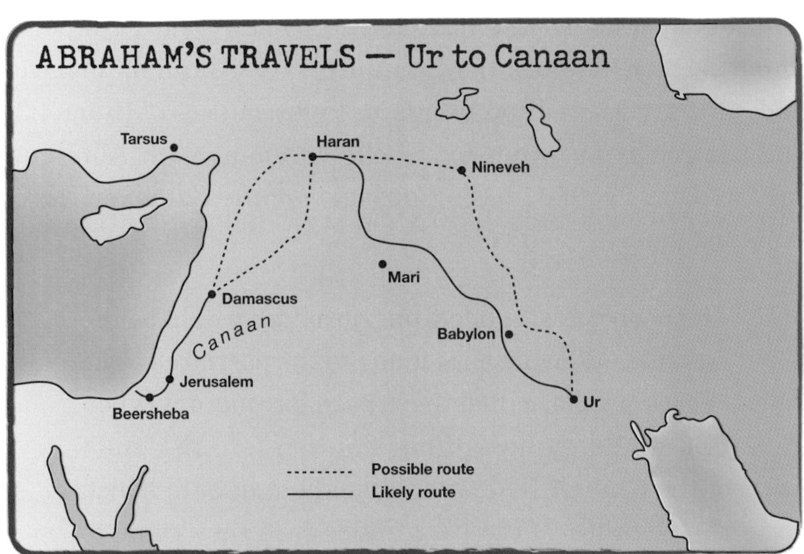

God's part of the agreement involved the promise of land, descendants, and a continuous friendship with Abraham's people. It is shared in the Book of Genesis:

> I will make of you a great nation,
> and will bless you;
> I will make your name great,
> so that you will be a blessing.
> I will bless those who bless you
> and curse those who curse you.
> All the communities of the earth
> shall find blessing in you. (Gen 12:2–3)

Understanding the promises God made to Abraham is an important lesson for followers of Jesus Christ. The Church teaches, for example, that God chose Abraham and made a covenant with him and his descendants and that by that covenant God formed his people. Abraham's faith in God's promises is considered an act of righteousness; that is, the "right" attitude a person should have toward God. As St. Paul pointed out, "For what does the Scripture say? 'Abraham believed God, and it was credited to him as righteousness'" (Rom 4:3). The Church is an extension of the covenant with Abraham, part of God's People. As the *Catechism of the Catholic Church* explains:

> The people descended from Abraham would be the trustees of the promise made to the patriarchs, the chosen people, called to prepare for that day when God would gather all his children into the unity of the Church. They would be the root onto which the Gentiles would be grafted, once they came to believe. (*CCC*, 61)

God Forms His People

After Abraham, the Book of Genesis tells the stories of the **patriarchs** of our faith, including Isaac and Jacob and Jacob's sons. But it is the Book of Exodus that formally introduces the Chosen People. God formed his people, Israel, by freeing them from slavery in Egypt. God taught the people to recognize him as a provident Father and a just judge. God also taught them to look for a promised Savior.

Through Moses, God gave Israel his Law so that the Israelites would not only know him, but also be able to serve him. The Law came through a covenant given to Moses and Israel at Mount Sinai. When the Israelites agreed to this covenant, they became a people united by the promise of a Savior. Their future liberation was only part of their agreement. Learning and keeping the Law made up the other part.

With the covenant came the Law of Moses, often called the "Torah." The Law of Moses expresses what human beings intuitively know to be right or wrong—the **natural law**. The basic principles of natural law extend to the entire human race. Natural law corresponds to three basic human drives and needs: 1) preserving life, 2) developing as individuals and communities, and 3) sharing life with others. The Ten Commandments provide the principal commandments of the natural law.

Israel, the Chosen People, was the first to hear the Word of God and to participate in this covenant. Through the prophets, God formed this people in the hope of salvation in expectation of the coming of the Messiah. But God also intended this covenant for all people and wanted it to be "written on their hearts." Israel was the channel of this revealed truth to the whole world. This truth was kept alive not only by the prophets, but also through other holy women of Israel. The greatest of these women was the Blessed Virgin Mary.

natural law
God's plan for human living that is written in the very way he created things. Binding on all people at all times, it is the light of understanding that God puts in us so we can discover what is good and what is evil.

Promises Fulfilled in Jesus

Chapter 1 of the Gospel of Matthew begins with a genealogy of Jesus. It begins by identifying Jesus as "the son of David, the son of Abraham." There is special significance in placing the names David and Abraham first.

Jewish expectations were that the Messiah would be a descendant of Israel's greatest king, David. The Lord had promised David that

> when your time comes and you rest with your ancestors, I will raise up your heir after you, sprung from your loins, and I will make his kingdom firm. It is he who shall build a house for my name. And I will make his royal throne firm forever. I will be a father to him, and he shall be a son to me. (2 Sm 7:12–14)

The reference to Abraham is also very important at the beginning of the genealogy. He was the father of Israel. But the Lord had promised that his "descendants of all the nations of the earth" would be especially blessed because he had obeyed God's commands.

The genealogy goes on to list generation by generation the ancestors of Jesus. Included in this genealogy are several women. Rahab and Ruth, David's grandmother, were Gentiles. Bathsheba, the mother of Solomon, had been the wife of Uriah, King David's top commander. These unusual and surprising circumstances in Jesus' family tree only highlight that his entrance into human history would be anything but predictable.

Another surprise is that the genealogy in Matthew's Gospel —and the one in Luke's Gospel as well—traces the family line of Jesus to Joseph, his foster father, and not Mary, his natural mother. Joseph was from the family of King David. His prominence in the genealogies shows both his faithfulness to Mary and the equal stature Jews assigned adoptive parenthood with natural parenthood.

However, it is the Virgin Mary who most perfectly embodies the obedience of faith. Mary was a young Jewish girl living in or around Nazareth when the angel of the Lord appeared to her with the monumental message. It was a call she was free to accept or reject: "Behold, you will conceive in your womb and

bear a son, and you shall name him Jesus" (Lk 1:31). Mary's unwavering answer of "yes" to the angel's news was given in obedience of her faith. St. Irenaeus later said of Mary's decision, "Being obedient she became the cause of salvation for herself and the whole human race."

Mary, a virgin, was unmarried but engaged to Joseph at the time she conceived her Son. Jesus was conceived solely by the power of the Holy Spirit, fulfilling the prophecy of the prophet Isaiah: "The virgin shall be with child, and bear a son" (Is 7:14). Mary's virginity was perpetual throughout her life; the Church holds that Jesus is Mary's only Son, but her spiritual motherhood extends to all.

With her faithful husband, Joseph, Mary raised Jesus in a loving home and taught him the Jewish faith of his ancestors. When Jesus began his ministry of preaching and healing, Mary supported him. And, eventually, when he was unfairly persecuted, tried, and hung on a cross to die, Mary was there. Finally, after Jesus' Resurrection, Mary remained with his disciples in the Upper Room in Jerusalem awaiting the promised coming of the Holy Spirit at Pentecost.

The birth of Jesus and his entrance into human history was the culmination of the Divine Revelation. "In times past, God spoke in partial and various ways to our ancestors through the prophets; in these last days, he spoke to us through a son, whom he has made heir of all things and through whom he created the universe" (Heb 1:1–2). In Jesus, God revealed everything the world needs to know in order to gain salvation and sanctification.

Yet, even though God's Revelation is complete, it has not been made magically clear. Christians from every age, including our own, are left to grow in understanding of the Revelation and to live it more deeply from now until the end of the world.

REVIEW

1. How was God's covenant with Noah a reprise of promises he had made to Adam?
2. What was God's part of the covenant with Abraham?
3. Explain how the Church has roots in God's covenant with Abraham.
4. On what occasion did God form Israel as his Chosen People?
5. What are two lessons learned about Jesus from his genealogy?
6. How does Mary most perfectly embody the obedience of faith?

WRITE OR DISCUSS

- How are you committed to responding in appropriate ways to natural law?
- How is your task in living today related to God's Revelation in Jesus Christ?

REDEMPTION THROUGH THE PASCHAL MYSTERY

The Paschal Mystery of Jesus Christ's Death on the cross and his Resurrection is not only the centerpiece of the Gospel, but also of human history. God's saving plan, promised immediately after the sin of Adam, was accomplished "once for all" (Heb 9:26) by the Death of Jesus. At first, it may seem incongruous or even absurd for God to redeem us in the way he chose. It is better understood through the lens of Scripture and Christ's ancestry in the Chosen People of Israel. Jesus lived his Father's plan perfectly. It was a plan the prophets of Israel had preached. After his Resurrection, Jesus chastised the disciples he met on the road to Emmaus. They did not connect what had happened to him to the Scriptures they had grown up learning and praying:

> Oh, how foolish you are! How slow of heart to believe all that the prophets spoke! Was it not necessary that the Messiah should suffer these things and enter into his glory? (Lk 24:25)

Next Jesus began with Moses and interpreted all that referred to him in the Scriptures. Through the eyes of faith and the perspective of history, it is easier to connect Jesus' Passion and Death with the promises God had made in the Old Testament covenants. It was not so easy to do that when Jesus walked the earth. In fact, from the beginning of his public ministry, some leaders of Israel were so put off by his actions—expelling demons, forgiving sins, healing on the Sabbath, offering novel interpretations of the Mosaic Laws regarding purity, and associating with public sinners—that he was suspected of being possessed by Satan. Many in Israel thought Jesus was acting against the essential beliefs and practices of the Chosen People. Eventually he was accused of **blasphemy** and false prophecy. These were religious crimes for which punishment according to the Law was death by stoning. Jesus' enemies believed he was indifferent to full obedience of the Mosaic Law and to the centrality of the Temple in worship. Jesus, they said, claimed authority reserved to God alone. These issues, further explained below, led to the events of the Paschal Mystery.

Events That Led to the Death of Jesus

There was no common understanding among first-century Jews that the Messiah would suffer and die. The Jews lived under Roman occupation. The more common belief was that the Messiah would be a military leader who would defeat the occupying enemies and restore Israel to its greatness as a nation. While the Hebrew Scriptures did call for a Messiah who would deliver the people from their sinfulness and bring everlasting life, this understanding was more directed to the people of Israel as a whole, not to individuals. It was believed that the people of Israel would live on in their descendants. Not many Jews in Jesus' time had any notion of personal salvation or resurrection for the individual person.

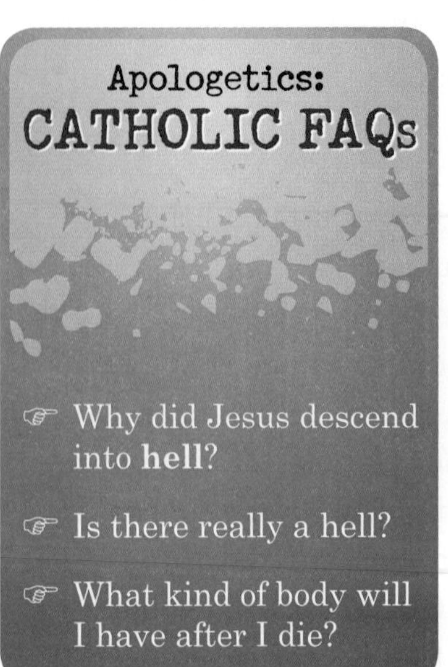

Apologetics:
CATHOLIC FAQs
☞ Why did Jesus descend into **hell**?
☞ Is there really a hell?
☞ What kind of body will I have after I die?

The Mosaic Law the Jews lived under was impossible to keep in its entirety without violating at least one law. That is why the Jews celebrated a **Day of Atonement** each year to ask God's forgiveness for their sins. Nevertheless, some zealous Jews, mainly from a religious sect called the Pharisees, did try to follow the Law to its letter and impose this impossible standard on others. It was in this setting that Jesus began his ministry. In the Sermon on the Mount he said:

> Do not think that I have come to abolish the law or the prophets. I have come not to abolish but to fulfill. Amen, I say to you, until heaven and earth pass away, not the smallest letter or the smallest part of a letter will pass from the law. (Mt 5:17–18)

As the "legislator" himself, Jesus was the only one who could fulfill the Law perfectly. Thought of by his contemporaries as a rabbi, Jesus argued with other teachers of the Law about their interpretation. He gave God's interpretation, which is summarized in the **Beatitudes**. He went beyond the letter of the Law to talk about a law written not on stone, but on the hearts of people. Jesus used the formula "You have heard that it was said . . . but I say to you" to explain this new understanding. For example, he said it was not enough to keep the Commandment "you shall not kill." A person should avoid anger as well. He said that not only should a person not commit adultery, "but I say to you, everyone who looks at a woman with lust has already committed adultery with her in his heart" (Mt 5:28). Jesus also perfected the many dietary laws that were so important in Jewish daily life by proclaiming all foods "clean" (see Mark 7:18–19). Jesus met

Beatitudes
Beatitude means "supreme happiness." The eight Beatitudes preached by Jesus in the Sermon on the Mount respond to our natural desire for happiness.

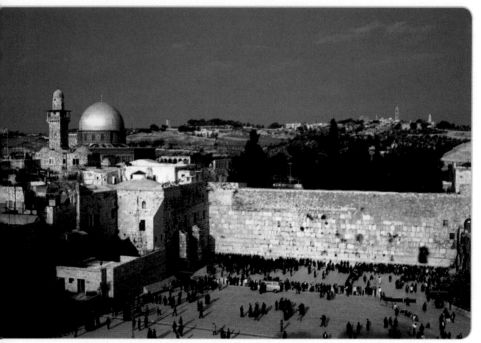

The Western Wall or "Wailing Wall" is the sacred remains of the Jerusalem Temple.

resistance to many of these teachings by some who questioned his right to act with the authority of God.

Likewise, just prior to the Passion, Jewish leaders misinterpreted what Jesus had taught about the sacred Temple. Throughout his life Jesus had shown only great respect and reverence for the Temple, where Joseph and Mary had presented him forty days after his birth. At age twelve, he decided to remain at the Temple to remind his parents that his mission was to do his Father's work. During his hidden life, Jesus would have gone to the Temple at least once a year to celebrate Passover. What's more, the public ministry of Jesus was linked to Jewish feasts held in Jerusalem. On one visit, Jesus was angered that the outer court of the Temple had become a place of commerce. He drove the merchants out because of his love

for his Father and his desire that the Temple be used only for worship.

Just prior to his Death, Jesus paid the highest compliment to the Temple and compared his own body to the Temple. Both would be destroyed, he said. Gathered around the Temple buildings, Jesus told his disciples, “You see all these things, do you not? Amen, I say to you, there will not be left here a stone upon another stone that will not be thrown down” (Mt 24:2). This was Jesus’ way of announcing the last days that would begin with his own Passion. Later, this prediction was thrown back in Jesus’ face when he was on the cross. Shaking their heads, passersby screamed at Jesus, “You who would destroy the temple and rebuild it in three days, save yourself, if you are the Son of God, [and] come down from the cross!” (Mt 27:40).

Ultimately, the forgiveness of sins—Jesus’ primary mission on earth—led directly to his Passion and Death. He scandalized the Pharisees by eating with tax collectors and sinners. He said, “I did not come to call the righteous but sinners” (Mt 9:13). But what angered the authorities most was that Jesus himself offered forgiveness for sins. They questioned, “Who but God alone can forgive sins?” (Mk 2:7). Besides forgiving sins, Jesus claimed his divine identity at other times and in other ways. Once while at the Temple, Jesus told those gathered that his origins preceded Abraham, the father in faith. When questioned about how this could be, he said, “Amen, amen, I say to you, before Abraham came to be, I AM” (Jn 8:58). That Jesus had explicitly equated himself with God—“I AM” translates to the Hebrew name for God, *Yahweh*—was more than the crowd could handle. They picked up stones to throw at Jesus, but he was able to slip away from them and the Temple area.

The Passion and the Death of Jesus

All of these events led to Jesus' being handed over first to the Sanhedrin, the formal assembly of chief priests, elders, and scribes, and then to the Roman governor Pontius Pilate, who would order his crucifixion. Jesus had predicted these events to his disciples. Like the first disciples, we wonder whether this had to happen.

The answer is that Jesus had to die to redeem humankind from sin. Because of the disobedience of Adam, all of his descendants were wounded by Original Sin. In this fallen condition, all men and women (except Mary), from Adam and Eve until our own generation, have committed personal sins as well. By freely giving his life on the cross, in complete obedience to his Father, Jesus atoned for both Original Sin and personal sins. His Death was an *expiation*—a purging or cleansing—of sin. The Apostle John wrote: "In this is love: not that we have loved God, but that he loved us and sent his Son as expiation for our sins" (1 Jn 4:10).

It was in this way that God's saving plan was accomplished "once for all" (Heb 9:26). There would be no more need for the animal sacrifices that were a main ritual of Mosaic Law. As Jesus pointed out, "the Son of Man did not come to be served but to serve and to give his life as a ransom for many" (Mk 10:45). This was the plan of God the Father. Jesus also said: "I am the good shepherd. A good shepherd lays down his life for the sheep. . . . No one takes [my life] from me, but I lay it down on my own. I have power to lay it down, and power to take it up again. This command I have received from my Father" (Jn 10:11, 18). The events of our salvation unfolded in this way:

The Entry of Jesus into Jerusalem. Jesus was greeted and hailed in Jerusalem as a prophet by the crowds as he entered the city gates during Passover. They waved leafy branches and called out, "Hosanna! Blessed is he who comes in the name of the Lord!" (Mk 11:9). Jesus entered the Temple area and then, because it was late in the day, retreated back outside the city walls to the small town of Bethany for the night.

Hostility toward Jesus. The mood in Jerusalem changed over the next two days. First, as mentioned, Jesus reacted strongly against the commerce taking place in the Temple courtyard. This was really business as usual. Jews coming from throughout Palestine had to exchange their secular money for the Jewish coin to be given as an offering. When Jesus drove out the money changers and those buying and selling, he was really making a statement against the leaders of the Temple—the elders and the priests. Jesus was criticizing their lack of attention to authentic religious matters, especially during Passover. These would be the people who later tried Jesus in the Jewish court and handed him over to the Romans. Besides these Jewish officials, Jesus was also challenged by others within Judaism—the Herodians and the Sadducees. Along with the Pharisees, these groups demanded to know where Jesus got his authority, his belief in the resurrection of the dead, and whether it was necessary to pay taxes to the government.

The Last Supper. At this Passover meal, Jesus gathered with his disciples. He broke bread and said, "This is my body" (Lk 22:19). He shared a cup of wine and said, "This cup is the new covenant in my blood, which will be shed for you" (Lk 22:20). This meal was in anticipation of the giving of Jesus' Body and Blood in his Passion and Death.

The Agony in the Garden and the Arrest of Jesus. After the Last Supper, Jesus retreated to the garden at Gethsemane. He prayed, "Abba, Father, all things are possible to you. Take this cup away from me, but not what I will but what you will" (Mk 14:36). His disciples were unable to stay awake with him. Jesus was betrayed by Judas, one of his Apostles. Then he was arrested in the garden by a crowd with swords and clubs who had come from the chief priests and the elders.

Arrest of Jesus

Jesus before the Sanhedrin. When the high priest asked Jesus, "Are you the Messiah, the son of the Blessed One?" Jesus answered, "I am" (Mk 14:61–62). The high priest then tore his own garments. Others spit on Jesus. He was soon convicted of blasphemy. The next day, in another council gathering, the Sanhedrin had Jesus bound and taken to Pilate. Legally, the Sanhedrin had no authority to carry out his conviction.

Jesus before Pilate. The details of the actual trial before the Roman governor vary among the Gospel accounts. Pilate is portrayed as one who had very little interest in the religious squabble between Jesus and the Jewish authorities. Yet it is clear he knew that Jesus was innocent but still sentenced him to death under the charge that he claimed to be a king. Hung on the cross were the words "Jesus of Nazareth, King of the Jews."

Jesus on trial before Pilate

The Death of Jesus. Jesus' entire life was an act of love. His final, greatest act of love was that he gave up his very life. This was also a perfect act of obedience to God the Father. Jesus' final words as he hung on the cross were, "Father, into your hands I commend my spirit" (Lk 23:46). Crucifixion was a form of capital punishment used in the Roman Empire until it was banned by the emperor Constantine in AD 315 for being too cruel. It was usually reserved for slaves and criminals convicted of the worst types of crimes.

Though as the First Letter to Timothy reminds us, there is "one mediator between God and the human race, Christ Jesus, himself human, who gave himself as ransom for all" (2:5–6), we, too, have a share in the Paschal Mystery. Jesus calls each of us to "take up [our] cross, and follow me" (Mt 16:24). We do this by following his example of total surrender to the will of God in our lives and by offering to God any sufferings we are handed with those of Jesus, just as Mary did at the foot of his cross. As St. Rose of Lima wrote, "Apart from the cross there is no other ladder by which we may get to Heaven."[6]

REVIEW

1. Why did Jesus chastise the disciples on the road to Emmaus?
2. Define *blasphemy*.
3. What is the Day of Atonement?
4. How did the Beatitudes go beyond the letter of Mosaic Law?
5. What was the highest compliment Jesus paid to the Temple?
6. What does it mean to say that Jesus' Death expiated our sins?
7. Why would Jewish leaders have been upset with Jesus' declaration of himself as "I AM"?

WRITE OR DISCUSS

- Being scrupulous can be defined as having an overly heightened sense of right and wrong. How does this attitude compare with that of the Pharisees? In what ways are you scrupulous?
- Do you know people who have followed the challenge to "take up their cross" for Christ? How have you taken up your own cross?

HE IS RISEN!

Three days after he died and was buried in a tomb cut out of a rock, Jesus rose from the dead. There were no witnesses to the actual Resurrection, but there were witnesses to the empty tomb and to the Risen Jesus.

The empty tomb was the first sign of the Resurrection. In itself, it was not direct proof that Jesus had risen from the dead. It could have been empty for a number of reasons. However, the empty tomb was still an essential sign for all. When the disciples discovered it, they began to understand and believe. Simon Peter and the beloved disciple John both ran out to the tomb when told by Mary of Magdala that the stone in front of it had been removed:

> When Simon Peter arrived after him, he went into the tomb and saw the burial cloths there, and the cloth that had covered his head, not with the burial cloths but rolled up in a separate place. Then the other disciple also went in, the one who had arrived at the tomb first, and he saw and believed. (Jn 20:6–8)

The belief of the Apostle John on discovery of the empty tomb suggests he knew that the body had not been stolen or even that Jesus had been revived and brought back to life as Lazarus had been (see John 11:1–44).

Many witnesses verified the appearances of Jesus after his Resurrection. There were Mary Magdalene and the other women who discovered the empty tomb and Peter and the other disciples to whom Jesus appeared in the Upper Room (the place of the Last Supper). Jesus also appeared to the disciples on the

The site of Jesus' tomb is Jerusalem.

road to Emmaus and to more than five hundred disciples gathered in one place (see 1 Corinthians 15:5–8). Given all the testimonies of Christ's Resurrection, it can be acknowledged as a historical fact and not as something the disciples made up. In fact, the disciples were demoralized and scared, and they originally discounted the stories of the empty tomb as nonsense. Even when they met the Risen Jesus face to face, they remained doubtful and thought they were seeing a ghost. This was hardly the attitude you would expect of people claiming a mystical experience or concocting a tale of encountering someone raised from the dead. Rather, their faith in the Resurrection was born, with the help of God's grace, from their direct experience of meeting the Risen Jesus.

What was Jesus like after the Resurrection? The disciples had trouble recognizing him. Mary Magdalene thought he was the gardener at first (see John 20:11–18). Though the disciples in the Emmaus story did not recognize him until the "breaking of the bread," he did function as a human being: "They gave him a piece of baked fish; he took it and ate it in front of them" (Lk 24:42–43). Yet he was able to pass into a room through locked doors (see John 20:19). Christ's resurrected body *was* different. "In his risen body he passes from the state of death to another life beyond time and space" (*CCC*, 646). Although he was truly the same Jesus the disciples knew before, he was glorified at his Resurrection. His body was transfigured, immortal, and able to move at will through space. St. Paul described the difference between the earthly and resurrected bodies this way:

> It is sown corruptible; it is raised incorruptible. It is sown dishonorable; it is raised glorious. It is sown weak; it is raised powerful. It is sown a natural body; it is raised a spiritual body. If there is a natural body, there is also a spiritual one. (1 Cor 15:42–44)

Belief in Jesus' Resurrection is central to our Christian faith. Christ, "the firstborn from the dead" (Col 1:18), makes our own resurrection someday possible.

We Believe in Everlasting Life

The Gospels were formed out of one sentence: Jesus is risen! All the rest of the Scriptures are somewhat of an exercise in filling in the details. In fact, if we do not believe this essential *kerygma*, or message, our faith is useless. As St. Paul put it,

> If Christ has not been raised, then empty too is our preaching; empty, too, your faith. . . . If Christ has not been raised, your faith is vain; you are still in your sins. Then those who have fallen asleep in Christ have perished. If for this life only we have hoped in Christ, we are the most pitiable people of all. (1 Cor 15:14, 17–19)

Christ's Resurrection was the work of the Holy Trinity. God the Father "raised up" Christ the Son and by doing so introduced the humanity of Jesus into the relationship of the Holy Trinity. The Resurrection has many implications for us, including bringing us into deeper relationship with Christ as his brothers and sisters. Christ's Resurrection and its accompanying grace make this possible.

Practically, what does Christ's Resurrection mean for us? Because of Jesus Christ, Christian death has a positive meaning. It helps dispel other ideas about what happens to human beings after they die. Philosophers through the ages have speculated on what takes place after death. Some have theorized that after death there is nothing; we cease to exist. Others presume that our soul lives on but without a body. Still others believe that we cease to exist as individuals but that God absorbs us. And some maintain that we become like ghosts, condemned to roam the world in misery, or that we are reincarnated and come back to earth to try life once again.

Pentecost
The day when the Holy Spirit descended on the Apostles and gave them the power to preach with conviction the message that Jesus is risen and is Lord of the universe.

The Good News of Jesus' Resurrection tells us that all these theories are false. Christ's Death was his final act of self-giving. With his Death, we are saved. In Baptism, we have already "died with Christ"; our physical death merely completes our incorporation into his act of Redemption. In death, our soul is separated from our body, the body decays, and the soul goes to meet God while awaiting reunion with its glorified body when we are "raised from the dead." We are called back to God and will live a life in glory with our friends, our family, and God. The goodness of the life that awaits us is impossible to imagine. Quoting the prophet Isaiah, St. Paul wrote:

> What eye has not seen, and ear has not heard,
> and what has not entered the human heart,
> what God has prepared for those who love him.
> (1 Cor 2:9)

We should prepare ourselves for the hour of our death. With many teenage deaths each year primarily because of car accidents and sometimes fatal disease, even at your age, you should keep your mortality in mind each day. An ancient Church litany of the saints asks to be spared from a "sudden and unforeseen death" so that we can finally return to God himself. It is our final communion with the Blessed Trinity, with Mary, the angels, and all the saints that is **Heaven**.

The Ascension of Jesus and the Coming of the Holy Spirit

Living with a glorified body, Jesus remained on earth for forty days after his Resurrection. Then, the Scriptures report, he was taken back to Heaven, where he was seated at the Father's right hand, signifying the start of the Messiah's Kingdom, one that will have no end.

When he left earth, Jesus had no intention of leaving his disciples as orphans. Nor did he want to abandon all the people who would be born later. Prior to his Death, he promised he would send the Holy Spirit: "I will ask the Father, and he will give you another Advocate to be with you always, the Spirit of truth" (Jn 14:16–17). Jesus' promise was fulfilled on the feast of **Pentecost**.

Once the Spirit came to them, the disciples were no longer afraid. Peter, who had denied he even knew Jesus in the chaos of his arrest and crucifixion, came out of hiding and began to address the Jews who had gathered from throughout the region in the streets of Jerusalem. He recounted for them the entire story of salvation, concluding with Jesus the Messiah and everything that had happened to him. The crowds were bewildered by what they heard. For one thing, even though they spoke several languages, each was able to understand Peter. Many thought Peter and the others were drunk, even though it was only nine in the morning!

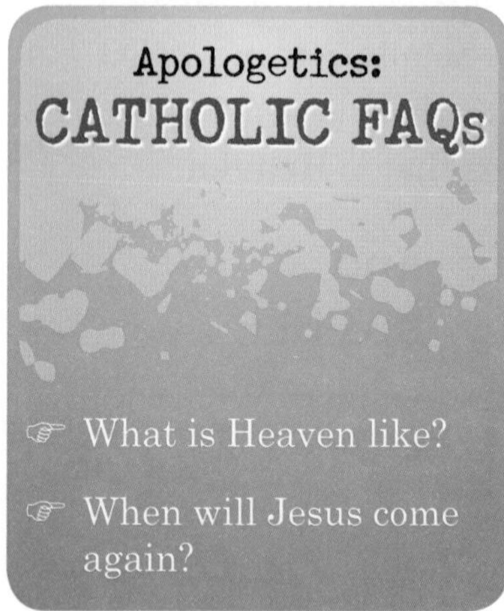

Apologetics:
CATHOLIC FAQs
☞ What is Heaven like?
☞ When will Jesus come again?

The result, however, was that about three thousand people were baptized that day. Through the coming of the Holy Spirit, the first Christians were able to look back and see the life of Jesus in a new light. They were able to preach confidently that "Jesus is Lord" and that Jesus was equal with the Father, true God from true God.

REVIEW

1. What was the first sign of the Resurrection?
2. Why is it more likely that the first desciples claimed Jesus had risen in response to a historical fact?
3. What was Jesus like after the Resurrection?
4. What does Jesus' Resurrection mean for us?
5. What happened on Pentecost?

WRITE OR DISCUSS

- How strong is your belief that Jesus is risen?

FAITH RETURNS

Life is filled with many challenges that rock the very core of our faith. Caitlin Riley, as a Michigan teenager at Lansing Catholic Central High School, decided to start her senior year standing in front of the student body explaining why she was bald.

Since age twelve, Caitlin has suffered from an autoimmune disorder called alopecia areata, which attacks hair follicles and can cause patchy hair loss or complete baldness. The condition can be temporary or permanent. The worst-case scenario developed for Caitlin. "At first I prayed that it would stop," she said. But when the condition did not go away, Caitlin blamed God for what was happening to her. "After a while, I didn't pray at all."

Caitlin took to wearing a wig at all times to hide her condition. The only place she felt comfortable enough to not wear the wig was at home. Only a few of her closest friends knew she was bald. The ongoing charade involved more than her physical appearance; Caitlin found that her natural personality of playfulness and fun was also compromised because she worried constantly about whether anyone would find out she was bald. "I just didn't feel like I was really me," she said.

During her junior year, Caitlin met a classmate's mother who was also bald. The woman was undergoing chemotherapy, and her hair had fallen out. But this woman did not seem self-conscious at all about walking around wearing a scarf or a hat that didn't completely hide her baldness. Seeing the woman at an Ash Wednesday Mass inspired Caitlin.

Caitlin attended a conference for people with alopecia. None of them wore a wig. Caitlin decided to take her wig off, too. She went swimming for the first time in years. She also decided not to wear a wig at school for her senior year.

At the opening assembly, after Caitlin explained what was going on to her classmates, they all responded with a long and tearful standing ovation, which Caitlin described as "surreal, amazing, awesome."

The affirmations did not stop there. In October she was voted homecoming queen and crowned with a tiara on top of her hairless head. Later, in the spring, she starred in a school musical. She wore a wig for that, as the costume demanded, but took it off once the show was over. Accepted at a small liberal arts college, she found out there was another woman at the school who also had alopecia and did not wear a wig. "That has to be a 'God thing.' It's really a small school to have two students with alopecia," Caitlin said.

Caitlin's attitude toward God also changed. "I still feel guilty that I stopped praying. It's not so much I forgave him—that doesn't feel like the right word. It is more that I finally let it all go. I used to think it was his fault, but it's not."

Caitlin planned a major in psychology and a minor in Spanish, but she would also like to be married and have a family. "I might be able to have a major influence. I might be able to help a lot of people—maybe as a motivational speaker."[7]

- **How is the Paschal Mystery modeled in Caitlin's life?**

GETTING TO KNOW JESUS

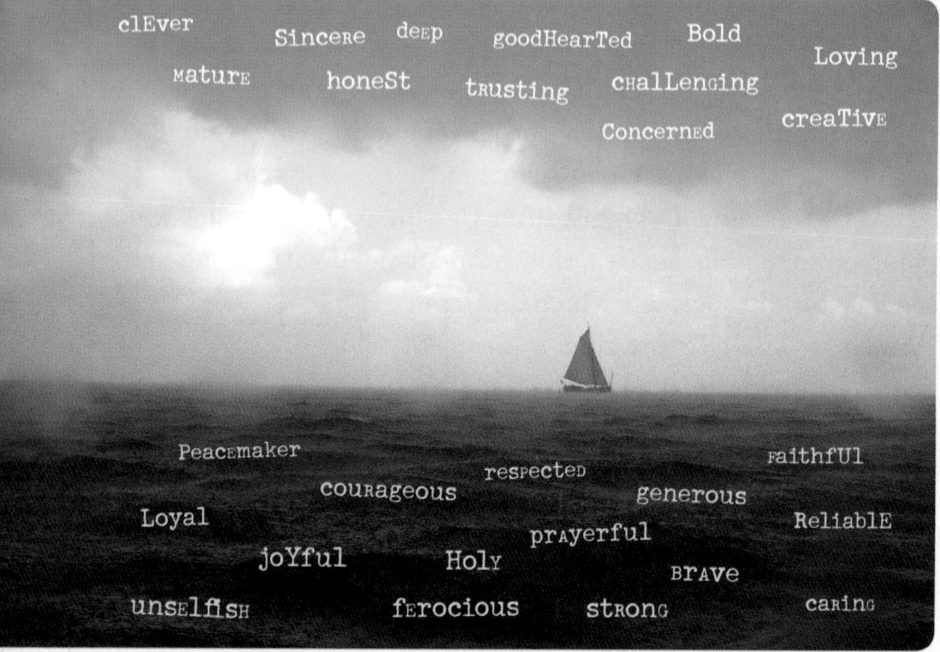

Do Not Be Afraid

When it was evening, his disciples went down to the sea, embarked in a boat, and went across the sea to Capernaum. It had already grown dark, and Jesus had not yet come to them. The sea was stirred up because a strong wind was blowing. When they had rowed about three or four miles, they saw Jesus walking on the sea and coming near the boat, and they began to be afraid. But he said to them, "It is I. Do not be afraid." They wanted to take him into the boat, but the boat immediately arrived at the shore to which they were heading. (Jn 6:16–21)

The part of the story where I find myself right now is:

- **In the dark.** I'm really not sure where my relationship with Jesus stands now or where it is going.
- **Blown away.** I didn't expect to have to get into a relationship with Jesus that could lead to danger and death.
- **Confronted.** I feel I am being challenged to a new way of life, and I am not sure I can handle it.
- **Not afraid.** I am truly comforted by Jesus and more content than ever to be his follower.

Choose one of the descriptions above as a title for a journal entry. Describe why your relationship with Jesus fits under that title. Use some of the affirmation words along the drawing on the facing page as part of your entry. Tell how you envision your relationship with Jesus evolving in the next three to five years and then throughout your life.

PRAYER

Act of Hope

O God,
I hope with complete trust that you
will give me,
through the merits of Jesus Christ, all
necessary grace in this world
and everlasting life in the world to come,
for this is what you have promised
and you always keep your promises.
Amen.

4

The Church: Christ's Mission Continues in the World Today

A SOURCE FOR TRUTH

St. Joan of Arc said Jesus is the light that allows the Church to shine. She also said, "About Jesus Christ and the Church, I simply know they are one thing, and we shouldn't complicate the matter."

The journey to know Jesus cannot be accomplished without the Church. St. Edith Stein, a convert from Judaism, discovered this while spending her formative years searching for the truth with high intensity. The German native was born on October 12, 1891, the Jewish Day of Atonement. Ultimately, she believed that "when you seek truth you seek God whether you know it or not."

The youngest of seven children of the widowed Frau Stein, Edith was a brilliant student and scholar. But she was also female and Jewish. Even at the turn of the century, this was a volatile combination in Germany. Edith experienced **anti-Semitism** in large doses. Nevertheless, at age nineteen she entered the University of Breslau and took up a philosophy major, claiming that she no longer believed in a personal God and that she practiced Judaism only to please her mother. She later said of that period, "The pursuit of truth was my only passion."

St. Edith Stein

How Edith came to know Jesus Christ is often attributed to two incidents. The first occurred in 1917. One of Edith's professors sent her to represent him at the funeral of colleague Adolf Reinach, who had been killed in World War I. She had respected the warm-hearted Reinach and dreaded being near his family, surely suffering in despair. Instead, Edith found that the professor's widow was consoling the guests rather than the other way around. Edith knew that the Reinachs had both been baptized in the Lutheran faith just a year earlier.

Frau Reinach further explained her demeanor: "I accept fully in my heart that Adolf now lives with God. He has reached his goal. It is my duty now to accept my loss and my portion of the cross of Christ, which brings healing and life to all."

The second incident occurred in 1921, when Edith spent the summer on a farm owned by another married couple from the university. One evening when her hosts were away, Edith looked in their library for a book to read and settled on *The Autobiography of St. Teresa of Avila*. To Edith, it seemed that Teresa's spiritual journey paralleled her own. In reading the book, Edith began to understand Teresa's conclusion that Christ is "the Way, the Truth, and the Light"—and that he draws us close to himself in prayer. She later recalled:

> This was my first encounter with the Cross and with the supernatural strength which it gives. For the first time I saw the redemptive suffering of Christ overcoming death. This was the moment when my unbelief broke down and Christ appeared to me in the mystery of the Cross.

What happened next was an amazing but common experience for someone who meets Jesus. Like many others before and since, Edith Stein sought out the Church. On New Year's Day 1922, she was baptized into the Catholic Church. She took the name Teresa as her baptismal name.

As a Catholic, Edith wanted to deepen her relationship with Christ. She resigned her position at the university and taught for less pay at a Dominican girls' school in Speyer, Germany, until 1932. While at Speyer, a priest who served on the staff there introduced her to the **Divine Office**, the official prayer of the Church. He wanted her to feel welcome as a Catholic. Edith recited the office daily in Latin.

Edith continued to face anti-Semitism, even as a Catholic. As a lecturer for a Catholic institute, Edith was eventually forced to resign because of her Jewish heritage. She concluded that God was calling her to a different path. She requested of the abbot of a Carmelite convent that she be able to enter as a nun. The request was accepted, and Edith broke the news to her mother

> **Divine Office**
> The official daily prayer of the Church; also known as the Liturgy of the Hours. The prayer offers prayers, Scripture, and reflections at regular intervals throughout the day.

on her own birthday, October 12. Frau Stein and Edith attended a synagogue service together that day. Afterward, as they walked home, Frau Stein told her daughter, "I have nothing against Christ. It is possible that he was a very good man. But why did he have to make himself God?"

Edith Stein took the name Sr. Teresa Benedicta of the Cross. Fearing for her safety, the sisters of the convent eventually transferred her to the Netherlands, but the Nazi persecutions reached there as well. Edith and her sister Rosa, also a convert, were captured and shipped to the Auschwitz concentration camp, where they died in the gas chambers on August 9, 1942.

In 1998, Pope John Paul II canonized Edith Stein. To the end of her life, Edith remained committed to seeking out the truth in Jesus Christ. Membership and public participation in the Catholic Church were essential to this journey. She wrote:

> The imperturbability of the Church resides in her ability to harmonize the unconditional preservation of eternal truths with an unmatchable elasticity of adjustment to the circumstances and challenges of changing times.

Put simply, Edith recognized in the Catholic Church the necessity to evolve and change through time as the Church continues to live the sufferings of Christ in each age. In the midst of anti-Semitism and the Nazi persecutions, Edith continually repeated the words of French philosopher Blaise Pascal, who had written: "Jesus is in agony until the end of the world."

This chapter explores how Christ is present in the Catholic Church. It examines the origins of the Church—Christ established the Church for all time—and how some biblical images of the Church reveal her meaning. Also, the four **marks of the**

Church—one, holy, catholic, and apostolic—are explained as ways in which Jesus Christ and the Holy Spirit work in and among the Church. Yet the marks also point out the weaknesses of the Church as her members often fall short of what they stand for. According to a favorite image of the Church Fathers, the Church is "like the moon, all its light is reflected from the sun." The strength of the Church is gathered from her efficiency in mirroring the life of Christ.

REVIEW

1. What two incidents led to Edith Stein's embracing Christianity?
2. Why did Edith feel that the Catholic Church was essential to her spiritual journey?
3. What do these words of the Church Fathers mean: "The Church is like the moon, all its light is reflected from the sun"?

WRITE OR DISCUSS

- Why do you think Frau Stein felt as she did about Christ?

WHAT IS CHURCH?

The story of the Church parallels salvation history. The Church *began* at the foundation of the world when Adam and Eve sinned and were promised a redeemer. The Church was *formed* with the call of Abraham and the Chosen People. Christ first *inaugurated* the Church in his preaching of the Good News and the coming of God's Kingdom. However, it wasn't until the soldier thrust his lance into Jesus' side as he hung on the cross and blood and water flowed out that the Church was really *born*. St. Ambrose wrote "that as Eve was formed from the sleeping Adam's side, so the Church was born from the pierced heart of Christ hanging dead on the cross" (see *CCC*, 766).

The chosen followers of Jesus—even the Apostles—did not recognize that the Church had been born on Good Friday. Finally, at the feast of Pentecost, the Church became visible to the whole world. It was on that day that the Holy Spirit came to make the Church holy and to lead her in her mission of preaching the Gospel of salvation to all people.

The word *church* itself comes from a Greek word meaning "belonging to the Lord." We belong to the Lord because we are attached to him as a body to a head. As the head of the Church, Christ gives the body direction and vision. The Holy Spirit is the soul of the Church. The Spirit lives in the baptized and provides the necessary gifts to be holy, alive, and Christ-like. Without Jesus Christ and the Holy Spirit, there would be no Church.

Pentecost is sometimes called the "birthday of the Church." It was on Pentecost that God, through the coming of the Holy Spirit, completed all covenants with humanity. Jesus prepared the Apostles for Pentecost during both his earthly ministry and the forty days between the Resurrection and the Ascension.

Apologetics:
CATHOLIC FAQs

Use this chapter and other sources to formulate your own answers to these questions. Then check your answers at "Catholic FAQs" at **www.avemariapress.com: Religious Education.**

- Is the Catholic Church really the only true Church?
- Why do we need organized religion?
- How can the Church preach holiness when many of her members, including clergy, are guilty of terrible wrongs?

Jesus' last words to his disciples were both an instruction and a promise. He said:

> Go, therefore, and make disciples of all nations, baptizing them in the name of the Father, and of the Son, and of the Holy Spirit, teaching them to observe all that I have commanded you. And behold, I am with you always, until the end of the age. (Mt 28:19–20)

The Descent of the Holy Spirit

The promises Jesus had made to send the Holy Spirit were fulfilled on the feast of Pentecost.

Pentecost is a Greek word that means "fiftieth day." Originally Pentecost was a Jewish feast called the "Feast of the First Fruits" or the "Feast of Weeks" that happened fifty days after Passover. Jews from all over the Roman Empire, many who spoke different languages and dialects, gathered in Jerusalem to celebrate this first harvest of summer.

Also in Jerusalem, Peter and the other disciples (including Mary, the Mother of Jesus) were holed up in the Upper Room, fearful of being arrested and possibly murdered just like Jesus was. The Acts of the Apostles describes what happened next:

> And suddenly there came from the sky a noise like a strong driving wind, and it filled the entire house in which they were. Then there appeared to them tongues as of fire, which parted and came to rest on each one of them. And they were all filled with the Holy Spirit and began to speak in different tongues, as the Spirit enabled them to proclaim. (Acts 2:2–4)

With the many new converts baptized that day (see pages 135–136), the Church did experience a birthday of sorts on that Pentecost in Jerusalem.

The Church Welcomes Gentiles

In the early days of the Church, it wasn't obvious that the salvation Jesus offered was intended for Gentiles as well as Jews. Only after God spoke to Peter in a vision did Peter become convinced that salvation in Christ was also for Gentiles. Peter explained his vision to the other Apostles: "If then God gave them the same gift he gave to us when we came to believe in the Lord Jesus Christ, who was I to be able to hinder God?" (Acts 11:17). When the other Apostles heard his explanation, they too began to offer Church membership to non-Jews.

The question then became which elements of Judaism were essential to Christianity. For example, did newly baptized Gentiles need to obey all Jewish dietary laws? Was it necessary for Christians to worship in the Jewish Temple? And was circumcision—the sign of the covenant between Abraham and his descendants—necessary for Gentiles who converted to Christianity? The answers came at a gathering of Church leadership at the Council of Jerusalem.

Under the inspiration of the Holy Spirit, Church leadership at the Council of Jerusalem decided Christians needed to keep only three basic Jewish laws. First, Christians were not to eat meat that had been sacrificed to idols because doing so would have been tantamount to honoring false gods. Second, Christians should continue to observe the law given to Noah that no one should eat the meat of strangled animals or eat blood. Finally, Christians were to avoid all illicit sexual practices. No matter what the influences of the world in the area of sexuality, Christians were to understand and practice sex only in marriage.

The Council of Jerusalem also emphasized that Christianity, like Judaism, was a religion of the body, not just of the spirit. Church leaders had the obligation to tell people what the Gospel required of them in terms of belief and behavior in all spheres of life. By the end of the first century, the Church had accepted that Christianity was a religion for both Jews and Gentiles. Anyone who converted to Christianity did not have to become Jewish first. However, all Christians, whatever their race or native land, were required to reject anything in their culture that would undermine or contradict faith in the one, true, Creator God.

The Good News Spreads

When the Gospel was being preached exclusively to Jews, Jewish Christians primarily preached in synagogues. Also, Jewish Christian merchants told about the "New Way" as part of business conversations (for example, when buying and selling merchandise). Using their own words, Jewish Christians gave the same explanation of the faith that Peter had shared on Pentecost: in the person of Jesus, God had fulfilled his promise to King David. The Messiah had come.

Christianity benefited by an elaborate system of roadways throughout the Roman Empire. Merchants were easily able to travel from town to town, region to region. The greatest missionary for the new faith was a person with several built-in advantages. Besides being a traveling merchant—a tentmaker—he had been raised a Pharisee and studied Jewish Law under the famous teacher Gamaliel in Jerusalem. Once a persecutor of Christians, he had a dramatic conversion. He was also a Roman citizen with expertise in Gentile religions, philosophies,

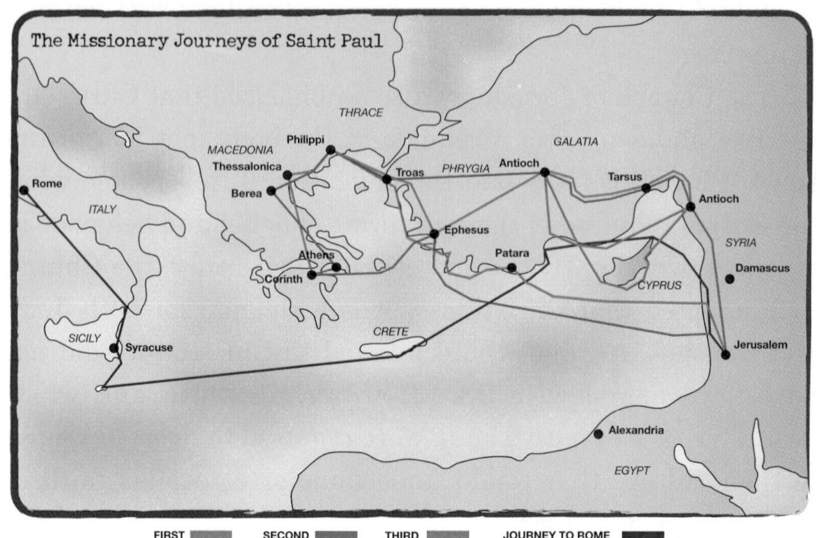

and customs. He could speak *Koine*, or common Greek, the language of the empire. This great missionary was St. Paul of Tarsus.

Paul took several missionary trips throughout the Roman Empire. The Acts of the Apostles divides Paul's missionary travels into three journeys. His second journey alone was nearly two thousand miles through the regions that now make up the modern countries of Macedonia, Turkey, Greece, and Syria. Along the way he founded several churches. When he left these places, he wrote the converts letters, instructing them further in the faith. These local churches were in places such as Corinth, Galatia, Ephesus, Colossae, and Philippi.

Paul was arrested and charged in Jerusalem with speaking out against Jewish Law and the Temple. However, as a Roman citizen, he had the right to be tried in Rome in the court of the emperor Caesar. A boat ride on rough seas followed. Paul got along amazingly well with his captors. He spent two years in rented lodgings in Rome, where he continued to preach the

Gospel to Jewish leaders. This is the point where the Acts of the Apostles ends, with Rome symbolizing the "ends of the earth" that Jesus had spoken of before ascending to Heaven. Tradition holds that Paul was beheaded in Rome in AD 67, but there was no stopping the spread of Christianity. By the early fourth century, Christianity had become the official religion of the Roman Empire.

At Pentecost, the Holy Spirit had given the Church—both the Apostolic leadership and all Christians in general—the gifts to proclaim Christ's Kingdom to all peoples. Thus, each Person of the Blessed Trinity had a role in the planning of the Church and her coming into historical reality.

Christ Proclaimed to All Generations

God wants everyone to be saved. He wants his revealed truth —that is, Jesus Christ—to be made known to all people in every generation. The Gospel is the source of God's truth. It was handed on in two ways: *orally*, by the spoken word of the Apostles in their preaching, and *in writing*, by both the Apostles themselves and those associated with the Apostles through the inspiration of the Holy Spirit.

In order that the Gospel would continue to be shared through the ages, the Apostles left **bishops** as their successors and gave them their own position of teaching authority. This mandate was initiated by Christ himself, who personally chose the Twelve Apostles but also commissioned Peter to a position of leadership or primacy among them:

> And so I say to you, you are Peter, and upon this rock I will build my church, and the gates of the netherworld shall not prevail against it. I will give you the keys to the kingdom of heaven. Whatever you bind on earth shall be bound in heaven; and whatever you loose on earth shall be loosed in heaven. (Mt 16:18–19)

Recall that there is no further Revelation after Christ and that God reveals himself through a single "deposit" of faith. Christ entrusted this deposit to the Apostles to be preserved and shared through the Church through their writings and preaching until Christ comes again. This single deposit is found in Sacred Scripture and in the Sacred Tradition of the Church.

As covered in Chapter 1, Sacred Scripture refers to the library of divinely inspired writings that make up the Bible. Sacred Tradition is the living transmission or "handing on" of the Church's Gospel message. This Tradition is contained in the Church's teaching, life, and worship. The Apostles, inspired by the Holy Spirit, were the first to receive the gift of faith. They in turn gave it to the care of their successors—the Pope and bishops—to "faithfully preserve, expound, and spread . . . by their preaching" (*Dogmatic Constitution on Divine Revelation*, No. 9, quoted in *CCC*, 81).

Christ commissioned the Apostles to interpret authentically God's Word—Scripture and Tradition. This Christ-appointed teaching authority, which extends to the Pope and bishops in communion with him, is known as the Magisterium (from the Latin word for "teacher"). With the help of the Holy Spirit, the Magisterium teaches with Christ's own authority. This is especially so when the Magisterium defines a dogma that Catholics are obliged to believe.

Today, our free response of faith to God's Revelation through what the Church teaches about Christ enables us to accept Jesus as Lord. We can also participate in the life of the Blessed Trinity and commit ourselves totally to God, with both our intellects and wills. Our saying "yes" to Jesus and the Good News makes us part of his Church.

REVIEW

1. When did the Church *begin*? When was the Church *formed*? When was the Church *inaugurated*? When was the Church *born*?
2. What were the origins of Pentecost?
3. What happened on the first Pentecost after Jesus' Resurrection?
4. How did Peter determine that Gentiles could be baptized?
5. What were three basic Jewish laws that Gentile Christians needed to follow?
6. What advantages did St. Paul have as a missionary?
7. How did each Person of the Blessed Trinity have a role in the Church's coming into historical reality?
8. How was the Gospel handed on?
9. How does God reveal himself through a single deposit of faith?
10. Define *Magisterium*. What is its purpose?

WRITE OR DISCUSS

- To Paul, Rome was the "ends of the earth." Where is God calling you to share the Good News?

A MISSIONARY TO THE EAST

St. Francis Xavier

Known as the "Apostle of the Indies," Francis founded missions in India and then moved on to Ceylon (today's Sri Lanka), a large island off India's southern coast.

Francis in Japan

Francis later went to Japan. He learned to speak Japanese in order to have influence with the daimyas, the 250 territorial lords. Francis and his fellow Jesuits appealed to the cult of honor. They incorporated local customs that were not in contradiction to Christianity.

St. Francis Xavier, a Jesuit priest, was instrumental in spreading the Gospel in Asia in the sixteenth century.

Thoughts on Missionary Work

His approach to missionary work is described by these words:

The better friends you are, the straighter you can talk, but while you are only on nodding terms, be slow to scold.

Take care not to frighten away by stern rigor poor sinners who are trying to lay bare the shocking state of their souls. Speak to them rather of the great mercy of God.

Death of a Saint

Francis wanted to travel to China but he died on a small island off its coast prior to beginning missionary work there.

THE MYSTERY OF THE CHURCH

As you recall, the term *mystery* was used to describe the Blessed Trinity. The Divine Mysteries, like the Trinity, both reveal and conceal God's ways, which are not our ways. Yet it is in the Mysteries that God continues to bless us with the knowledge and the truth of his plan. The Church is also a mystery of faith. The Church is both a means and a goal of the great mystery of God's love for us.

Pope Paul VI described the Church as a reality filled with God's hidden presence. This definition points to two essential ingredients in the Church: the human and the divine; the visible reality that we can see along with the spiritual reality that brings us God's life. This definition also teaches that like Jesus, the Church is a sacrament. Mystery and sacrament are intimately connected. With the eyes of faith, we proclaim that in the Church, Heaven and earth come together. The Church is a visible sign of Christ Jesus in the world. How are these truths so? The Church is at the same time:

- a **society** organized hierarchically as well as the mystical Body of Christ
- the visible society and the spiritual community
- an earthly community blessed with heavenly riches

Apologetics:
CATHOLIC FAQs

- Did Jesus found the Catholic Church?
- Why is the Church called Roman Catholic?
- How is the Church able to maintain unity even though her unity is lived out in many different cultures?

contemplation
Wordless prayer whereby a person's mind and heart rest in God's goodness and majesty.

As sacrament, the Church is the mystery where the human and the divine meet. The Church is visible, but she is endowed with invisible realities. The Church is both committed to action and dedicated to **contemplation**. The Church is a pilgrim in this world but also directs her members to the next world. Because the Church is the place where the human and the divine meet, Scripture uses many vivid images to describe the Church. Each of the images described in the sections that follow aids our appreciation and understanding of the mystery of the Church.

The People of God

"The People of God" is the name for the Church that is unlike any title used for a group in all of history. The People of God is much more than an ethnic, a political, or a cultural group that one can find in any nation. Rather, the Church has her origins in the Chosen People of Israel. The Church was brought into fullness by Christ, who called together a race of all people to participate in the New Covenant made in his blood. The description of the Church as the People of God is marked by several distinct characteristics:

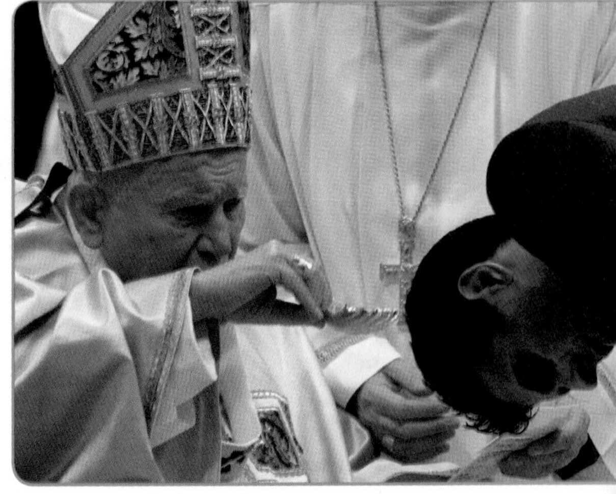

Pope John Paul II baptizes a man during the Holy Easter Vigil Mass in St. Peter's Basilica.

- The Church is *of God*. God is not the property of any one nation, race, or religion. Those who are called to the Church by God are to be "a chosen race, a royal priesthood, a holy nation."
- Church membership is not by birth. Rather, a person becomes a member of the Church through faith in Christ and Baptism by "water and Spirit."
- The Church has Jesus Christ as her head.
- The People of God have the Holy Spirit living in them, and they have dignity and freedom as God's children.
- The law that the Church is to follow is "love one another as Christ loved us."
- The mission of the Church is to be "the salt of the earth and the light of the world" (see Matthew 5:13–16).
- The destiny of the Church is God's Kingdom, which will be brought to fullness at the end of time.

Membership in the Church through faith and Baptism allows Christians to be more like Jesus. We participate in three offices of Christ—priest, prophet, and king. Each of these offices helps us be more like Jesus and know him more deeply.

In Baptism, we become sharers in Christ's priesthood. We are able to offer ourselves with Christ in his sacrifice to the Father. In doing so, we become "living stones" in building up the structure of the Church. Life on earth is often difficult. In their quest for holiness, Christians experience some of the same challenges and persecutions met by Christ. Only by aligning ourselves with Jesus can we live up to this priestly vocation.

The First Letter of Peter directs us to

> Come to him, a living stone, rejected by human beings but chosen and precious in the sight of God, and, like living stones, let yourselves be built into a spiritual house to be a holy priesthood to offer spiritual sacrifices acceptable to God through Jesus Christ. (1 Pet 2:4–5)

The People of God also share in Christ's prophetic office. This means we are Christ's witnesses in the world. Think about what *witness* means in another arena, a court of law. A witness is a person called to testify on behalf of another or on behalf of a cause. In court, a person might also be called as a "character witness," that is, someone called to the stand to testify to a person's good ethical qualities and moral standing. A Christian is to be a witness to the world on behalf of Jesus Christ. This is done by our words but primarily by our actions. Consider the life of any saint as an example of one who lives out this gift of prophecy.

Jesus' royal identity was not one of richness, power, and glory in an earthly sense. Christ, the King and Lord of the universe, made himself a lowly king, one who served the least and the lowly. In doing so he "did not come to be served but to serve and to give his life as a ransom for many" (Mt 20:28). We share in this royal commissioning when we unite the suffering—big and small—that inevitably befalls us all with the cross of Christ.

The Body of Christ

As the Church, not only do we gather *around* Jesus, we are also united *in* him. We are his body. Jesus spoke of this intimate communion with him in two direct ways.

He described himself as the "vine" and the Father as the "vine grower." We, the Church, are the "branches." Jesus said:

> You are already pruned because of the word that I spoke to you. Remain in me, as I remain in you. Just as a branch cannot bear fruit on its own unless it remains on the vine, so neither can you unless you remain in me. (Jn 15:3–4)

While the image of the vine and the branches is clear, Jesus also presented another description of the mysterious communion between himself and the Church that some of his first disciples found more difficult to understand. He said:

> Whoever eats my flesh and drinks my blood remains in me and I in him. Just as the living Father sent me and I have life because of the Father, so also the one who feeds on me will have life because of me. (Jn 6:56–57)

Both of these descriptions of the Body of Christ provide built-in challenges for us today as we seek to know Jesus in the most familiar and loving way. As a branch connected to a vine, we can only live in our relationship with Jesus. As the vine, Jesus is the head of the body. He makes our growth possible. Not only that, we are only a single branch among many. Our faith must be communal as well as personal. We must believe and relate to Jesus not only as individuals but also in the context of groups—families, friends, parishes, dioceses, and the worldwide Church. We cannot know Jesus intimately unless we live and function in these groups shaped by Christ. Together, Jesus and the Church make up the "whole Christ."

The second description of the Body of Christ is also difficult. Some of the disciples who heard about eating the flesh of Jesus and drinking his blood found it too hard to believe and accept. They returned to their former way of life and no longer followed him. Jesus then asked Peter if he also wanted to leave. Peter responded: "Master, to whom shall we go? You have the words of eternal life" (Jn 6:68).

In the Eucharist, "The body and blood, together with the soul and divinity, of our Lord Jesus Christ, and therefore, *the whole Christ is truly, really, and substantially* contained" (*CCC*, 1374, quoting the Council of Trent). This teaching of the "real presence" of Christ in the consecrated species of bread and wine remains difficult for some outside the Church to believe in today. Jesus is present wholly and entirely in each species from the moment of consecration for as long as the Eucharistic species exist. The Eucharist unites us with Christ and forms us into his body, the Church.

Also, the unity of Christ with the Church is deeply personal. It has been described by the image of a Bridegroom and a bride. Jesus once referred to himself as the Bridegroom (see Mark 2:19), and he described the Kingdom of God like a wedding feast (see Matthew 22:1–14). The Church herself has also been described as the "Beginning of the Kingdom" and the "Way to Salvation."

virtues
Good habits that help us live a moral life.

Finally, when we think of our human body, we also consider our **soul**. Just as the soul is the spiritual part of human beings that together with the body forms one human nature, the Holy Spirit is the agent of the spiritual part of the Church. The Holy Spirit brings life to the Body of Christ, the Church, and enables the Church to grow through the sacraments, the **virtues** infused by the Spirit, and the charisms he offers. The Holy Spirit makes the Church "the temple of the living God" (2 Cor 6:16).

REVIEW

1. Why is the Church a mystery?
2. How is the Church a visible sign of Christ Jesus in the world?
3. Name three ways the Church is the People of God.
4. How is Jesus in communion with his Body, the Church?

WRITE OR DISCUSS

- How are you called to participate in the three offices of Christ—priest, prophet, and king?
- Which Scripture passage helps you understand how the Church is the Body of Christ?

THE MARKS OF THE CHURCH

At the First Council of Constantinople in 381, the words "[we believe] in one, holy, catholic, and apostolic church" were officially added to the Nicene Creed. The Council Fathers understood that the nature of the Church is an expression of Christ.

Through the Holy Spirit, Jesus makes the Church one, holy, catholic, and apostolic. These characteristics are known as the four marks of the Church. The Church does not possess these marks on her own, but only from Christ, their source.

The Church is the first sacrament of Christ. This means that the Church is the symbol and the instrument of God's presence on earth and through history. It is in and through the Church that Christ is visible and present. Christ remains active in the Church through the Holy Spirit, constantly shaping the Church by making these marks present in different ways. The four marks do help us understand *how* the Church is the sacrament of Christ and ways that Christ remains present and visible in the Church and the world today.

The Church Is One

The Church is one first and foremost because of her source: the unity in the Trinity of the Father, the Son, and the Holy Spirit in one God. The Church's unity can never be broken or lost because this foundation itself is unbreakable. The Church is also one because of her founder, Jesus, who died on the cross to restore the unity of all. Christ's gift of the Holy Spirit continues to join all believers together in him.

The gift of love given by the Holy Spirit to Christians is the "bond of perfection" (Col 3:14). Other visible signs of the Church's unity include:

- The same Creed. The Church professes one faith as received from the Apostles.
- A common celebration of divine worship, especially the sacraments. The Church respects diversity in this area. For example, Mass is celebrated in many languages, incorporating the traditions of

several cultures. Seven non-Roman Church rites are in union with the Roman Catholic Church. The Armenian, Byzantine, Coptic, Ethiopian, East Syrian (or Chaldean), West Syrian, and Maronite rites are all part of the one Catholic Church.

- Recognition of the bishops ordained in the Sacrament of Holy Orders as successors to the Apostles.

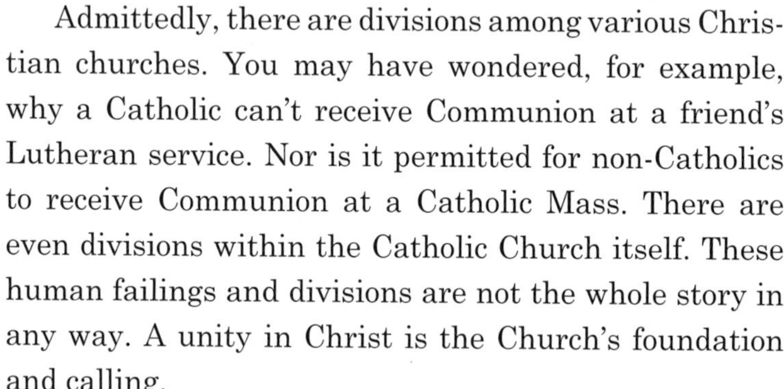

Admittedly, there are divisions among various Christian churches. You may have wondered, for example, why a Catholic can't receive Communion at a friend's Lutheran service. Nor is it permitted for non-Catholics to receive Communion at a Catholic Mass. There are even divisions within the Catholic Church itself. These human failings and divisions are not the whole story in any way. A unity in Christ is the Church's foundation and calling.

It's important to understand that from the beginning the Church has been diverse within its unity. Consider that people of countless races, cultures, and nations represent the Church. These people have different gifts, traditions, and ways of life. A 2007 statement by the Vatican's doctrinal congregation stated that "these separated churches and communities . . . are deprived neither of significance nor importance in the mystery of salvation." In fact, the spirit of Christ has not refrained from using these other churches as instruments of salvation, "whose power derives from the fullness of grace and of truth that Christ has entrusted to the Catholic Church" (*CCC*, 819). The Second Vatican Council taught that "those who believe in Christ and have been

properly baptized are put in a certain, although imperfect, communion with the Catholic Church" (*CCC*, 838).

The Pope, the successor of Peter, and the bishops, who are in communion with the Pope, govern the Church. In discussing the Church's unity, several questions need to be addressed. How are the separated churches part of the one Church founded by Christ? What is the history of some of the divisions within the Church that have taken place? How can these wounds be repaired? The succeeding sections trace these issues.

Ruptures in Christian Unity

From the very beginning of the Church's history, there were rifts in her unity. St. Paul spoke of it when some of the local Corinthian church began to align themselves exclusively with different Christian leaders and consider some people to be superior to others. Jealousy was at the root of most of these early disagreements.

In later centuries, the divisions were more severe and lasting. Large communities became separated from the Catholic Church. Sinfulness on both sides contributed to these divisions, but the primary causes were ***heresy*** (denying essential truths of the faith), ***apostasy*** (abandoning the faith), and ***schism*** (breaking the Church's unity).

For about the first thousand years, Christians belonged to one Church. This was the Church that took her moral and spiritual direction from the Bishop of Rome. These Christians believed he was given this role of primacy because St. Peter had been the first Bishop of Rome and Jesus had personally commissioned Peter to be the leader of the Apostles and the Church.

A major schism in 1054 took place between the churches of the West (centered in Rome) and the East (centered in the

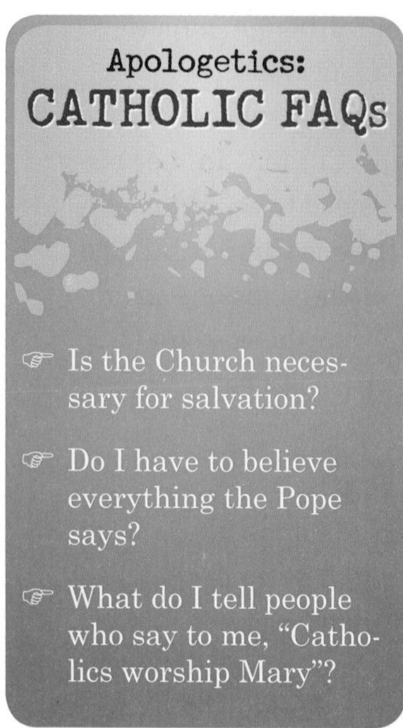

Greek city of Constantinople). The Roman Church had added the expression "and the Son" to the article of the Nicene Creed referring to the Holy Spirit ("he proceeds from the Father and the Son") without seeking approval for such a change from a Church-wide council of bishops. Though other issues were involved, this controversy led to a split that lasts to this day between what are now known as the Eastern Orthodox churches and the Roman Catholic Church. These eastern churches have many of the same doctrines, sacraments, Mass, and devotions as the Roman Catholic Church, but they do not accept the Pope as the universal leader of the Church. Still, great strides have been made in recent years to repair this rift.

Apologetics:
CATHOLIC FAQs
Is the Church necessary for salvation?
Do I have to believe everything the Pope says?
What do I tell people who say to me, "Catholics worship Mary"?

A second major rupture in the Church's unity occurred in the Protestant Reformation of the sixteenth century. The root word of ***Protestant*** is *protest*, and several Church leaders protested against perceived abuses in the Church. Several of these issues involved the mixing of the spiritual and political realms. Martin Luther, a Catholic priest from Germany, was the first to protest. Other protestors included John Calvin in Switzerland and John Knox in Scotland. These individuals and their followers broke from the Roman Catholic Church and formed their own branches or denominations of Christianity that came to be known as Lutheran, Calvinist, Presbyterian, Anglican, Baptist, and more. From that time on, Christians who continued to accept the authority of the Pope were known as Catholics; those who did not were called Protestants. While the authority of the Pope was a focal point of the disagreements, there were many other important issues as well. One was the way in which God's grace works in our lives. Others were the celebration of the sacraments and the nature of the priesthood.

Nevertheless, the Catholic Church has a great deal in common with most Protestant ecclesial communities, including belief in the Trinity, acceptance of the Bible as God's inspired Word, a life of prayer, Baptism, a moral code, and service of the needy.

Catholics accept Christians in these churches as brothers and sisters in faith. The Holy Spirit uses these churches as means of salvation "whose power derives from the fullness of grace and truth that Christ has entrusted to the Catholic Church" (*CCC*, 819). The Catholic Church is understood as being governed by the Pope—the successor to St. Peter—and the bishops, who are in communion with him.

Repairing Christian Unity

Jesus prayed for the unity of his disciples on the night before he died "so that they may all be one, as you, Father, are in me and I in you, that they also may be in us" (Jn 17:21). The Church will always be one because of her source (one God: Father, Son, and Holy Spirit), founder (Christ), and soul (the Holy Spirit). However, because of the ruptures due in part to human sinfulness, the Church must continue to work toward unity and repair any damage to the unity that has taken place.

The *Catechism of the Catholic Church* lists seven things required of Catholics to help in this movement toward Christian unity:

1. Being faithful to his or her own vocation (e.g., especially toward charity).
2. Living holier lives. This example will work oppositely from unfaithfulness of Church members that often plays a part in divisions.
3. Common prayer with other Christians. We can pray for Christian unity and with Christians in other ecclesial communities.
4. Fraternal knowledge of each other. This often takes place through participation together in social and service activities.
5. Formation of all the faithful—especially of priests—in this charge to develop greater unity. A first task is for us is to study our own faith so we can comfortably share our knowledge of it with others.
6. Dialogue between theologians and meetings among Christians of different ecclesial communities.
7. Collaboration with other Christians in efforts of service to all people, for example, to the poor.

Ecumenism is the name given to the efforts to build unity among all Christian denominations. Ecumenism encourages understanding among the various Christian churches and avoidance of needless opposition to one another. Interreligious dialogue is a related effort to foster religious understanding. There are dialogues between the Church and non-Christian religions in order to improve those relationships as well.

Ecumenism
The movement, inspired and led by the Holy Spirit, that seeks the union of all Christian religions and eventually the unity of all peoples throughout the world.

We can all participate in the ecumenical effort. However, the reconciliation of all Christians to the one and only Church of Christ, the Catholic Church, is something that "transcends human powers and gifts." We place our hope "in the prayer of Christ for the Church, in the love of the Father for us, and in the power of the Holy Spirit" (*Decree on Ecumenism*, 24).

The Church Is Holy

Holiness means "to be set apart" or "of God." The Church's holiness does not come about because of anything her members do, no matter how well intentioned. For example, the Church's holiness is not dependent on actions of individual members such as praying more, being extra kind, or even being more forgiving.

While these actions are holy and good, the Church is holy because she is the Body of Christ. The Church is also holy because the Holy Spirit dwells in her. All holiness has its roots in God, who alone is truly holy. God alone is completely set apart from all creation because God alone is uncreated. The Church is holy or set apart from the rest of creation because of her intimate connection with God.

With Christ and together with the Church, we strive to make ourselves and all the world holy in Christ for the glory of God. Though our holiness is imperfect now, we are each called—through whatever course our lives take—to the perfect holiness by which God the Father is himself perfect.

The Way to Holiness

The way to holiness is love. Loving actions are the fruit of a person's holiness. St. John of the Cross wrote that "at the end of our life, we shall be judged by love." St. Thérèse of Lisieux called love "the vocation which includes all others; it's a universe of its own, comprising all time and space—it's eternal." According to St. Augustine:

> Love is itself the fulfillment of all our works. There is the goal; that is why we run: we run toward it, and once we reach it, in it we shall find rest.

Jesus gave us the most difficult criteria for love. We are to love others as we love ourselves. We are to have special love for children and the poor. We are to love even our most contemptible enemies. We do this because Jesus loved in these ways. Though we are sinners, Jesus loved us so much he willingly died on the cross for us.

We are still a Church of sinners. One of the first characteristics of holiness is to acknowledge this fact, and also to know that the Church gathers us up in our sinfulness and carries us through the life of grace to holiness. As Pope Paul VI put it, "The Church is therefore holy, though having sinners in her midst, because she herself has no other life but the life of grace" (see *CCC,* 827).

Taking steps to overcome our sinfulness is part of the life plan to be holy. We do this through acts of penance and by seeking forgiveness for our sins. Participation in the Eucharist is a way to be fed and strengthened in our pursuit of conversion and penance. The Eucharist frees us from daily faults and preserves us from mortal sins. The Sacrament of Penance offers the opportunity for forgiveness and absolution of grave sins. The Church Fathers described the Sacrament as "the second plan [of salvation] after the shipwreck which is the loss of grace" (quoted in *CCC*, 1446).

A Communion of Saints

The Church is known as the "People of God," and its members are called **saints** or "holy ones" (see Acts 9:13). "Who, me? A saint?" You may be questioning whether you measure up. Keep in mind that a saint is simply a person who chooses to be holy. And all Christians are called to be holy.

The term **communion of saints** refers to the unity of all those living on earth (the pilgrim Church), those being purified in **Purgatory** (the Church suffering), and those enjoying the blessings of Heaven (the Church in glory). In this sense, we are, in fact, all saints.

Raphael's La Disputa
(Disputation of the Holy Sacrament)

The Church also has a process of **canonization** in which she recognizes the particular examples of Christians who have led good and holy lives and died in faithfulness to Jesus. The process includes careful study of the person's life and a sign from God (usually in the form of miracles) that this person is truly with God in Heaven. When the process is completed, the Church can call these people "saints." We can seek them out to intercede to God on our behalf and imitate their good examples.

Some non-Catholics criticize Catholics for "praying to saints" as if saints were God. We *honor* saints for their holy lives, but we do not pray to them as if they were God. We ask the saints to pray with us and for us as part of the Church in glory. We can ask them to do this because we know that their lives were spent in close communion with God. We also ask the saints for their friendship so we can follow the examples they have left for us. Mary, the Mother of God, is the Queen of the Saints and the most worthy model of faith. (See pages 118–119 for more information on Mary.)

The Church Is Catholic

The mark of the Church *catholic* with a small *c* means that the Church is "universal" or "for everyone." The totality of the Body of Christ is present in the Church. This means that the Church is whole; she is complete. Nothing that is good—no virtue, no spiritual gift, no cure for sin—exists outside the Church but not inside the Church. Nothing of God is lacking in Christ. Therefore, nothing is lacking in the Church, Christ's Body. To call the Church "catholic" also means she is for all people. Jesus offers salvation to all people, and he established the Church that she might be the "universal sacrament of salvation" (*CCC*, 849, quoting *Ad gentes*, 1).

All people are called to this catholic unity of the Church. However, although the Church is for everyone, not everyone belongs to the Church in the same way. There is a certain ordering of people in the Church. Full members are those who are baptized Catholics and accept all the tenets of the Church, besides behaving in a loving way.

The Church also knows that other Christians, for various reasons, do not profess the Catholic faith in totality. Or they have had their unity with the Pope severed but are still joined in many ways with the Church. Still others have not received the Good News of Jesus Christ but are related to the Church in some ways.

For example, Jewish People were "the first to hear the Word of God," as we hear in the Good Friday liturgy. Both Jews and Christians await the coming of the Messiah, though the Jewish understanding of the Messiah remains hidden and mysterious, while Christians await the **Second Coming** of a Messiah they know

Second Coming
The final judgment of all humanity when Christ returns to earth. It is also known by its Greek term, Parousia, which means "arrival."

to be the Risen Christ. With Muslims, the Church shares a belief in the one Creator God and the faith of Abraham, to whom God spoke. Finally, the Church shares a bond with people of all non-Christian religions because of our common humanity. The Church recognizes that all people are searching for the God who gives them life.

Why is the Church universal? First and foremost, because Christ is present in the Church. As St. Ignatius of Antioch wrote, "Where there is Christ Jesus, there is the Catholic Church." Because Christ is present in the Church as the head while the Church is the body, all salvation comes through the Church. For this reason it is absolutely necessary for all Catholics to help lead others to Christ through the Church and to work to repair Christian unity.

To the Ends of the Earth and Nearby

The Church's missionary mandate to share the Good News of Christ with *all people* began with Christ's own words at the time of his Ascension to Heaven: "Go, therefore and make disciples of all nations" (Mt 28:19).

The love of God spurs us onward for Christ. The Holy Spirit is the fuel driving our missionary efforts. The Church always reaches out to people, in all times, in all places, and in several ways. For example, in the sixteenth and seventeenth centuries, the Church was involved in spreading the Gospel to the Americas.

Whenever explorers went into the New World, missionaries followed. Their motto was "cross and crown." History has recorded several abuses by missionaries who did not bother to learn the native languages and forced conversion on the populace. Yet many good missionaries fought against this tide of ill will. For example, Bartolomé de Las Casas worked vigorously for the rights of native people in the New World. St. Peter

Claver worked among the slaves in Colombia and the West Indies. St. Martin de Porres earned the nickname "the wonder worker of Peru" for his ceaseless devotion to lessen the evils of slavery. Jesuits set up model communities in Paraguay and Brazil that tried to preserve the native cultures while providing education and the benefits of civilization. These are but a few of the examples of how the Church has shared the Gospel in a particular time and place. In fact, missionary efforts have flourished in every generation.

The Second Vatican Council mandated ongoing missionary activity of the Church, describing it as

> nothing else, and nothing less, than the manifestation of God's plan, its epiphany and realization in the world and in history; that by which God, through mission, clearly brings to its conclusion the history of salvation. (*Ad gentes divinitus*, 9)

Today, in places all over the world, including the fertile nations of Africa, the Church couples her missionary activities with a focus on social justice, being careful not to risk economic exploitation of native peoples at the expense of religious conversion.

While the Church is universal in the scope of her missionary activities, her care for and welcome to all people extend to local areas as well. The Church in a particular area, called a ***diocese*** ("house"), is also truly catholic as long as she is united to her local leader, the bishop. The sum of all the dioceses in the world is more than simply a federation in which each is a chapter. Rather, they are catholic through their communion with the Church of Rome, the Church where St. Peter himself was the first bishop.

Within a diocese are parishes with given physical boundaries that include a place of worship, a church. In these parishes, where the Gospel is preached and the Eucharist is celebrated, a variety of levels of income, cultures, languages, and traditions exist. Yet each of these particular churches is catholic in each of the senses described: It draws on the whole of Revelation—all of Scripture, the teachings of the Apostles, and the understanding and the witness of Christians from all times and places—in union with the Magisterium. Also, it is welcoming of all and cognizant of its mission to share the Good News of Jesus.

The Church Is Apostolic

The Apostles chosen by Jesus are the foundation on which the Church began and developed and will always remain. Jesus himself sent them on their mission.

Through the ministry of the Apostles, Jesus' mission on earth continued. As Jesus told the Apostles, "Whoever receives you receives me" (Mt 10:40). Through Jesus, the Apostles were united to the mission Jesus received from God the Father and were given the power to carry it out. The Apostles were given other titles in the New Testament; they were called "servants of God" and "ambassadors of Christ."

The Church remains apostolic because she still teaches the same things the Apostles taught. And the Church is apostolic because she is led by leaders who are successors to the Apostles and who help guide us until Jesus returns.

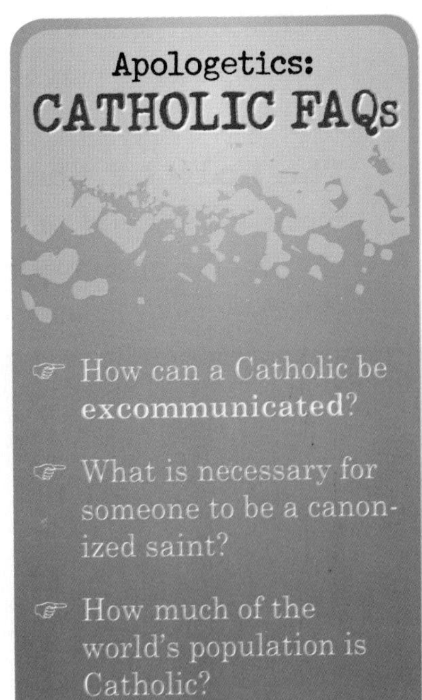
Apologetics:
CATHOLIC FAQs
How can a Catholic be excommunicated?
What is necessary for someone to be a canonized saint?
How much of the world's population is Catholic?

laity
All the members of the Church who have been initiated into the Church through Baptism and are not ordained (the clergy) or in consecrated life. The laity participates in Jesus' prophetic, priestly, and kingly ministries.

The bishops are the successors to the Apostles. The Church teaches that "the bishops have by divine institution taken the place of the Apostles as pastors of the Church, in such ways that whoever listens to them is listening to Christ and whoever despises them despises Christ and him who sent Christ" (*Dogmatic Constitution on the Church,* 20). It is the bishops who confer the Sacrament of Holy Orders in three degrees—the degrees of priestly participation (bishops and priests) and the degree of service (deacons).

Yet not only the bishops (and priests) are called to be apostolic. The entire Church, including religious and **laity**, are to take up the apostolic call to bring God's Kingdom to all the earth.

The next sections explain more about how these groups work together as part of the one Body of Christ in the apostolic mission.

The Role of the Hierarchy

Simon Peter was clearly the leader of the Twelve Apostles. Jesus confided in him personally on several occasions. In fact, Peter's name is mentioned more than any other besides Jesus' in the Gospels. Jesus said: "You are Peter, and upon this rock I will build my church, and the gates of the netherworld shall not prevail against it. I will give you the keys to the kingdom of heaven" (Mt 16:18–19).

Jesus gave Peter the "keys to the Kingdom."

Peter may have lived for more than twenty-five years after Jesus' Death and Resurrection. He traveled extensively around the Roman Empire and eventually founded, with St. Paul, the Church in Rome. Because of Peter's primacy among the Apostles, the Church at Rome came to enjoy the same primacy over other local churches. Thus, the Bishop of Rome, or the Pope, is respected with authority over the universal Church in the same way Peter once was.

All the bishops—and in a lesser way priests—share with the Pope the authority to teach in Jesus' name in the teaching office called the Magisterium. The "college" or body of bishops has the authority to teach in union with the Pope. Magisterial teaching of the Pope and the bishops can be found in their writings. These include council documents, papal encyclicals, pastoral letters, and sermons. The goal of these teachings is to build up the Church, administer the sacraments, and correctly proclaim the Gospel for the current age.

Infallibility is a gift of the Holy Spirit to the Church that enables the Pope and the bishops to teach and proclaim a doctrine without error. This gift is grounded in the fact that Jesus promised to send the Holy Spirit to remain with the Church for all time. Infallible teachings are given with the guidance of the Holy Spirit. One form of infallible teaching is when the Pope teaches "from the chair" of St. Peter. The Latin term for "from the chair" is *ex cathedra*. This type of teaching is very rare. The last time a Pope issued an *ex cathedra* teaching was in 1950, when Pope Pius XII proclaimed the **Assumption**, that Mary was assumed body and soul into Heaven after her death.

Infallibility
A gift of the Spirit whereby the Pope and the bishops are preserved from error when proclaiming a doctrine related to Christian faith or morals.

Another form of infallibility is found in the teaching of the entire body of bishops, in union with the Pope, especially in an **Ecumenical Council**. Finally, infallibility refers to the beliefs of the Church as a whole: those things that have always and everywhere been taught and believed by the Church, for example, the beliefs expressed in the Apostles' Creed.

Lay Faithful and the Consecrated Life

The term *laity* comes from the Greek word *laos*, which means "of the people." Lay people are not second-class citizens in the Church. The laity has its own role or mission in the world to share in the priestly, prophetic, and kingly offices of Christ. The laity includes any baptized Catholic who has not received Holy Orders and does not belong to a Church-approved religious state. The laity has the special call to be involved in the social, political, and economic affairs of the wider human community and to direct them according to God's will. Laymen and laywomen are to be the light of the world and the salt of the earth.

The consecrated or **religious life** refers to Catholics who make a public profession of the **evangelical counsels** of poverty, chastity, and obedience. Those in consecrated life can be members of the **hierarchy** or lay people and include hermits, consecrated virgins, secular institutes, different apostolic societies, and men (brothers) and women (sisters) in religious orders such as Jesuit, Franciscan, Dominican, Benedictine, and many more. Those living in religious life serve as special gifts to other Catholics and to all people. They are unique witnesses to Jesus' union with the Church and a sign to the world that God's salvation is taking place in our midst.

Both committed lay people and consecrated religious have done much to strengthen the witness of Christ through the Church's two-thousand-year history. Led by the hierarchy, the Church, as Christ's Body, will exist until the end of time.

REVIEW

1. What are the four marks of the Church?
2. Name three signs of the Church's unity.
3. What were the causes of the schism of 1054?
4. What does the Catholic Church have in common with most Protestant churches?
5. Why will the Church always be one?
6. How is love the true test of holiness?
7. Define *communion of saints.*
8. What are two ways the Church is catholic?
9. What did the missionaries of the New World mean by the motto "cross and crown"?
10. How do the Church's missionary efforts extend to local areas?
11. Why does the Church remain apostolic?
12. Why does the Church at Rome have primacy over other local churches?
13. Define *infallibility.*
14. Name the evangelical counsels.

WRITE OR DISCUSS

- Of the ecumenical efforts listed on page 170, what is the one you feel most comfortable participating in? Why?
- What can you say to someone who criticizes you for "praying to saints"?
- What does it mean to be "the light of the world and the salt of the earth"? Who is someone you know who lives this call?

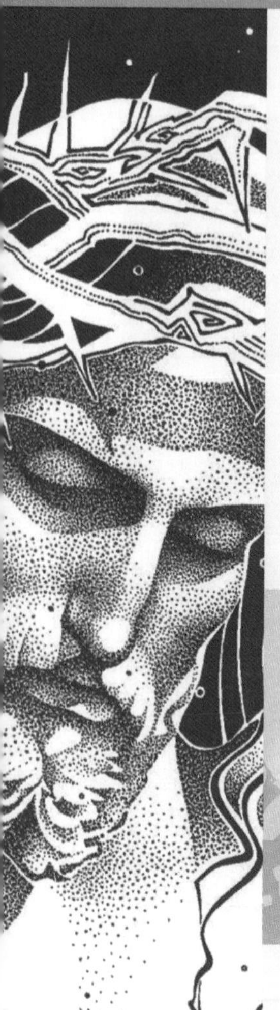

REVERSING TRENDS

A recent collection of survey statistics[8] revealed disarming trends in the spiritual and religious practice of young adult Catholics. For example, it found that young adult Catholics are less likely to say that their Catholic faith is "the most important" or "among the most important parts" of their lives than Catholics from older generations. Young adult Catholics gave the following responses to the question "How important is your Catholic faith in your daily life?":

- The most important part of your life—**14%**
- Among the most important parts of your life—**28%**
- Important, but so are many other areas of your life—**41%**
- Not too important in your life—**14%**
- Not important in your life at all—**3%**

Young adult Catholics also had wide-ranging responses, from "essential" to "not important at all," when asked how important different aspects of the Catholic faith are to their sense of what it means to be a Catholic. For example:

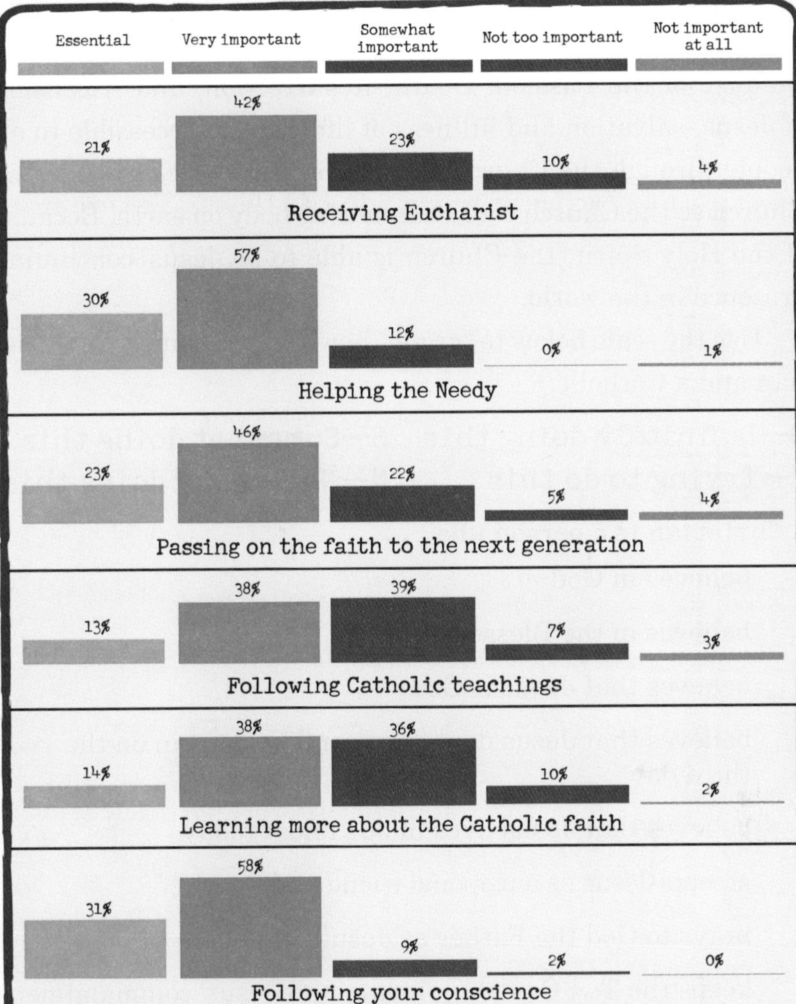

Do two things:

- Administer the two surveys from above among twenty Catholic peers. Graph your results to each survey. Write a summary of the surveys. Note and speculate on reasons for variation in the results.
- Research other issues involving the spiritual, prayer, and religious life of Catholic teenagers and young adults. Summarize and share your findings.

GETTING TO KNOW JESUS

Because of the Passion, Death, Resurrection, and Ascension of Jesus, salvation and fullness of life became accessible to all people through the Church. Jesus breathed his Spirit into the Church so the Church could become his body on earth. Because of the Holy Spirit, the Church is able to be Jesus' continuing presence in the world.

Use the scale below to "grade" how you are doing as a Christian and a Catholic.

D—Definitely doing this **S—Somewhat doing this**
T—Trying to do this **N—Not really doing this**

A Christian is a person who . . .

____believes in God

____believes in the Blessed Trinity

____believes that Jesus is God

____believes that Jesus died for us and rose again on the third day

____believes that Jesus lives in our midst today

____accepts Jesus as a personal friend and Savior

____prays to God the Father as Jesus taught

____keeps the Ten Commandments and Jesus' commandment to love

____tries to live according to the teachings of Jesus

____reads and prays with the Bible

A Catholic is a person who, besides the things listed above . . .

____accepts the Pope as Christ's vicar or representative on earth

____celebrates the Eucharist every Sunday and holy day with other Catholics

____believes that Jesus is present in the Eucharist

____receives Holy Communion frequently

____goes to confession at least once per year and after committing a mortal sin

____contributes to the support of the Church with gifts of time, talent, and tithing

____observes special days of fasting and abstinence

____honors Mary as the Mother of God and the saints and asks for their **intercession**

____holds that salvation comes from Christ through the Catholic Church

____receives the sacraments within the Catholic Church

Choose one of your strongest responses (D or T) and write a statement that shares the depth of your belief.

Choose one of your weakest responses (S or N) and write an action plan with both immediate and long-term steps for improving in these areas.

PRAYER

Ave Crux, Spes unica!
Hail Cross, Only Hope
The world is in flames.
The conflagration can also reach our house.
But high above all flames towers the cross.
They cannot consume it.
It is the path from earth to heaven.
It will lift one who embraces it
in faith, love, and hope into the bosom of the Trinity.
The eyes of the Crucified look down on you asking, probing.
Will you make your covenant with the Crucified anew
in all seriousness?
What will you answer him?
"Lord, where shall we go? You have the words of
eternal life."
Ave Crux, Spes unica!
—St. Edith Stein

5 The Sacraments of Christ

SIGN, SYMBOL, SACRAMENT

Why are there seven sacraments in the Catholic Church? An easy answer is that Jesus instituted exactly seven.

In the thirteenth century, St. Thomas Aquinas expanded on the reasons and taught that human development is likewise marked by a similar seven stages. While it was not mandatory for Christ to institute exactly seven sacraments, it was reasonable because:

- We are born (**Baptism**)
- We grow (**Confirmation**)
- We are fed (**Eucharist**)
- We are healed (**Penance**)
- We recover (**Anointing of the Sick**)

- We need and form family (**Matrimony**)
- We need and respond to leaders (**Holy Orders**)

This chapter defines the sacramental nature of the Church in relationship to the sacramental nature of Christ. It discusses who is eligible to receive and minister the sacraments, their essential elements, as well as the effects and the implications of the Seven Sacraments. It examines sacraments in the natural flow of human development and experience.

sacrament
An outward (visible) sign of an invisible grace; an "efficacious" symbol that brings about the spiritual reality to which it points. This term applies to Christ Jesus, the great sign of God's love for us; to the Church, his continuing presence in the world; and to the Seven Sacraments.

To begin, it's important to break open three traditional definitions of sacrament. St. Paul provided a first definition. In Scripture the Latin word for ***sacrament***—*sacramentum*—is used to translate the Greek word *mysterion* ("mystery"). When Paul used the term *mystery*, he referred to God's hidden plan of wanting to save, renew, and unite all things in Christ. Speaking of our fulfillment through Christ, Paul wrote to the Ephesians:

> In him we have redemption by his blood, the forgiveness of transgressions, in accord with the riches of his grace that he lavished upon us. In all wisdom and insight, he has made known to us the mystery of his will in accord with his favor that he set forth in him as a plan for the fullness of times, to sum up all things in Christ, in heaven and on earth. (Eph 1:7–10)

St. Augustine's definition of sacrament stressed sign and symbol. Think about what you already know from everyday

experience about signs and symbols. A symbol can be defined as "something concrete that points to something else." It is a sign that points to another reality. For example, an American flag represents democracy and freedom. Yet for enemies of the United States, an American flag may represent imperialism. Another symbolic thing is a stop sign. Its red octagonal shape is a sign that drivers should put on their brakes and stop their cars! Things such as flags and road signs are not the only common symbols. Events such as Independence Day or Thanksgiving typically symbolize family, food, and fun besides their national significance. People can also be symbols. For example, in the early 1960s President John F. Kennedy was a symbol in the United States for idealism and hope. Muslim leaders—for example, an ayatollah in Arab countries—often symbolize the same thing, albeit from different perspectives and with different means.

Augustine understood a sacrament to be a sign of a sacred reality. A sacrament is a holy sign, a symbol through which the believer can both perceive and receive an invisible grace. The sign or symbol points to the deeper reality of the spiritual world, where friendship and communion with God can be realized. For example, the waters of Baptism point to a rebirth of communion and friendship with God. The waters help Christians perceive the reality of rebirth, but because Baptism is a sacrament, the grace of the rebirth truly occurs.

Aquinas went even further to delineate the meaning of sacrament. He defined sacrament as an efficacious ("truly effective") symbol or sign of grace. This means that a sacrament effects what it symbolizes and symbolizes what it effects. An ordinary symbol does not do that. For example, a stop sign does not cause a person to stop. It only points to the idea of stopping. A sacrament does in fact bring about what it symbolizes and symbolizes what it brings about. A sacrament confers the particular grace that is proper to it.

For example, in the Sacrament of Eucharist, the bread and wine are symbols that point to the Body and Blood of Jesus. But the Eucharist is more than just an ordinary symbol. It is a sacrament, and the bread and wine *are* the Body and Blood of Christ *and* visible signs.

God reveals himself in many, countless ways. We can know and feel God's presence in unlimited people, events, and places. But God has chosen some ways to be more present, some ways to reveal himself more clearly, in a way even more real and powerful than others. The sacraments are unique signs we can perceive through our senses and put us into real contact with the saving Jesus. In a sacrament there is a "pointing to" and an "effecting of" the reality symbolized. A sacrament is a very special kind of symbol.

REVIEW

1. What did St. Paul stress in his definition of sacrament?
2. Share an example of a symbol. Explain why it is so.
3. How is a sacrament an efficacious sign? Explain how the Eucharist is an efficacious sign.

WRITE OR DISCUSS

- If you could devise a symbol for your life, what would it be? What would it tell about you?

THE SACRAMENTAL NATURE OF CHRIST AND THE CHURCH

The sacraments are tangible signs and symbolic actions by which the presence of Christ and the power of the Holy Spirit enable us to be the People of God. The sacraments are the action of Christ living through us. As Pope John Paul II put it:

> What else are the sacraments (all of them), if not the action of Christ in the Holy Spirit? When the Church baptizes, it is Christ who baptizes; when the Church absolves, it is Christ who absolves; when the Church celebrates Eucharist, it is Christ who celebrates it: "This is my body." And so on. All the sacraments are an action of Christ, the action of God in Christ. (*Crossing the Threshold of Hope*)

Though a sacrament is a sign, not all signs are sacraments. To be a sacrament, a sign must not only lead us to God, as all sacraments do, but it must come from God and be an action of God. Using this understanding, Jesus Christ is the original sign and the primordial, or prime, sacrament. Jesus is not only a sign of God the Father in our midst, he is the very presence of God.

The Scriptures support this view. The beginning of the Letter to the Hebrews expresses it clearly:

> In times past, God spoke in partial and various ways to our ancestors through the prophets; in these last days, he spoke to us through a son, whom he made heir of all things and through whom he created the universe. (Heb 1:1–2)

In John's Gospel, Jesus said to his disciples:

> I am the way and the truth and the life. No one comes to the Father except through me. If you know me, then you will also know my Father. From now on you do know him and have seen him. (Jn 14:6–7)

The next section explains more about how Christ is the primordial, or prime, sacrament.

Jesus as Sacrament

Jesus is God in the flesh. His whole life, all of his words and actions, reveals God the Father. The Paschal Mystery—Jesus' Passion, Death, Resurrection, and Ascension—most clearly reveals God.

The Paschal Mystery is a unique event in history. Like other historical events, it really happened at a definite time and in a specific location. Unlike other historical events, the Paschal Mystery transcends time and place. Because through this event Jesus was able to destroy death and bring about salvation, the Paschal Mystery is present to every generation since. Christ is truly present in the Paschal Mystery.

Christ's presence in the Paschal Mystery is made known to us in the **liturgy**, which comes from a Greek

Apologetics: CATHOLIC FAQs

Use this chapter and other sources to formulate your own answers to these questions. Then check your answers at "Catholic FAQs" at www.avemariapress.com: Religious Education.

- Did the early Church baptize infants?
- Is Baptism all that is needed for salvation?
- What happens to children who die without Baptism?

word that means "work of the people." The liturgy is the work of the Holy Trinity. God the Father is the source of the liturgy in the same way he is the source of all creation. The blessings of the liturgy are the words and the gifts of God the Father to us. We respond to his blessings by responding to his grace. Christ's presence in the liturgy is sacramental. God the Father gave us his Son so we might really experience what it is to be in his presence. The Holy Spirit is the teacher who enlightens our faith and inspires our response. When we do this, the Holy Spirit unites us in a loving community, the Church, and gives us life in the Risen Lord.

liturgy
The official public worship of the Church. The sacraments and the Divine Office constitute the Church's liturgy. Mass is the most important liturgical celebration.

Pope Leo the Great explained it this way: "Whatever was visible in our Redeemer has passed over into the sacraments."

Christ Is Really Present

To be able to accomplish such a great work as our salvation, Christ must be and always is present in the Church, especially in the sacraments. This is most clearly expressed and understood in the Eucharist. How is this so?

First, Jesus is present in the priest, the minister of the sacrament, who received a personal calling by Christ to his ministry through the Sacrament of Holy Orders. In the same way, through the Sacrament of Holy Orders, Christ is present in the minister who baptizes, hears confessions, anoints the sick, and presides at marriage. Christ, in point of fact, is the minister of the sacraments. The priest or the deacon only acts in his name.

How is this so? One way to understand this reality is to think about representatives who stand in for others. For instance, substitute teachers take the place of—or act in the name of—regular teachers. Babysitters stand in for parents. So when teachers or parents aren't present, representatives take their places to help students or sons and daughters experience their teachers' or parents' presence through sharing lessons or through giving care and protection.

Second, Jesus is present when the Holy Scriptures are read. The Scriptures are the Word of God and inspired by the Holy Spirit. Think of a letter—especially one that is handwritten—you have received from a close friend. In a way, you can experience the person's presence through what is written and even how it is written. This is similar to how Jesus is present in the Scriptures read at Eucharist and in the other sacraments.

Third, Jesus is present in the community that has gathered in his name. Jesus once told his disciples, "For where two or three are gathered together in my name, there am I in the midst of them" (Mt 18:20). He is present in the Church when we pray and sing. Jesus promised to be with the Church until the end of the world (Mt 28:20).

Finally, and specifically, in the Eucharist, Jesus is really present in the consecrated species of bread and wine. This presence is known as "real presence" because it is Jesus' presence in the fullest sense. According to the *Catechism of the Catholic Church*, "It is a substantial presence by which Christ, God and man, makes himself wholly and entirely present" (*CCC*, 1374). For many years, the Church has used the term ***transubstantiation*** to express how the reality (substance) of bread and wine changes into the reality of Jesus' risen and glorified Body and Blood.

The Second Vatican Council taught:

> Christ indeed always associates the church with himself in the truly great work of giving perfect praise to God and making men holy. The church is his dearly beloved Bride who calls to her Lord, and through him offers worship in the Eternal Father. (*Sacrosanctum concilium*, 7)

The earthly liturgy is a foretaste of the heavenly liturgy, which is the celebration of God's praises by the whole company of angels and saints in the city of Jerusalem. Christ is present there, sitting at the right hand of God. It is our hope that someday we will participate in the heavenly liturgy and share in Christ's glory.

The Church as Sacrament

Like Christ, the Church is also a sacrament. The Church is a sign of our inner union with God. Because we are also in community with other people, the Church is also a sign of our union with each other. This unity is taking place now, in the diverse gathering of people of all races and cultures in the catholic, or universal, Church. At the same time, the unity is not yet complete. The Church is also a sign of the full unity of people that is to come in the future.

Jesus is no longer physically present with us. Yet, as a sacrament, the Church is Christ's instrument. Christ, the head of the Church, uses the Church to dispense the graces necessary for salvation. One way this is done is through the Seven Sacraments—"signs and instruments by which the Holy Spirit spreads the grace of Christ the head throughout the Church which is his Body" (*CCC*, 774).

How else does the Church fit in with our understanding of sacrament?

First, like Christ, the Church is a mystery. The Eastern churches still refer to the sacraments as "holy mysteries." The Church is the visible sign of the hidden reality of salvation.

Second, Christ loves the Church. He always has and always will. He gave up his life for the Church, and he has remained present in the Church in all the days since. The Gospels describe the faithful as a bride attached to Christ. In Mark 2:19,

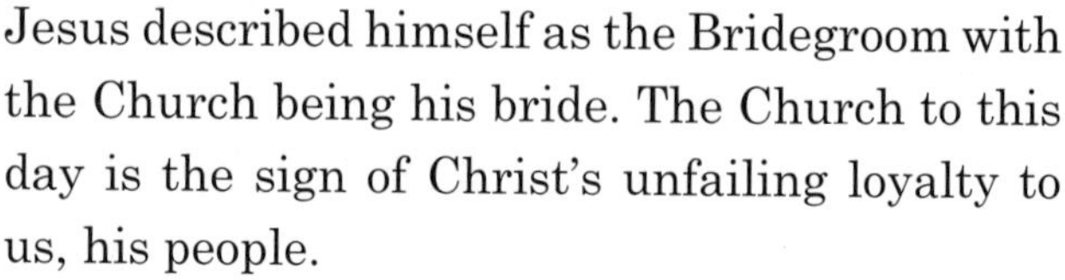

Jesus described himself as the Bridegroom with the Church being his bride. The Church to this day is the sign of Christ's unfailing loyalty to us, his people.

Third, the Church is an efficacious symbol. That means it is a symbol that not only points to a reality—in this case, our salvation—but also causes it. Recall that this is different from other symbols or signs. For example, the traditional peace sign of the 1960s was a symbol for an effort mostly by young people of that era to bring an end to the Vietnam War and violence in the streets of their own country. The young people did things like march in protest and petition government officials. It was these efforts, not the peace sign, that helped bring about an end to the war and some of the violence. The Church is different. It not only points to our deeper union with God and our salvation, it also causes them to happen. Mainly they happen through the invisible graces of the Seven Sacraments.

Seven Sacraments Instituted by Christ

Just as the Church developed the canon of the Scriptures and the other doctrines of faith through the Holy Spirit, the Church has gradually recognized that, among its various liturgical celebrations, there are exactly Seven Sacraments instituted by Christ: Baptism, Confirmation, Eucharist, Penance, Anointing of the Sick, Holy Orders, and Matrimony.

This is a common statement: Christ instituted the sacraments. What does it mean?

First of all, when the first Christians baptized (see Acts 2:41), laid on hands (see Acts 6:6; 8:17), healed the sick (see James 5:14), and broke bread together (see Acts 2:46), they were doing exactly as Jesus had commanded them to do. This is the explanation of how Christ instituted the sacraments. Note, too, as St. Thomas Aquinas did, how the Seven Sacraments correspond chronologically with human development and experience (see explanation on page 187).

Though for the first two centuries there was no one term to describe the sacraments, from the very earliest times, the Church realized that when Christians practiced these liturgical actions, they were also learning more and more about Jesus when they did so. They recognized that Jesus was present with them in these actions. Moreover, they understood that Jesus was, in fact, the minister of these actions.

Already long in use, eventually the Seven Sacraments were formally named at the Council of Florence in 1439. The council also explained that three things are necessary for each sacrament:

1. *Proper matter.* The Magisterium determines the essential elements used in the sacraments. For example, Eucharist can be celebrated only with recently made, unleavened, wheat-based bread and natural wine of the grape. Ensuring proper matter helps keep the integrity of the sacraments in line with Jesus' intentions.
2. *Correct words or form.* Likewise, the order of the rites and the words spoken in the sacraments are entrusted to the Magisterium, which makes sure they are observed universally in the Church. No priest, for example, may change or alter the approved liturgical texts.
3. *Designated minister.* An ordained minister—a bishop, a priest, or a deacon who has received the Sacrament of Holy Orders—is at the service of the community of faith in the sacraments. "The ordained minister guarantees that it really is Christ who acts in the sacraments through the Holy Spirit for the Church" (*CCC*, 1120).

The Seven Sacraments are also grouped and understood by designations: the Sacraments of Christian Initiation (Baptism, Confirmation, and Eucharist), the Sacraments of Healing (Penance and Anointing of the Sick), and the Sacraments at the Service of Communion (Holy Orders and Matrimony). The rhythm of the sacraments takes place as part of a daily, weekly, and yearly calendar, which helps us plunge more deeply into the mystery of salvation. Further explanation of the sacraments and the liturgical year follows.

REVIEW

1. How is Jesus the primordial sacrament?
2. How is the Paschal Mystery more than a historical event?
3. Name four ways Jesus is really present in the Eucharist. How is he present in the fullest sense?
4. What are three ways the Church is a sacrament?
5. Name and explain three things the Council of Florence said are necessary for each sacrament.

WRITE OR DISCUSS

- Describe a time when you have experienced Jesus' presence when gathered together with others in his name.
- Explain in your own words what it means to say, "Christ instituted the sacraments."

SACRAMENTS OF INITIATION

From the earliest days of the Church, Christian initiation has been celebrated in different ways.

For example, consider the day of Pentecost after the Apostles received the Holy Spirit. Peter stepped out on the balcony of the Upper Room (where Jesus had shared his Last Supper) and spoke convincingly to the crowds gathered in the streets below. Jews from many different regions neighboring Jerusalem were there to celebrate the Feast of the Firstfruits. By the end of the day, the Scriptures report, about three thousand of those who listened to Peter accepted the message of Jesus Christ and were baptized.

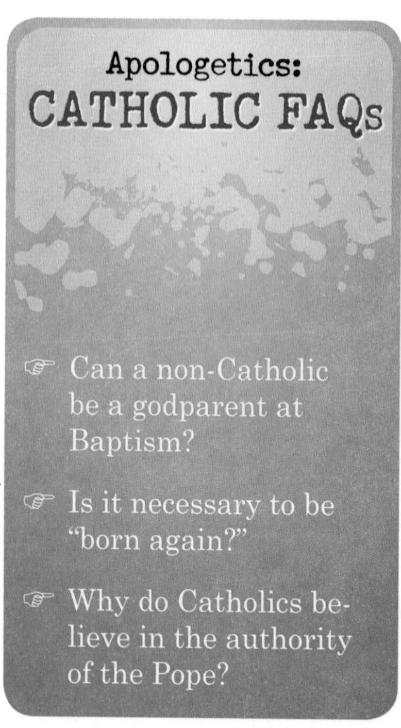

Apologetics:
CATHOLIC FAQs
Can a non-Catholic be a godparent at Baptism?
Is it necessary to be "born again?"
Why do Catholics believe in the authority of the Pope?

This relatively easy road to becoming a Christian is contrasted by countless more difficult routes to Christianity in the first centuries of the Church. From the time of Pentecost onward, Jesus' disciples began to carry out his command to "make disciples of all nations, baptizing them in the name of the Father, and of the Son, and of the Holy Spirit" (Mt 28:19). This task was complicated because initially, the "New Way," as the Church was described, was thought of only as an extension of Judaism. When Gentiles began to be baptized, there were disagreements about how many laws and customs of Judaism the Gentiles would have to follow once baptized. Recall that Church leaders determined that Gentile Christians could be spared some of the more difficult requirements of Judaism (i.e., dietary laws and circumcision). In the process, Christianity left behind some of its Jewish roots. But that didn't mean the process of Christian initiation became significantly easier.

Until AD 313 it was illegal to be a Christian in the Roman Empire. Those who sought initiation were faced with persecution and often martyrdom. Also, the **catechumenate**, or "period of instruction," was a three-year process. The candidate—sponsored by a baptized Christian—studied Christianity, prayed, fasted, and

catechumenate
A process of formation and instruction for an unbaptized person to prepare to receive all the Sacraments of Christian Initiation.

proved himself or herself up to the challenge of choosing a lifestyle that could bring death.

There were always essential steps to the process of becoming Christian. The initiation took place in several stages and included the following:

- the hearing and acceptance of the Good News of Christ
- the making of a profession of faith
- Baptism ("the basis of the whole Christian life, the gateway to life in the Spirit, and the door which gives access to the other sacraments," *CCC*, 1213)
- Confirmation, which more perfectly binds the Christian to the Church and enriches him or her with a special strength of the Holy Spirit (*CCC*, 1285)
- full welcome into the Church through receiving Holy Communion.

Initially, the three-year catechumenate mostly proceeded in the order described above, with culmination being the reception of all three sacraments on the vigil of Easter. Confirmation was a rite of laying on of hands directly connected with Baptism. A key point in the process was that it was reserved for adults.

The process changed with the advent of more infant Baptisms in the fifth century. At that time, St. Augustine used the term "Original Sin" to explain how all humans are born with the sin of Adam on their souls. One of the graces of Baptism is that all sins, personal sin and Original Sin, are forgiven. Thus in a time of high infant mortality, Christian parents sought Baptism for their children to purify them from sin, make them children

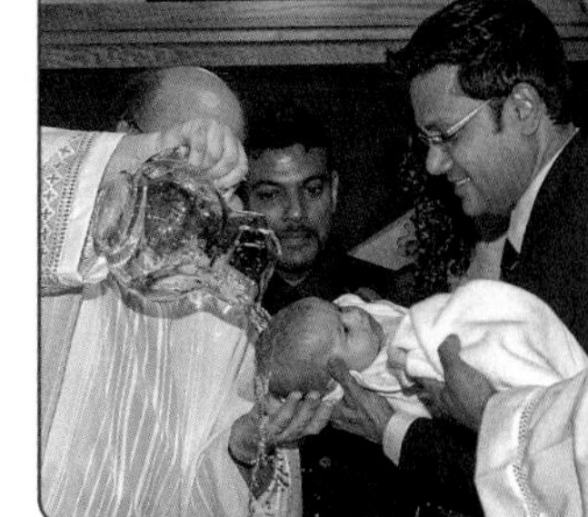

of God, and give them a share in God's life, called "sanctifying grace." Though this was a time of increased infant Baptisms, it was not a new practice. From the time of the Apostles, young children had been baptized. In fact, when Peter spoke from the Upper Room on Pentecost, he said:

> Repent and be baptized, every one of you, in the name of Jesus Christ for the forgiveness of your sins; and you will receive the gift of the Holy Spirit. (Acts 2:38)

Both infant Baptism and adult Baptism have continued to have a place in the Church; Christian initiation is for all. The Second Vatican Council restored the catechumenate for adults, with four distinct steps, much as it had been in the early Church. The four steps are these:

> ***Evangelization.*** A person hears the Word of God and initially responds to it. Prayer, reading, and questioning accompany this stage. At the end of this period, a rite of acceptance is celebrated.
>
> *Catechumenate.* Today, this step may take a full year or longer. The catechumens receive instruction in special classes held at the parish, are accompanied by a sponsor who answers their questions, do service work, and participate at Mass through the time they are dismissed at the Liturgy of the Word. On the first Sunday of Lent, the candidates travel to the diocesan cathedral, where the local bishop enrolls them in the book of the elect, naming those who will receive the Sacraments of Initiation.

Purification and Enlightenment. This step also takes place during Lent. Rituals known as scrutinies help the catechumens look closely at—scrutinize—their lives and do penance for their sins. They are gifted with the Lord's Prayer and the Creed and promise to make these central to their lives. As in earlier times, this period culminates with the reception of the Sacraments of Initiation—Baptism, Confirmation, and Eucharist—at the Easter Vigil Mass.

Mystagogia. The newly baptized—called **neophytes**—continue to meet with one another after Easter and at least until Pentecost. They gradually take their place in the life and the ministries of the Church.

The Church also has a second initiation rite, the Rite of Baptism of Children. This is the process most Catholics are initiated in, at least the so-called "cradle Catholics," who are born and raised in Catholic families. The difference in this rite is that **catechesis**, or instruction, takes place after the reception of Baptism. The child's parents and godparents speak in the name of the child, promising the infant's future commitment to faith. Gradual formation takes place as the child grows. The other Sacraments of Initiation are typically received at a later time. Eventually the child is able to accept for himself or herself the gift of faith.

Evangelization
To bring the Good News of Jesus Christ to others.

The three Sacraments of Initiation—Baptism, Confirmation, and Eucharist—are explained in more detail in the following sections.

Baptism

The **essential rite** of Baptism consists of a triple immersion of the candidate in water or a triple pouring of water on his or her head while the words "I baptize you in the name of the Father, and of the Son, and of the Holy Spirit" are said by the normal minister of the sacrament—a bishop, a priest, or a deacon. In an emergency, however, anyone can baptize. As mentioned, the first disciples did not refuse Baptism to anyone who professed faith in Jesus; both Jews and pagans who confessed in him received Baptism.

Baptism is the essential sacrament for us because of what it brings: new life in Christ. St. Paul wrote that in Baptism we are "clothed" with Christ (Gal 3:27). With Baptism, Christ lives in us and permeates our entire selves. We share in the **common priesthood** of Christ with the task of participating in his mission of salvation. Another way to describe a person baptized is to say he or she is "configured" to Christ. That means we can know and recognize Christ in the baptized Christian. Others can recognize Christ in us.

Baptism makes us part of Christ's Body, the Church. Like the Church, Baptism is necessary for our salvation. St. Irenaeus wrote that "Baptism indeed is the seal of eternal life." Baptism marks us with a spiritual character that will be with us until the day of our death. This spiritual mark will be with us as we prepare to meet God face to face.

Celebration of the Sacrament

Besides the essential rite of Baptism, there are several other important rituals and symbols. The candidate is also anointed with sacred chrism. This is perfumed oil consecrated by the bishop of the diocese on Holy Thursday or at a special Mass during Holy Week. The chrism signifies that the Holy Spirit is given to the baptized and that this person is now incorporated into Christ. This post-baptismal anointing with chrism announces that the bishop will confer a second anointing later at the Sacrament of Confirmation, the completion of the baptismal anointing.

The newly baptized puts on a white garment to symbolize that the person has put on Christ and is risen with Christ. A candle lit from the Easter candle signifies that, in Jesus, the baptized are "the light of the world."

Baptisms of both adults and infants usually take place at Mass in the presence of the faithful community, the Body of Christ. This is the community to which the person will belong. Whereas the Baptism of adults is reserved for the Easter Vigil and is followed by Confirmation and Eucharist, the Baptism of an infant may take place on any Sunday. In the Roman rite, the child will return for First Communion at the age of reason. To show Baptism's connection with Eucharist, the infant may be brought to the altar for the praying of the Our Father.

Confirmation

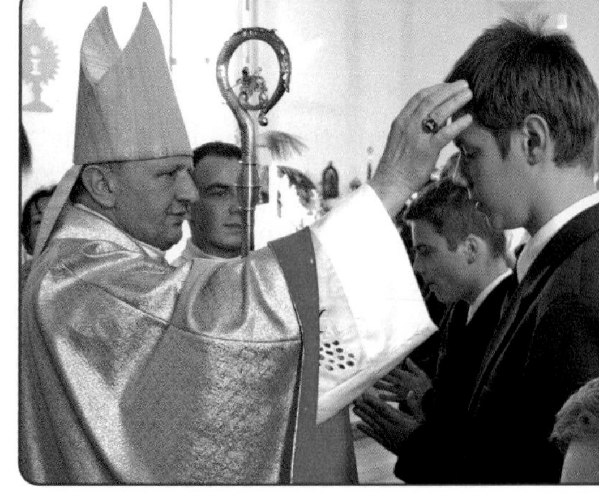

In the Sacrament of Confirmation, the bishop lays his hand on the forehead of the candidate and anoints him or her with chrism while saying, "Be sealed with the gift of the Holy Spirit." This is the essential rite of the sacrament.

From the time of the Apostles, the laying of hands on the newly baptized was understood to impart the gift of the Holy Spirit and complete the grace of Baptism. The Letter to the Hebrews (6:2) describes Baptism and the laying on of hands as one of the basic teachings of the Apostles. The Church understands this laying on of hands as the origin of the Sacrament of Confirmation and as a way to bring to Christians in all generations the fullness of grace that was present on the day of Pentecost.

Early in Church history, an anointing with chrism was added to the laying on of hands. These gestures were meant to highlight the name "Christian" the person takes on at the time. In the Eastern churches, the sacrament is called *Chrismation*, meaning "anointing with chrism," and is administered immediately after Baptism (and is followed by participation in the Eucharist). In the Roman Catholic Church, the sacrament is Confirmation, highlighting that the sacrament both confirms the promises made at Baptism and strengthens baptismal grace.

Gifts of the Holy Spirit
An outpouring of God's gifts to help us live a Christian life. The traditional seven gifts of the Holy Spirit are wisdom, understanding, knowledge, counsel (right judgment), fortitude (courage), piety (reverence), and fear of the Lord (wonder and awe).

Confirmation was originally part of a single ritual that included the other Sacraments of Initiation, Baptism and Eucharist. For those who are baptized after they have reached the age of reason (age seven or so), Confirmation is still celebrated that way today as part of the Easter Vigil liturgy. However, for Catholics baptized as infants, Confirmation is usually reserved for a later time, either in adolescence or around the time of a person's First Communion. Received in either order, Confirmation is the sacrament that completes Baptism. Eucharist is the sacrament that completes both Baptism and Confirmation and brings about full initiation into the Church.

To receive the Sacrament of Confirmation, a person should be prepared. This means growing in a more intimate union with Christ and becoming more familiar with the Holy Spirit —recognizing his actions, gifts, and callings—so that once confirmed, the person can assume the responsibilities of Christian life. The candidate should also be in a state of grace. This means the person should receive the Sacrament of Penance to be cleansed from any serious sin. Even if one is in a state of grace, celebrating the Sacrament of Penance prepares us to receive the gift of the Holy Spirit.

Confirmation brings about a special outpouring of the Holy Spirit. Because of this, the graces of Baptism are perfected at Confirmation. Like Baptism, Confirmation is given only once, for it also imprints on the person a spiritual mark or an indelible character that cannot be removed. This seal of the Spirit leads the Christian to profess Christ and be his witness to the world.

Other effects of the Sacrament of Confirmation:

- It roots us more deeply in God's love, leading us to call out to God, "Abba! Father!"
- It unites us more firmly with Christ.
- It strengthens our bond with the Church.
- It gives us the special strength of the Holy Spirit to spread and defend the faith by word and action, to confess the name of Christ boldly, and never to be ashamed of the cross.

Another effect of Confirmation is it increases the **gifts of the Holy Spirit** in us. The traditional list of the seven gifts comes from a description of the Messiah from the Book of Isaiah (11:1–5).

Celebration of the Sacrament

In the Roman rite, Confirmation is typically celebrated during Mass to further strengthen its connection with Eucharist, the third Sacrament of Initiation. The bishop is the ordinary minister of the Sacrament, and he fittingly celebrates the Sacrament to connect our experience of the coming of the Spirit with that of the Apostles who received the Holy Spirit at Pentecost. The bishop's presence unites the candidates more deeply with the mission of the universal Church and to the mission of sharing Christ with all.

Words, symbols, and concrete actions also make up the rite. After the Gospel, the pastor of the parish or the catechist responsible for Confirmation preparation presents the candidates to the bishop, usually by name. The bishop then gives a homily on the readings and explains the meaning of the sacrament.

The candidates then stand and renew their baptismal promises before the bishop and the community of faith.

The bishop extends his hands over the entire group of candidates and prays for the outpouring of the Holy Spirit and the seven gifts on them. The essential rite of Confirmation follows. In the Latin rite, it is the anointing of the candidates with chrism on the forehead, which is done by the laying on of hands and through the words, "Be sealed with the Gift of the Holy Spirit."

After this Rite of Confirmation, the Eucharist continues. Perhaps the first effect of the sacrament is that the newly confirmed can approach the altar to receive the Body and Blood of Christ with a new understanding of their oneness with Christ and his Church.

Apologetics:
CATHOLIC FAQs

- Why can't priests be married?
- Why do you have to confess your sins to a priest in the Sacrament of Penance?
- What are the rules for receiving Holy Communion?

Eucharist

The Second Vatican Council document *Constitution on the Church* describes the Eucharist as the "source and summit of the Christian life" (11). All the other sacraments and the other Church ministries are bound up in the Eucharist. To put it simply, the Eucharist is the sum and summary of our faith. St. Irenaeus wrote, "Our way of thinking is attuned to the Eucharist, and the Eucharist in turn confirms our way of thinking."

By the Eucharist, we are united with the heavenly liturgy and anticipate eternal life. At the beginning of the twentieth century, Pope St. Pius X was dismayed that more people did not regularly receive Communion, even when they attended Mass, so he encouraged weekly and even daily Communion. He lowered the age of First Communion from twelve to the age of reason (seven) so even more people could receive the Body and Blood of Christ at the Eucharist table. Pope Pius explained:

> Holy Communion is the shortest and safest way to heaven. There are others: innocence, but that is for little children; penance, but we are afraid of it; generous endurance of trials of life, but when they come we weep and ask to be spared. The surest, easiest, shortest way is the Eucharist.

The Eucharist is the sacrament that completes Christian initiation. Those who share in the priesthood of Christ through

Baptism and are configured more closely to him through Confirmation form community through their participation in the Eucharist. Reception of Holy Communion increases the communicants' union with the Lord, wipes away venial sins, protects them from mortal sin, and joins them more intimately with the Church, which is the Mystical Body of Christ.

Development of the Sacrament

Christ instituted the Eucharist during the Passover meal held at the Last Supper as a memorial of his Death and Resurrection. In doing so in the context of Passover, Jesus gave the Jewish Passover ultimate meaning. The passing over to God the Father at the Death of Jesus was anticipated in the Last Supper meal and is celebrated to the end of time whenever the Eucharist is shared.

Jesus offers an everlasting gift of himself, for he is truly present in the consecrated species of bread and wine that are his Body and Blood. We see this in the recitation of Christ's words, "This is my body, which will be given for you. . . . This cup is the new covenant in my blood, which will be shed for you" (Lk 22:19–20). When he told the gathered Apostles to "do this in memory of me," he was making them priests of the New Testament, responsible for celebrating the Eucharist until his return.

From the beginning, the Eucharist had references to the past and the future, in addition to its place in the present. In the Eucharist, the participants are removed from the constraints of time so the saving events of the Paschal Mystery are made present in the here and now.

In the first century, Christians would gather in homes to celebrate the Lord's Day, Sunday. Eventually some of these homes became churches. Preaching, prayer, and the breaking of the bread were essential parts of the Eucharist from the beginning. In AD 155 Justin Martyr wrote the earliest outline of the rite of Eucharist that survives today.

Justin Martyr's outline began with the Liturgy of the Word, the sharing of readings from the memoirs of the Apostles (New Testament) or the writings of the prophets (Old Testament). These readings, which at times were quite lengthy, were followed by a sermon. After the sermon everyone stood for the prayers of the faithful. The prayers were followed by a kiss of peace. Then the people brought forward bread and wine (and water on the occasion of Baptism) they had brought from home. The presider (bishop or priest) accepted these gifts and offered prayers of thanksgiving "at some length." When he finished praying, the congregation gave their assent by saying "**Amen**." The deacons were then called forward to distribute the consecrated elements to all who were present. Justin made it clear in his *First Apology* that the bread and wine were no longer "common bread or common drink." He wrote:

> Just as our Savior Jesus Christ . . . took flesh and blood for our salvation, so too we have been taught that the food over which thanks have been given by a word of prayer is from him . . . is both the flesh and blood of that incarnate Jesus.

Many of the prayers we use today at Eucharist date back to the time of Justin Martyr. The introductory dialogue of the Liturgy of the Eucharist ("The Lord be with you. And also with you. Lift up your hearts. We lift them up to the Lord . . .") is all found in Justin's account.

The Apostolic Tradition, generally believed to be written by Hippolytus around 215, outlines prayers and an order of worship that are even closer to today's liturgy. Other liturgical rites of the third and early fourth centuries reflect the same basic structure. The only differences are that the *Sanctus* ("Holy, holy") and the preface to the Eucharistic prayer were added later in the fourth century.

In these early centuries, the prayers of Eucharist varied from region to region. By the Middle Ages, however, the emperor Charlemagne attempted to unify the liturgy as a way to bring greater unity to people under his reign. Then, at the Council of Trent (1545–1563), the Church reaffirmed the sacrificial nature of the Eucharist. The doctrine of transubstantiation was defined. Pope Pius V published a Roman Missal that brought uniformity to the official rite of Eucharist. This Missal was used in the Church for the next four hundred years, until the Second Vatican Council.

The Second Vatican Council emphasized the actions and the elements Jesus had begun at the Last Supper. These elements included the community as a sign of the Lord's presence, the call to forgiveness and penance, the Scripture readings proclaimed and understood by the people, the reception of both the consecrated species of bread and wine by all the baptized, and the command to go forth from the Eucharist to serve others.

Celebration of the Sacrament

Many people of all ages lament that they don't want to go to Mass because "it's boring" or they "don't get anything out of it."

This attitude can change only when we begin to view liturgy as its name intends, as the "work" of the people. The work we are meant to do is coming to know God and to participate with God in the salvation of the world. The work of the priest, "acting in the person of Christ the head" (CCC, 1348), is to preside over the assembly, proclaim the Gospel, and consecrate the bread and wine into the Body and Blood of Christ. Our work places us in an active role as well, perhaps as readers, gift bearers, or those who give Communion, but always through our active participation expressed in our responses and prayer. Even more important than our presence at Mass is our understanding that God has chosen to be present there and to act through the Mass to give us grace.

The Mass has a fundamental structure with two main parts—the Liturgy of the Word and the Liturgy of the Eucharist—that together are united as one single act of worship. God is present and acting in each of these parts and all of their elements. The order of the Mass and each of its major elements are described below.

Introductory Rites. All gather in the name of Christ. Jesus Christ himself is the High Priest who presides over every Eucharist. The bishop or the priest represents Christ and presides over the assembly, speaks the readings, receives the offerings, and says the Eucharistic prayer. The priest and other ministers process to the altar and bow. The priest kisses the altar out of respect. The Mass always begins with the Sign of the Cross. Just as it would be improper for you to join any celebration without healing divisions between you and the host or you and the other invited guests, it would not be right to participate in the celebration of the Eucharist without asking forgiveness for wrongs we have

Mass at St. Peter's Square at the Vatican

done. A penitential rite follows in which we ask for mercy and forgiveness from God and from the community. The ancient song of praise, the *Gloria*, comes next. The introductory rites end with an opening prayer written especially for the day or the feast being celebrated.

Apologetics:
CATHOLIC FAQs

- Why do Catholics believe that Jesus is really present in the consecrated species of bread and wine and that they are not just symbolic of his presence?
- Why can't I receive Communion in another Christian church? Why can't my friend who is Christian but not Catholic receive Communion at my church?
- Am I really required to go to Mass every Sunday?

The Liturgy of the Word. On Sundays, there are three readings from the Scriptures. The first is usually taken from the Old Testament, the second from one of the New Testament letters. In between, a Psalm is sung as a response. The high point of the Liturgy of the Word is the Gospel reading. It tells us directly about the life of Jesus. There is an intended common theme between the first reading and the Gospel. The assembly stands for the Gospel out of reverence and signs themselves three times, on their forehead and lips and over their heart. This gesture symbolically shows the commitment to make God's Word come alive in our thoughts, in what we say, and in what we do. A homily, given by the priest, helps the congregation understand more about the readings and apply them to their daily lives. The reciting of the Nicene Creed and the offering of prayers of intercession conclude the Liturgy of the Word. The prayers of the faithful are said for the needs of all people.

The Liturgy of the Eucharist. The preparation of the altar and the presentation of gifts of bread and wine as well as monetary donations begin the Liturgy of the Eucharist. The offertory has always been part of the liturgy. The *Catechism of the Catholic Church* reminds us:

> From the very beginning Christians have brought, along with the bread and wine for the Eucharist, gifts to share with those in need. The custom of the *collection*, ever appropriate, is inspired by the example of Christ who became poor to make us rich. (1351)

The Eucharistic prayer is the high point of the Liturgy of the Eucharist and of the Mass itself. The Church has several Eucharistic prayers, but each has certain common elements:

- offering thanksgiving to the Father, through Christ and in the Holy Spirit, for all his works
- asking the Father to send the Holy Spirit (or **blessing**) on the gifts of bread and wine so they may become the Body and Blood of Christ
- through the words of Christ at the Last Supper, making him present under the species of bread and wine

- offering his sacrifice on the cross once and for all, and recalling the Passion, the Resurrection, and the return of Christ
- offering intercessions for the Pope, the bishops, the clergy, and the living and the dead

Though the Eucharistic prayer seems a long recitation by the priest, it is really a dialogue with the assembly, and we respond with our agreement to all that was prayed with our resounding "Amen," or "I agree."

Communion Rite. In the Communion Rite, the people prepare to receive Jesus in Holy Communion by reciting the Our Father and sharing a sign of peace. These words and actions reinforce our unity and highlight our communion with God and one another. The Lamb of God reminds us of our sinfulness and our need for God's mercy. The priest breaks the bread as another sign of our unity that we will all share from the one loaf. Then we share in Communion, eating and drinking the Body and Blood of Christ. A prayer after Communion asks God to grant the effects of the mystery just celebrated.

Concluding Rite. Visitors to a Catholic Mass once commented how "everything seems to end so quickly" after Communion. Really, their observation is accurate. After such a climax, the liturgy can really go no other place except to a conclusion. After the priest blesses the people, he asks them to "go in peace to love and serve the Lord." We are to carry the graces received at Eucharist out into our world.

REVIEW

1. Why was it difficult to become a Christian in the Roman Empire of the first three centuries?
2. Explain how a deeper understanding of the doctrine of Original Sin led to an increase in infant Baptisms.
3. Name and briefly explain the four steps of today's catechumenate.
4. What are the differences in catechesis and reception of the Sacraments of Initiation between those in the adult catechumenate and babies or children initiated in the Rite of Baptism for Children?
5. Why is Baptism the essential sacrament?
6. What are the effects of Baptism?
7. How is Confirmation intimately connected with the Holy Spirit?
8. What is the essential rite of the Sacrament of Confirmation?
9. Briefly trace key developments of the Eucharist in four eras or events: the first century, the Middle Ages, the Council of Trent, and the Second Vatican Council.
10. At Eucharist, what is the high point of the Liturgy of the Word? What is the high point of the Liturgy of the Eucharist and of the Mass itself?

WRITE OR DISCUSS

- Describe a Baptism you most recently attended. Which symbol of Baptism was especially meaningful to you? Why?
- If you were designing a process of preparation for Confirmation for teenagers, what would it be like? Be creative with your response.
- "Holy Communion is the shortest and safest way to heaven." What does this statement mean to you?
- How can you "get more" out of Mass?

WHERE IS THE LITURGY CELEBRATED?

The Tabernacle

The tabernacle is the case or box that contains the Blessed Sacrament. It is located in a place of great honor in the church. A tabernacle light burns near it as a sign of Jesus' Real Presence there.

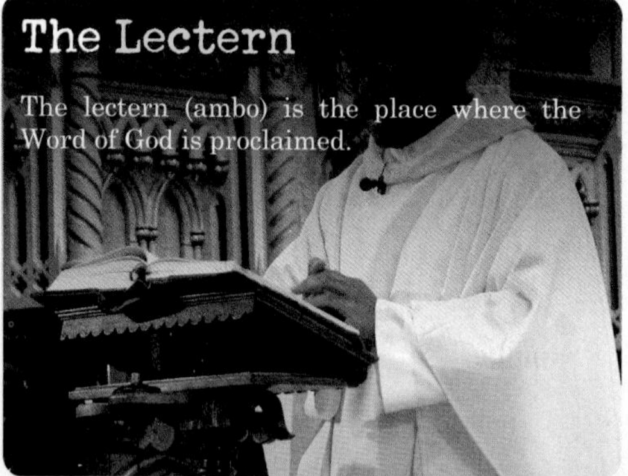

The Lectern

The lectern (ambo) is the place where the Word of God is proclaimed.

The Altar

The altar is placed at the center of the sanctuary because this is where Christ's sacrifice of the Cross is made present. The altar is also the table of the Lord to which the community of faith is invited.

The liturgy is not limited to any one place. However, in places where liberty is not compromised, Catholics do construct churches for worship. Churches are houses of prayer. The inside of a Catholic Church contains several elements key to liturgy:

The Baptistery

The baptistery is a place for the celebration of Baptism. It may be in several different places in a church. In some churches it is near the entrance to symbolize the entrance of a person into the Church.

The Presider's Chair

The presider's chair of the bishop or priest is placed in the sanctuary to express his role in leading the assembly and directing prayer.

The Confessional

The reconciliation chapel or confessional are open areas to receive penitents for the Sacrament of Penance and to provide for private confession.

The Holy Oils

The holy oils, which include the oil of the catechumens, oil for the Sacrament of Anointing of the Sick, and the sacred chrism, are kept in a special place called the ambry.

SACRAMENTS OF HEALING

Through the Sacraments of Christian Initiation, we are reborn to new life in Christ. However, we are still in our human bodies, which are prone to suffering, illness, and death. Our new life in Christ can be weakened by these ailments and many other challenges of human existence—physical, mental, and emotional. Our life in Christ can even be lost to the wages of sin.

Jesus Christ is the "physician of our souls and bodies" (*CCC*, 1420). He was once asked why people have to suffer. He never responded with a clear answer. Instead of explaining the situation, whenever he encountered a person in need of either physical or spiritual healing, Jesus simply healed the person or forgave the person's sin. In one Gospel story—the cure of the paralytic in Mark 2:1–12—Jesus did both. After witnessing the faith of the people who had lowered the man into the home, Jesus said to the paralytic, "Child, your sins are forgiven." Later, to show he had been given the power to forgive sins by God the Father, he said to the man, "I say to you, rise, pick up your mat, and go home." The man did just as Jesus said.

Through the power of the Holy Spirit, Jesus continues his work of healing and salvation, even among members of the Church. This is the purpose of the two Sacraments of Healing—the Sacrament of Penance and the Sacrament of Anointing of the Sick.

Penance

Penance is the sacrament of renewed faith. It is the sacrament that renews, restores, and strengthens our relationship with God and the community after it has been damaged by sin. While Baptism reveals the mystery of God's love for us, the Sacrament of Penance shows that God's love is without limits. Christian life is marked by lifelong conversion. That is why Christ gave us this Sacrament as a sign of his love and to show in a personal way his merciful forgiveness to individual sinners.

The name *Penance* is given to this sacrament because it consecrates the steps of conversion, penance, and satisfaction the person takes individually and through the Church. The sacrament is also known by several other names. Each of these names reveals something important about its meaning. It is called a sacrament of *conversion* because it makes present sacramentally Jesus' call to conversion and because it marks the person's first step in returning to God after committing a sin. It is a sacrament of *confession* because the essential element of the sacrament is the penitent's confession of his or her sins to a priest. Also, it is a "confession" or acknowledgment of God's holiness, mercy, and compassion in his forgiveness of sin. It is a sacrament of *forgiveness* because by the priest's sacramental **absolution**, the penitent's sins are forgiven. The Sacrament of Penance is also commonly known as ***Reconciliation*** because it restores God's merciful love to the penitent.

The history of the Sacrament of Penance begins, of course, with Jesus, who ministered to, loved, and forgave sinners. He stated that his mission was to sinners:

> Those who are well do not need a physician, but the sick do. Go and learn the meaning of the words, 'I desire mercy, not sacrifice.' I did not come to call the righteous but sinners. (Mt 9:12–13)

Jesus lived his words. There are many examples of his forgiveness offered to sinners besides his healing of the paralytic.

> **works of mercy**
> Charitable actions that remind us how to come to the aid of a neighbor and his or her bodily and spiritual necessities.

For example, he forgave the woman caught in adultery but told her to avoid the sin in the future (see John 8:1–11). He praised the faith of the woman who approached him as he dined at the house of the Pharisee and forgave her many sins (see Luke 7:36–50). He offered forgiveness to the criminal who hung next to him on the cross (see Luke 23:32–43). Jesus even forgave his persecutors as he hung on the cross, despite their taunts and jeers (see Luke 23:34).

Jesus gave the power to forgive sins to the Apostles. He told Peter: "Whatever you bind on earth shall be bound in heaven; and whatever you loose on earth shall be loosed in heaven" (Mt 16:19). The early Church continued to minister to those who committed sins after being baptized. St. Paul urged the community to "forgive and encourage" the sinner so the person would not bring a bad example to others (see 2 Corinthians 2:5–11).

The history of the sacrament reveals differences in the practice, though not the essential elements. From the second to fifth centuries, the forgiveness of **venial sin** took place through participation in the Eucharist, prayer, and **works of mercy**. However, the forgiveness of **mortal sin** required a long and difficult time of penance, and forgiveness was granted just once in a lifetime. The sacrament also took place in public. For this reason, many penitents put off seeking reception of the sacrament until they were near death. Around the sixth century, the practice of private confession took hold in Irish monasteries, where an older, wiser monk typically counseled and offered forgiveness to a younger monk.

St. Thomas Aquinas helped define the nature of the Sacrament of Penance in the thirteenth century. He said the sacrament is both the sign and the cause of the sinner's forgiveness. God's grace gives love to the sinner to turn his or her heart to the sacrament. **Contrition**—true sorrow—wipes out the sin. Sacramental confession is necessary for the forgiveness of mortal sin. Both the penance and the absolution together form the sacrament.

Recent reforms in the sacrament emphasize its healing aspect. Dark confessionals with a screen separating the priest and the penitent have been redesigned with an additional opportunity for face-to-face confession. The priest further acts in the person of Jesus Christ by helping the sinner experience the Lord's healing touch and conversion to God and the Church.

Celebration of the Sacrament

The essential elements of the Sacrament of Penance are part of its celebration. The sacrament consists of two equally necessary elements: the acts of the person who undergoes conversion and the intervention of the Church.

The person has three tasks as part of the sacrament: contrition, confession, and satisfaction.

Contrition is the heartfelt sorrow and aversion for the sin committed. It must be accompanied by the intention not to sin again. When we love God above all else, we experience what is known as "perfect contrition." We willingly let go of all those things that pull us away from God.

True contrition results in *confession*. Confession is the external expression of our sorrow and our willingness to accept responsibility for damaging or breaking the covenant. When we confess our sins to God, we proclaim our belief in God's love and mercy. When we confess our sins within the Church, we express our belief in the goodness of the community. When we confess our sins to a priest, we admit we have caused harm to other members of the Body of Christ and are asking the priest to forgive us in the name of Christ. All Catholics are required to confess all serious sins and to go to confession at least once per year.

A person who is contrite and confesses his or her sins must then work to build up new life again with God and the Church. This is done through *satisfaction*, or penance: offering recompense for injustices caused or working to rebuild what was lost.

When the person is forgiven, all obstacles to a complete union with God and the Church are removed. The person is reconciled with the Church. At least some of the temporal punishments resulting from sin are removed. God's love once again flows through the repentant sinner. The person is filled with peace and serenity of conscience and increased spiritual strength for the Christian battle. The person's own efforts are again effective because they are united with Christ's love.

Finally, it is important to remember that even though forgiveness is expressed through the Church and this sacrament, God alone forgives sins. The Church is the Body of Christ. Christ is the head of the Body. If Christ has forgiven the sinner, the Church must reestablish that relationship. The Church is the sign of what God has done and the instrument through which God acts. Each time the priest offers sinners God's forgiveness, he also welcomes them back to the life of the Church.

Anointing of the Sick

Physical weakness and illness are an inevitable part of the human situation. Whether a person is temporarily out of commission with the flu, more seriously ill with a life-threatening illness, or just weakened by old age, sickness can claim a person's total being. It can separate us from others and throw us into **despair**. It is just this situation of brokenness that Jesus confronted. Jesus ministered to the sick and called them to wholeness they had never known. He reminded them that this transformation was not magic, but an experience of God's grace.

After Jesus returned to Heaven, the Church continued to obey Jesus' command to heal by preaching, repentance, casting out demons, and anointing and healing the sick. Today, Jesus continues to bring healing through the prayers of the Church and through the sacraments, especially the Eucharist and the Anointing of the Sick. The foundation of the Anointing of the Sick has roots in the Letter of James:

> Is anyone among you sick? He should summon the presbyters of the Church, and they should pray over him and anoint (him) with oil in the name of the Lord, and the prayer of faith will save the sick person, and the Lord will raise him up. If he has committed any sins, he will be forgiven. (Jas 5:14–15)

Anointing and prayer for the sick were common in the early Church (see Acts 9:34 and Acts 28:8–9). However, by the Middle Ages, this sacrament was usually administered only to the dying. The term for the sacrament became *extreme unction*, that is, "last anointing" before death. Penance and ***viaticum*** ("food for the way"), the final reception of the Eucharist, are received before the sacramental anointing of a dying person.

Jesus ministered to the sick.

With the liturgical reforms of the Second Vatican Council, the Sacrament of Anointing of the Sick is intended for others besides the dying: for those suffering from serious illness, for the elderly, for those facing major surgery, as well as for the dying. Also, the sacrament may be repeated more than once if the sick person has a relapse or the condition worsens.

The spiritual effects of the Sacrament are:

- the reception of grace to be able to accept the trials of illness
- the forgiveness of sin if the sick person has not been able to obtain it in the Sacrament of Penance (this is true even if the person has lapsed into unconsciousness)
- the grace to unite oneself to the redemptive Passion of Christ
- the gift of sharing in the merits of and contributing to the holiness of the Church
- the restoration of health, if it would help the salvation of the soul
- offering dying persons the supernatural strength, offered in both the anointing and the viaticum, that is necessary to prepare for eternity

Only a priest or a bishop may administer the Sacrament of the Anointing of the Sick. However, prayerful support of the entire Church is necessary as it shows the unity of the Church with the person who is sick and his or her family and friends.

Celebration of the Sacrament

Anointing of the Sick is sometimes celebrated during Mass. This reminds the parish community of the presence of sick people. In a special way, the whole community can support those who are suffering. More typically, however, the sacrament is celebrated with the priest, the person who is ill, and the person's family.

The essential elements of the sacrament are part of the celebration. They include:

- the priest's laying his hands on the sick person
- his prayer for the person in the faith of the Church
- the anointing of the forehead and hands (in the Roman rite) or other body parts (in the Eastern rite) with oil ideally blessed previously by a bishop or, if necessary, by the priest himself

Also part of the celebration of the sacrament are an introductory rite and a Scripture reading. The priest greets and blesses the sick person and guests with holy water, saying: "Let this water call to mind your baptismal sharing in Christ's redeeming Passion and Resurrection." The priest may hear the person's confession at this point. The priest or a guest shares a Scripture reading with words of hope, healing, and restored dignity. The anointing follows as the priest, imitating the actions of Jesus, silently lays his hands on the sick person. At the time of the anointing, he prays:

> Through this holy anointing may the Lord in his love and mercy help you with the grace of the Holy Spirit.

The sacrament encourages those who are sick to overcome the alienation caused by sickness, to grow to wholeness through the illness, to identify with the sufferings of Jesus Christ, and to enter more fully into the Paschal Mystery.

REVIEW

1. How did Jesus address the issue of human suffering?
2. In early centuries of the Church, why did people typically put off receiving the Sacrament of Penance until a time near their death?
3. Explain each part of the Sacrament of Penance: contrition, confession, and satisfaction.
4. What are the scriptural roots of the Sacrament of the Anointing of the Sick?
5. Name the essential elements of the Sacrament of the Anointing of the Sick.

WRITE OR DISCUSS

- Which name of the Sacrament of Penance best resonates with your experience of the sacrament? Explain.
- What would you say if your parent or grandparent was hesitant to receive the Sacrament of the Anointing of the Sick because he or she associated it only with dying?

SACRAMENTS AT THE SERVICE OF COMMUNION

Baptism, Confirmation, and Eucharist are the Sacraments of Christian Initiation. They confer the vocation of holiness and the mission of evangelizing the world on Christians. They provide the necessary graces needed for this lifetime that will help us reach Heaven.

Two other sacraments—Holy Orders and Matrimony—also confer a particular mission in the Church and serve to build up God's People. The difference is that these sacraments are directed toward the salvation of others, not of those receiving the sacraments. If they contribute to personal salvation as well, it is because of the service to others that they do so. For example, those who are ordained work for the salvation of all by sharing the Word and the grace of God. Those who are married cooperate as husband and wife for the holiness of each other and in the continuation of the faith through having children and raising them in the faith.

The Sacrament of Holy Orders and the Sacrament of Matrimony are called the Sacraments at the Service of Communion because of their focus on others. Those who receive these sacraments can themselves be made holy and be saved, but the primary focus of each of these vocations is to reach out to others.

Holy Orders

Through Baptism and Confirmation, Catholics share in the common priesthood of the faithful. Holy Orders is the Sacrament for which certain members of the Church have been entrusted with the **ministerial priesthood** first entrusted to the Apostles. Through the ministerial priesthood, Christ himself becomes visibly present to the Church as the head of the Body and as the High Priest who offers the gift of his redemptive sacrifice on the cross.

Bishops and priests receive the ministerial or hierarchical priesthood through the Sacrament of Holy Orders. Sacramental ordination consecrates certain baptized men to one of three degrees of a sacred order: ***episcopate*** (bishops), ***presbyterate*** (priests), and ***diaconate*** (deacons). Deacons do not participate in the priesthood, which Christ exercises through bishops and priests.

The Church's authority allows only baptized men to be ordained. This follows the teaching and the Tradition of the Church, which extend from Jesus and his ministry. For example, Jesus chose only male Apostles even though while on earth he associated with and emphasized greatly the dignity of women. He did not even choose the Blessed Mother, Mary, to serve as an Apostle, a bishop, or a priest. The Apostles followed Jesus' example when they chose only males to succeed them in ordained ministry. Also, recall the importance of sacramental signs. Not only objects but also persons should represent what they signify by natural resemblance. The priest is a sign of Christ. Because Christ was male, a priest must also be male.

The blessing of candidates at the ordination Mass

The Sacrament of Holy Orders remains essential to the Church. Bishops, and by extension priests, connect the line of succession in the Church back to the Apostles. Holy Orders offers a gift of the Holy Spirit that allows bishops and priests to exercise a "sacred power" on behalf of Jesus for the Church. The effects of the sacrament are that bishops and priests proclaim and teach God's Word to all people, lead the Christian community in worship, and govern God's People by imitating Jesus' role of humble service.

Apologetics: CATHOLIC FAQs

- ☞ Is the reception of Confirmation necessary for salvation?
- ☞ What is the sin against the Holy Spirit spoken of in Matthew 12:31–32 that cannot be forgiven?
- ☞ Aren't the sacraments just celebrations to mark significant moments in our lives?

Priesthood is not something anyone can choose. No one has a right to be ordained. The call to priesthood is a call by God to serve the Church in a very special way. Anyone who thinks he recognizes God's call to the ordained ministry must humbly submit his desire to the authority of the Church. The Church then takes the responsibility and the right to call someone to receive Holy Orders.

Celebration of the Sacrament

The essential rite of the Sacrament of Holy Orders consists of the laying on of hands by the bishop accompanied by a specific prayer of consecration asking for the grace needed for the particular ministry to which the person is being ordained. The prayer for priestly ordination concludes with these words:

Almighty Father,

Grant to this servant of yours the dignity of the priesthood. Renew within him the Spirit of holiness. As a coworker with the order of bishops may he be faithful to the ministry that he receives from you, Lord God, and be to others a model of right conduct. May he be faithful in working with the order of bishops, so that the words of the Gospel may reach the ends of the earth, and the family of nations, made one in Christ, may become God's one, holy people. We ask this through our Lord Jesus Christ, your Son, who lives and reigns with you and the Holy Spirit, one God forever and ever. Amen.

With Holy Orders, an indelible spiritual character is conferred on the ordained man. As with Baptism and Confirmation, the fundamental identity of the person is changed with ordination and allows him to act in the person of Christ in a unique way. The Sacrament of Holy Orders cannot be repeated, nor can the character it confers ever be taken away, even if a man discontinues serving as a minister in the Church.

Sacrament of Matrimony

Marriage is an institution established by God, not by man, from the time of creation. The Book of Genesis tells us that God intended for man and woman to cling together and become one body (Gn 2:23–24). Genesis also teaches about human sexuality in marriage, which God found to be "very good" (Gn 1:31). He commanded us to "Be fertile and multiply; fill the earth and subdue it" (Gn 1:28).

Jesus blessed the relationship between a husband and wife and restored the ideal of marriage: "So they are no longer two, but one flesh. Therefore, what God has joined together, no human being must separate" (Mt 19:6). Marriage was modeled on the relationship between Christ and the Church; hence, Christ raised it to a sacrament.

The Church has always presided over marriages between Christians and contracted the marriage within the Church. In the fifth century, St. Augustine wrote some of the most definitive work of the Church Fathers on marriage, emphasizing its goodness, including:

- the procreation of children by the conjugal act
- the **chastity** of the spouses and their fidelity to one another
- the indissoluble union of the marriage

In the twelfth century, the Church made it explicit that marriage is one of the Seven Sacraments. The Councils of Florence (1439) and Trent (1563) reaffirmed this teaching. The Second Vatican Council emphasized the essential element of the sacrament: the mutual consent to marry. In the rite of the Sacrament of Matrimony, the time of consent takes place:

immediately after the Liturgy of the Word when the couple literally gives themselves to one another by saying:

> "I take you to be my wife."
> "I take you to be my husband."

For the words of consent to be valid, they must be given freely. No one can force someone into marriage. Unlike in the other sacraments, the spouses themselves are the ministers of the Sacrament of Matrimony. They mutually confer upon each other the graces of the sacrament by expressing their consent in public before the Church. Catholics must marry in the presence of a priest or a deacon and in the presence of two witnesses.

The Sacrament of Matrimony offers the couple a gift of unconditional love, which freely binds them for life. Marriage remains indissoluble. The effects of the sacrament can be witnessed in several ways, including:

- The man and the woman are given the grace to love each other unselfishly as Christ has loved the Church.
- The man and the woman are given the grace to remain faithful in their union to death.
- The man and the woman are given a grace that strengthens them for eternal life.
- The man and the woman are blessed with children and are given the grace to raise them in faith and love. The Christian home is where the children first hear the story of the faith and practice it with their parents through worship, celebrating the sacraments, and witnessing to Christ and the Church

through acts of holiness, self-denial, and active charity. For this reason the family is often called the **domestic church**.

Besides these graces, the Sacrament of Matrimony bestows directly on the couple the grace to witness Christian marriage in society. The living testimony of the couple (and their children) is a witness to the world of eternal, unbreakable, and boundless love.

Celebration of the Sacrament

Marriage is a sacred covenant that is an agreement between the couple themselves and the couple and God. Therefore it is fitting that the spouses seal their consent and give themselves to each other through the offering of their own lives. They do this by uniting their lives to the offering Christ makes present at Mass for the Church. The couple also receives the Eucharist so they can become one Body in Christ.

In the celebration of the wedding liturgy, certain elements are emphasized besides the giving of mutual consent of the bride and groom. The Liturgy of the Word focuses on the importance of Christian marriage in salvation history. The priest or the deacon offers a special nuptial blessing, and Holy Communion is received by the groom and bride and by all Catholics present who are properly prepared.

In summary, the Seven Sacraments celebrate Jesus as “the Way, the Truth, and the Life.” They celebrate the Paschal Mystery. The sacraments are a definite way we can come in contact with Jesus today. Jesus is the way for us to live life to the fullest, and the sacraments are the way to allow Jesus to touch our lives.

REVIEW

1. Why are Holy Orders and Matrimony called "Sacraments at the Service of Communion"?
2. Why does the Church ordain only males?
3. What are the effects of the Sacrament of Holy Orders?
4. How are the spouses themselves the ministers of the Sacrament of Matrimony?
5. What are ways in which the effects of the Sacrament of Matrimony are witnesses in the life of the couple?

WRITE OR DISCUSS

- Which priest has had the most influence on your life? How so?
- How is living in a family a preparation for the Sacrament of Matrimony?

PRESENCE AND ADORATION

A teenage boy heading home from school used to cut through the church from the side door to the front door to save a few steps to the bus stop. The church was darkened on those weekdays except for the red glow of the sanctuary lamp. The boy knew this light was a sign Jesus was in the church, reserved in the tabernacle behind the altar. That is, he knew this from his religion lessons over the years, but he didn't really *know* this. More information was about to come.

Out of rote respect, the boy paused and faced the tabernacle. Then he genuflected. He did this every time he walked through the church on the way to the bus.

One day when he was in a particular hurry, the boy did not pause. He did not face the tabernacle. And he did not genuflect. He kept going.

When he was almost to the front door and out of the church, he heard a woman's voice: "Hey, boy. Stop!" It was a homeless woman sitting off to the side in a rear pew. She had grocery bags with clothing and other belongings next to her.

"What?" the boy answered.

"Were you not going to acknowledge your God today?" she asked him.

"What do you mean?" said the boy.

"You did not bow before the Lord. You did not look at him," said the woman.

"I'm in a hurry. I do it most days. Why do I need to look at him today?" the boy continued.

"Well, maybe *you* don't need to look at him. Maybe *he* needs to look at you."

The tabernacle is where Jesus remains in our midst, available in his Eucharistic presence to communicate his love for us. Pope John Paul II wrote:

> The Church and the world have a great need for Eucharistic worship. Jesus awaits us in this sacrament of love. Let us not refuse the time to go to meet him in **adoration**, in contemplation full of faith, and open to making amends for the serious offenses and crimes of the world. Let our adoration never cease. (*Dominicae cenae,* 3)

Here are more quotations about Jesus' presence in the Blessed Sacrament, stored in the tabernacle:

> "God dwells in our midst, in the Blessed Sacrament of the altar."
>
> —St. Maximilian Kolbe
>
> "When I am before the Blessed Sacrament I feel such a lively faith that I cannot describe it. Christ in the Eucharist is almost tangible to me. To kiss the wounds continually and embrace him. When it is time for me to leave I have to tear myself away from his sacred presence."
>
> —St. Anthony Mary Claret
>
> "I throw myself at the foot of the tabernacle like a dog at the foot of his master."
>
> —St. John Vianney

> "Do you realize that Jesus is there in the tabernacle expressly for you—for you alone? He burns with desire to come into your heart."
>
> —St. Thérèse of Lisieux

Spend at least fifteen minutes in quiet prayer and reflection before the Blessed Sacrament.

Describe being in God's presence.

What does Jesus see when he looks at you? (Answer from Jesus' perspective, not your own or any other person's.)

GETTING TO KNOW JESUS

Christians are to imitate the values of Jesus in their own lives. Here are some of the things Jesus valued:

> Conversion • Commitment • Service • Community
> Fellowship • Forgiveness • Healing • Love
> Leadership • Reconciliation • Trust • Family • Life

Jesus instituted the sacraments from his own life and values. Read the following Gospel passages. Determine which sacrament each one points to. Name some values of Jesus that each passage represents:

Matthew 3:13–17; 9:35–36; 16:15–16; 28:16–20

Mark 1:40–45; 8:22–26

Luke 7:36–50; 12:8–12; 22:14–20

John 2:1–11; 6:47–58; 16:5–16; 20:19–23

PRAYER

Tantum Ergo

"Tantum ergo" begins the last two verses of the Eucharistic poem Pange Lingua written by St. Thomas Aquinas. It forms the opening words of the vespers sung during **Benediction** to honor and adore the Blessed Sacrament. The English translation follows the Latin version.

Tantum ergo Sacramentum
Veneremur cernui:
Et antiquum documentum
Novo cedat ritui:
Praestet fides supplementum
Sensuum defectui.

Genitori, Genitoque
Laus et iubilatio,
Salus, honor, virtus quoque
Sit et benedictio:
Procedenti ab utroque
Compar sit laudatio.
Amen.

Down in adoration falling,
Lo! the sacred Host we hail,
Lo! or'e ancient forms departing
Newer rites of grace prevail;
Faith for all defects supplying,
Where the feeble senses fail.

To the everlasting Father,
And the Son Who reigns on high
With the Holy Spirit proceeding
Forth from each eternally,
Be salvation, honor blessing,
Might and endless majesty.
Amen.

6
Our Life in Christ

RADICAL DISCIPLESHIP

If you were a teenager in the 1960s, your parents probably would not have wanted you to choose the life of a "hippie." Why? Hippies were countercultural, that is, they were mainly opposed to the culture and the values of the adult generation. They were mostly fifteen- to twenty-five-year-olds who typically dissented against middle-class and religious values, used illegal drugs, and practiced promiscuous sexual habits. And hippies of the 1960s were different from teens in most other generations, who kept their dissenting behaviors compartmentalized while continuing along a conventional academic and career path. Hippies often dropped out of their families and communities altogether while forming their own alternate social group.

Peaceful protestors prior to Selma to Montgomery march for voter's right in 1965

On the other hand, several other teenagers and young adults of the 1960s took on some of the elements of radicalism from the hippies but without the other destructive behaviors. Look closely at photos or films of civil-rights marches and protests, from Selma, Alabama, to Washington, D.C. You can usually find white, middle-class teens and Catholic nuns and priests integrated with the African Americans whose civil-rights struggle was at issue. Similarly, many young people of that era disagreed with their parents' values and beliefs in the area of war with constructive and peaceful protest of American military involvement in Vietnam.

It's worth imagining the cultural and social revolution of the 1960s as one way to understand the nature of Christian discipleship. Certainly the first disciples—primarily Jews who practiced their religion—were similarly radical in leaving behind some of their families' traditions and lifestyles in order to follow Christ. You've read this text and probably spent a lifetime learning about Jesus and praying to know him better. As this process continues, you are challenged to live the life of a disciple of Jesus Christ. Christian discipleship is itself a radical choice, albeit without destructive or immoral elements. It is a choice for positive living that parallels the life of Christ with both hardships and rewards. The disciples of Jesus gave up their professions, left their families, and practiced a faith that some of their Jewish neighbors found blasphemous. Remember some of the specific words and actions of the first Christian disciples.

Simon Peter and his brother Andrew were casting their fishing nets. Jesus approached and said, "Come after me, and I will make you fishers of men" (Mt 4:19). This rather obscure request convinced them to leave their property and follow him. Next, Jesus called James and his brother John. He called them, and they immediately followed. They not only discarded their boat, they left their father in it!

Nothing could distract Jesus from his mission. When James and John insisted on retribution for the people of Samaria who had given Jesus a cold welcome, Jesus could not be bothered. Rather, Jesus rebuked his disciples for their suggestion. Then someone who wanted to follow Jesus said, "Let me go first and bury my father." Jesus answered him, "Let the dead bury their dead. But you, go and proclaim the kingdom of God" (Lk 9:60). Jesus demanded that faith and preaching the Gospel come before anything else in life.

Another time, Jesus forgave a woman caught in adultery while religious leaders around them wanted to stone her based on the letter of Mosaic Law. Though he did not condemn her, Jesus told the woman, "From now on do not sin any more" (Jn 8:11).

Jesus most clearly defined discipleship in Mark's Gospel. James and John had foolishly been arguing over who would get to sit at Jesus' right hand when they reached God's Kingdom. (It was foolish because Jesus had already taught that

God's Kingdom was not about earthly power and riches.) He then told them:

> You know that those who are recognized as rulers over the Gentiles lord it over them, and their great ones make their authority over them felt. But it shall not be so among you. Rather, whoever wishes to be great among you will be your servant; whoever wishes to be first among you will be the slave of all. For the Son of Man did not come to be served but to serve and to give his life as a ransom for many. (Mk 10:42–45)

This type of difficult and, yes, radical discipleship is the vocation of anyone who claims to be a Christian, of anyone who is a baptized member of the Church. You are not called to "put off" discipleship as something you might pay attention to "after college" or "when you get married" or "after you've raised a family" or "when you are old and near death."

You are called now to the single-minded determination that Jesus demanded of the first disciples. St. Thérèse of Lisieux knew that a person cannot be "half a saint. . . . You must be a whole saint or nothing at all."

This chapter discusses what it takes to have life in Jesus Christ. As with doing that in any human era, the challenges are many. The reality of sin still clouds the world. Nevertheless, the Blessed Trinity provides the graces for living in Jesus Christ. The natural law, the Ten Commandments, the Beatitudes, and Church teachings are among the helps. These and other facets of Christian living are covered in more detail in the sections that follow.

WRITE OR DISCUSS

- For you, which adjective best describes Christian discipleship: radical, idealistic, hopeful, difficult, or rewarding?
- Practically, what would be the difference between being "half a saint" and being a "whole saint"?

OUR VOCATION TO BEATITUDE

Why would we want to leave everything behind for Jesus? The answer is happiness. St. Augustine wrote, "In seeking you, my God, I seek a happy life."[9] Or, as St. Thomas Aquinas succinctly put it, "God alone satisfies." We all want to be happy.

In fact, *beatitude* means "supreme happiness." The Beatitudes, preached by Jesus in the Sermon on the Mount, respond to our natural desire for happiness. This type of happiness is not temporal or fleeting. This desire for happiness comes from God himself. It is placed in our hearts to draw us to God, the only one who can ever fulfill this desire.

In the New Testament, the supreme happiness is described in several ways but most typically as "the coming of the Kingdom (or reign) of God." The Beatitudes make us like God and able to share eternal life.

From the Beatitudes themselves (Mt 5:3–10), we know of Jesus' love and the kind of love to which we are called. Good enough. But when you've read or heard the Beatitudes, you might have wondered what they could have to do with happiness.

Meaning of the Beatitudes

In many ways, the Beatitudes put a face on Jesus Christ in the world today. The Beatitudes help us recognize Christ's continuing to live in our midst. The "blessed" he spoke of may be members of our own family, nondescript classmates, or aged and ill grandparents, besides the countless number of poverty-stricken people who live in our country and elsewhere on this planet. The Beatitudes do something else as well: They provide a road map to our own holiness and happiness. They express our own vocation as connected with Christ's Paschal Mystery. They are promises made to us that allow us to sustain hope for God's Kingdom amid the trials of life on earth. A deeper examination reveals how.

Sheep graze on the Mount of Beatitudes overlooking the Sea of Galilee.

Blessed are the poor in spirit, for theirs is the Kingdom of Heaven.

In the Jewish Bible, the poor are described by their Hebrew name, *anawim* (ah-nah-weem). These were people without material possessions who nevertheless kept a positive attitude, realized their helplessness, and sought God for all their needs, material and spiritual. Most importantly, they trusted that God would take care of all their needs.

Blessed are they who mourn, for they will be comforted.

The ache of mourning can seem inconsolable. Imagine suffering through the death of a parent or a child. But when we mourn even in the worst of situations, we also pause to think about others who are experiencing even worse situations than ours. We empathize with them. We move deeper into the human community. And from our deep mourning, we receive comfort for our aching selves that only God can provide.

Blessed are the meek, for they will inherit the land.

Meekness is not considered a strength in most settings today. Aristotle thought of meekness as the midpoint between too much anger and too little anger. Anger is a natural human emotion. The gift of meekness helps us know the most appropriate times to feel and express anger.

Blessed are they who hunger and thirst for righteousness, for they will be satisfied.

Righteous people are bothered when things are not fair or just, not only for themselves but for others. A person who seeks righteousness or justice literally craves that each person's just needs will be met and can't be satisfied until that happens. God rewards this desire with satisfaction.

Blessed are the merciful, for they will be shown mercy.

This Beatitude urges empathy. We are to think, feel, and act from another's perspective rather than our own. When we show mercy, we live this petition of the Our Father: "Forgive us our trespasses as we forgive those who trespass against us."

Blessed are the clean of heart, for they will see God.

Those who are clean of heart are opposite from the "two-faced" people who say one thing and do another. The clean of heart do not have ulterior motives for their actions. Rather, they are honest, unselfish, and sincere.

Blessed are the peacemakers, for they will be called children of God.

We tend to think of peace as an absence of war or trouble. The Hebrew understanding of peace—*shalom*—means helping others enjoy all the good that life has to offer. This means a peacemaker is active, not passive. A peacemaker looks for a variety of ways to make the local and larger community a better place to live.

Blessed are they who are persecuted for the sake of righteousness, for theirs is the Kingdom of Heaven.

The life of a Christian on earth is not easy. Jesus, our model, experienced pain, suffering, abuse, and death on behalf of God's Kingdom. We must be prepared for much of the same; others, even family members, may shun us for standing up for what we believe in.

The happiness promised in the Beatitudes is not all future oriented. God's reign is happening now. Our life here on earth is the beginning of our eternal life, which will culminate in paradise. Making decisions based in the Beatitudes readies us for that time.

REVIEW

1. How does the New Testament define happiness?
2. Who were the *anawim*? How are they connected with the first Beatitude?
3. How does the Beatitude that speaks of peacekeeping mean more than the absence or war or trouble?
4. How are the Beatitudes connected with Christ's Paschal Mystery?

WRITE OR DISCUSS

- Describe someone you know whose happiness is centered in the Beatitudes.
- Which Beatitude do you find most closely connected with happiness?

CHALLENGES TO A LIFE IN CHRIST

Morality, or living a moral life, is another way to describe Christian discipleship. A moral life is made possible only by Jesus Christ, who in his Passion "delivered us from Satan and sin" and "merited for us the new life in the Holy Spirit" (*CCC*, 1708). Morality involves putting your faith into action. No one appreciates a person who only preaches about something ("I am such a great basketball player" or "I have an aptitude for math," etc.). When we don't see actions backing up the words (actually making the team or scoring high in precalculus), we tend to write off such a braggart.

Morality
Putting your faith and religion into practice through making good decisions in word and action.

Living a moral life means being responsible for:

- what you say and do
- your inaction as well as your action
- the motives for your behavior

Living a moral life also means being free. God gave you the freedom "to act or not to act, to do this or that, and so to perform deliberate actions on your own responsibility" (*CCC*, 1731). God is not a master programmer or puppeteer high above the

Apologetics:
CATHOLIC FAQs

Use this chapter and other sources to formulate your own answers to these questions. Then check your answers at "Catholic FAQs" at www.avemariapress.com: Religious Education.

- How can the Catholic Church maintain that certain moral teaching applies to everyone and not only to Catholics?
- If God knows everything about us, how can we really be free?
- Where does the Bible name the difference between mortal and venial sins?

earth, pulling every string, controlling all your actions. You were made free. You can initiate and control your own actions. The more you choose good, the freer you become.

Unfortunately, Satan's allure and the effects of Original Sin remain. When we freely choose against reason, truth, and right conscience, we sin. Sin is an offense against God. Sin turns our hearts away from God's love for us. There are different kinds of sins, and their effects vary as well.

Different Kinds of Sins and Their Effects

Scripture provides names and descriptions of a variety of sins.

In the Letter to the Galatians, St. Paul names fornication, impurity, licentiousness, idolatry, **sorcery**, enmity, strife, jealousy, anger, selfishness, dissension, factions, envy, drunkenness, carousing, and the like as works of the flesh that contrast with the fruit of the Spirit (Gal 5:19–21).

These kinds of acts are personal sins and can also be described by their degree of seriousness.

Mortal sin is the most serious kind of personal sin. When we speak of mortal sin, we use words such as *destroy* and *kill*. Mortal sin effectively destroys our relationship with God and kills our ability to love. It's easy to see how **adultery** could kill the ability of a husband or a wife to love a spouse who has been unfaithful. Adultery can seriously damage the relationship of the adulterous spouse with God. Disregard for the covenant of marriage is profoundly destructive.

However, mortal sins cannot be committed by accident. For a sin to be mortal, these three conditions must exist:

1. The moral object must be of grave or serious matter. Grave matter is specified in the Ten Commandments (e.g., do not kill, do not commit adultery, do not steal, etc.).
2. The person must have full knowledge of the gravity of the sinful action.
3. The person must completely consent to the action. It must be a personal choice.

An additional and maybe obvious condition for mortal sins is that the action must be completed. Desiring to do something evil is certainly wrong but is not of itself mortally sinful. Instead, it reflects a serious breach in the person's relationship with God.

Let's look at an example of an action that presents a grave or serious matter—the abuse of illegal drugs. When an action constitutes a grave or serious matter, it meets the first condition of a mortal sin.

The second condition, however, could diminish a person's culpability in this area. Take the situation of a teenage boy raised in an impoverished environment who uses illegal drugs. The use of illegal drugs is a serious sin against one's own health, a violation of the Fifth Commandment. But is the boy fully aware of the moral gravity of his actions? What if he

capital sins
Sins that are the root of other sins and vices. There are seven capital sins: pride, covetousness, envy, anger, gluttony, lust, and sloth.

witnessed his own parents using the same drugs on many occasions? Is it possible the boy does not have the full and broad picture about the serious immorality of illegal drug use? However, if the boy pretends he does not know that illegal drug use is a serious sin and really does, his guilt is increased. Faked or "feigned" ignorance, as the *Catechism* describes (1859), can increase the voluntary character of a sin.

What about the third condition, freedom of consent? If a person's choice is limited by things such as peer or parental pressures, physical force, or extreme emotions, the degree of guilt for the sin may be lessened. This condition could apply to sins such as murder or stealing.

To be forgiven, all mortal sins must be confessed to a priest in the Sacrament of Penance because reconciliation of mortal sin "necessitates a new initiative of God's mercy and a conversion of the heart" (*CCC*, 1856).

Less serious sin is called venial sin. Examples of venial sins are petty jealousy, disobedience, and "borrowing" a small amount of money from a parent without the intention to repay it. Venial sins, when repeated and unrepented, can lead us to commit mortal sins.

Vices are bad habits linked with **capital sins**—pride, avarice, envy, wrath, lust, gluttony, and sloth.

Sinning is a personal action. But we also have a responsibility for sins committed by others when we cooperate with or praise them. For example, when we protect or fail to stop someone we know who has vandalized school property. Or suppose we praise someone ("wow, you're cool") for stealing or for engaging in premarital sex.

Children begging in Egypt

Sinful behavior multiplies. It can affect social situations and institutions. For example, lust and gluttony for profits can cause a large corporation to underpay its employees in third-world nations. Or they can lead to pollution of the environment. Each person must take stock of his or her responsibility in these types of "social sins."

REVIEW

1. What are the responsibilities for living a moral life?
2. How does living a moral life equate with freedom?
3. What are the conditions for mortal sin?
4. Define *venial sin.*

WRITE OR DISCUSS

- Report how two of the sins St. Paul described in Galatians 5:19–21 have affected your life personally or societal life you've observed.
- How can we have responsibility for sins committed by another person or by society at large?

BLESSED ARE THE POOR IN SPIRIT

Poor among us

There are people who are literally poor among us. A recent study found over 37 million Americans living below the poverty line.

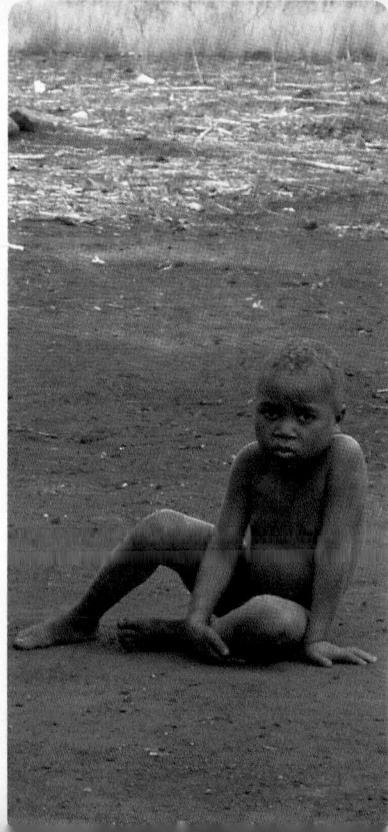

The "poor in spirit" whom Jesus calls "blessed" in the first Beatitude were known as the *anawim* (ah-nah-weem) in the Old Testament. The prophet in Isaiah 61:1 called them "lowly" and "brokenhearted." The *anawim* were those without material possessions who were dependent on God for their very lives. To be "poor in spirit" is to be a person who realizes his or her own helplessness and puts all trust in God.

The poverty line

The government calculates the poverty line by determining the minimum amount families or individuals need for food, shelter, clothing, health care, and transportation (certainly not the only expenses people incur).

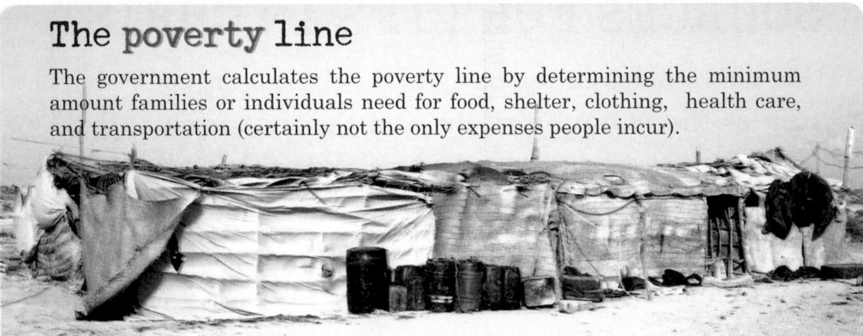

A response to poverty

The United States Bishops have offered a three-point plan for people to begin a response to poverty. They are:

- **LEARN**. The first step to solving a problem is to understand it. Work to understand the root causes of poverty.
- **ACT**. Some of the ways to begin action are to share information about poverty, talk to elected officials, and support social justice principles.
- **GIVE**. Donating time, money, and resources are effective ways to give of yourself.

For more information see: **www.usccb.org/cchd/povertyusa/index.htm**

SOURCES FOR LIFE IN CHRIST

God offers helps to combat sinful behavior through supports such as the natural law, the Ten Commandments, the New Law—or Law of the Gospel—(including the Beatitudes), and Church teaching. Good laws such as these guide human freedom. Remember that freedom makes us responsible for our choices and actions, good or evil. Law also serves as an objective standard outside ourselves. Too often today people claim that morality is subjective, that is, each person has the right to determine what is right or wrong according to personal preferences. Rather, the moral law is the work of God and emanates from the Divine Law, the source of all laws. St. Thomas Aquinas defined *law* as "an ordinance of reason for the **common good**, promulgated by the one who is in charge of the community" (quoted in *CCC*, 1976). Moral law finds its fullness and unity in Jesus.

The different expressions of the moral law, all of them interrelated, are described in the sections that follow.

Natural Law

Natural law is our participation in Divine Law. Natural law refers to what human reason can discover about human nature and its moral duties independent of God's gift of Revelation.

Natural law teaches us what to do and what to avoid. It corresponds to three basic human drives and needs:

- preserving life
- developing as individuals and communities
- sharing life with others

The natural law expresses human dignity and serves as the basis for all human rights. It is the foundation of both civil laws and moral rules. The natural law is universal, and its principles unify the human race. It is unchangeable, and its basic principles can never be destroyed.

The norms expressed by the natural law can be positive or negative, general or specific, dealing with our actions (what to do) or governing our character (what to be). Examples of behaviors derived from natural law include the following:

- "Do good and avoid evil."
- "Love your neighbor."
- "Don't murder."
- "Don't steal."
- "Don't commit adultery."

Natural law is present in the heart of each person and established by reason. However, the precepts and the behaviors that flow from the natural law (such as those listed above) have not been realized by everyone due to sin. Because of sin and our weakened intellects, we cannot always correctly discern the natural law.

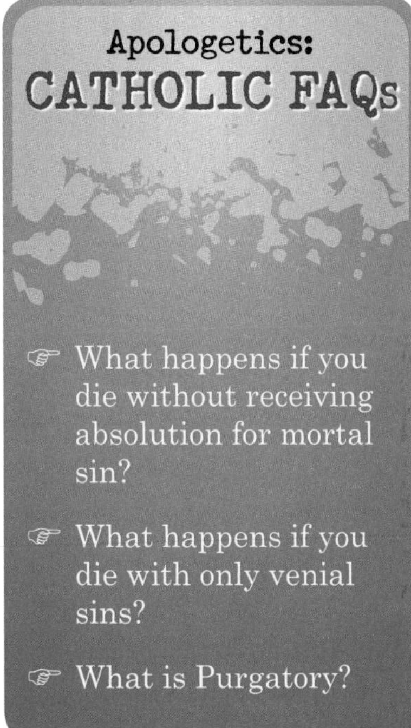

Apologetics:
CATHOLIC FAQs
What happens if you die without receiving absolution for mortal sin?
What happens if you die with only venial sins?
What is Purgatory?

What humans lack, God provides. God has revealed himself through history and gives us the moral law of the Old and New Testaments. The Law of Moses, summarized in the Ten Commandments, contains the major precepts of the natural law. The Law of Moses, or Old Law, sets the stage for the New Law, the Law of Christ.

The Ten Commandments

The Law of Moses is the first stage of God's revealed law. The Ten Commandments (or Decalogue) summarize the major precepts of the Old Law, expressing the truths of the natural law that human reason can discover on its own. The Ten Commandments prohibit what is contrary to the love of God and neighbor and teach what the demands of love require.

The Ten Commandments have always been a source for Christian morality. Revealed by the Father, they were recognized by Jesus himself. He told the rich young man, "If you wish to enter into life, keep the commandments" (Mt 19:17). Since the time of St. Augustine (fourth century AD), the Ten Commandments have been used as a source for teaching baptismal candidates.

The first three Commandments have to do with love for God. The last seven refer to love for neighbor. As you review the Commandments below, think about how each applies to decisions you make daily in your own life.

1. I am the Lord your God: You shall not have strange gods before me.

To worship God means we accept God as our Creator and ourselves as made in his image. To understand what it is to worship, think of some sins against the First Commandment: **idolatry** (worship of false gods), atheism (denial of God's existence), and **agnosticism** (the belief that no one knows for sure whether God exists). On the other hand, the First Commandment asks us to practice the virtues of faith, hope, and love. Practicing our religion also helps us keep the First Commandment.

II. You shall not take the name of the Lord, your God, in vain.

We must respect God's name and never use the name of God, Jesus, Mary, or the saints improperly. This means that when we take an **oath** or make a promise in God's name, we must be true to it. We should also respect our name and strive for holiness. God made us and knew us from the beginning of time. Our name will be with us into eternity. This commandment forbids blasphemy, a sin that involves hateful words against God, Jesus, or even the Church. Cursing also violates this commandment.

III. Remember to keep holy the Lord's Day.

God set aside the Sabbath to remind us of the time at creation when God rested on the seventh day. It is a day intended for people to rest from their work and to praise God for his works of salvation.

Catholics celebrate by worshiping God through attending Sunday Mass and by observing rest on Sunday, the day of Christ's Resurrection. Sunday is linked with the Paschal Mystery, the Passion, Death, Resurrection, and Ascension of Jesus, commemorated in the Eucharist. Church law—stemming from the law of the Lord—requires Catholics to participate in Sunday Mass or the Sunday vigil, which is on Saturday. To deliberately miss Sunday Mass is mortally sinful. We also make Sunday holy by spending time with our families, visiting our other relatives, helping the poor, or doing other charitable acts.

IV Honor your father and your mother.

The Fourth Commandment begins the second part of the Ten Commandments, having to do with love for neighbor. This is appropriate, for love truly begins at home. How can you be loving to your friends and teachers at school if you lambasted your mom or were rude to a sibling on the ride to school? You owe your parents (and other family members) respect and obedience for as long as you live at home. When you are older, you still must respect your parents and care for them when they are old, ill, or lonely. Teachers, civil authorities, religious leaders, and other adults are also owed your respect according to this commandment.

V You shall not kill.

All human life is of immense value. This statement applies to human life from the moment of conception until natural death. For this reason, this commandment forbids **abortion** (killing an unborn baby) and **euthanasia** (mercy killing of the aged or the sick).

There are times when killing is morally permissible—for example, in self-defense or when protecting the life of another. Killing in war may be morally permissible if the nation is defending itself against aggressors. Also, the traditional teaching of the Church does not exclude the use of the death penalty if this is the only way to defend innocent lives against an unjust killer. However, the Church continues to teach that today there are very few, if any, situations in which execution of a person is necessary. Held in a secure prison, the offending person is kept away from society and has the chance to seek redemption and conversion.

This Commandment also tells us not to "kill" our own bodies and requires us to live healthy lives of exercise, wholesome eating, and rest and to avoid harmful addictions such as alcohol and drugs.

VI. You shall not commit adultery.

The Sixth Commandment encompasses the whole of human sexuality. In the Old Testament, the offense of this commandment primarily involved a husband's having sexual intercourse with a married woman other than his wife. Jesus took the command further, saying that "everyone who looks at a woman with lust" (Mt 5:28) has already committed adultery.

Apologetics:
CATHOLIC FAQs

- Are Christians always obliged to obey civil law and authorities?
- How can I tell if I made the right decision in the area of morality?
- Isn't it wrong to judge other people by telling them something they are doing is wrong?

For people of any age or state in life, keeping this commandment involves practicing the virtue of chastity. Chastity involves self-mastery over one's sexuality and rejects lust (inordinate enjoyment of sexual pleasure), masturbation (deliberate self-stimulation of genital organs to derive sexual pleasure), fornication (sex between unmarried persons), pornography (displaying sexual acts for a third party to see), prostitution (selling of sexual acts), rape (forcing another to have sex), and homosexual acts (sexual activity between persons of the same gender).

Rather, this Commandment teaches us that sexual love must be shared only in the intimacy of a loving marriage, where sexual intercourse strengthens the unity of the marriage and results in the procreation of children in a stable, loving setting.

VII. You shall not steal.

The Seventh Commandment forbids theft, which is the taking of another's property against his or her will. This is a violation of justice since we must respect the property rights of others.

Stealing, however, is more encompassing than just the unlawful taking of someone else's things. Stealing also includes cheating (e.g., on taxes or a test), doing shoddy work on the job, and vandalism.

VIII. You shall not bear false witness against your neighbor.

We are to be truthful in our words and actions. Any misrepresentation of the truth violates this commandment. A lie is the most direct offense against the truth. "To lie is to speak or act against the truth in order to lead someone into error" (*CCC*, 2483). There are other violations against this commandment that are sins against truth. For example, it is sinful to give false testimony in court and make the evil worse by committing **perjury**. Another sinful action is **detraction**, which reveals a person's faults and failings to someone who did not previously know about them and has no right or need to know them. And **calumny** is lying about others so people will make false judgments about them.

IX. You shall not covet your neighbor's wife.

Covet means to "desire something that is not one's own." In this case, like the Sixth Commandment, it directly refers to the covenant of marriage. But this commandment addresses purity of heart and the struggle for modesty. It forbids all internal sins of thought and desire against chastity. It does not allow our flesh to control our spirit. Recall that the Sixth Commandment addresses sexual *acts* that are forbidden.

The commandment tells us to purify our hearts in these ways: by the virtue and the gift of chastity, by purity of intention (sincerely trying to do God's will in everything), by purity of vision (disciplining our emotions, imagination, and thoughts), and by praying (for the grace of chastity).

modesty
The virtue of temperance that applies to how a person speaks, dresses, and conducts himself or herself. Related to the virtue of purity, modesty protects the intimate center of a person by refusing to unveil what should remain hidden.

Purity requires **modesty**, which "protects the intimate center of the person" (*CCC*, 2521). Modesty guides us as to how one looks at others and behaves toward them in conformity with their dignity and our solidarity with them.

X. You shall not covet your neighbor's goods.

Similar to the Seventh Commandment, the Tenth Commandment opposes greed, envy, and avarice (the seeking of riches and the power that comes with them).

The Tenth Commandment makes it clear we desire things that give us pleasure. These desires are morally permissible as long as they do not lead us to crave things that belong to others.

Christians believe that the Old Law, including the Ten Commandments, is holy, good, and spiritual. It is meant to be followed. However, the Old Law does not offer the grace and the strength of the Holy Spirit. According to St. Paul, the special function of the Old Law is to reveal and condemn what is sinful. Therefore, it prepares us for conversion in Jesus Christ. The Old Law lays the groundwork for the Gospel, for the coming of the New Covenant in Jesus Christ, and for his New Law of love.

The New Law, or Law of the Gospel

The New Law, or Law of the Gospel, is the perfection of Divine Law. The New Law is the work of Jesus Christ and is represented in the Sermon on the Mount, especially, as mentioned, the Beatitudes.

The New Law is a law of love. Love is the fulfillment of the Old Law. The New Law does not offer any new precepts for us to follow. Rather, it focuses on the attitudes and the motivations we have when we act. It teaches us to be sincere when we perform religious duties such as fasting, praying, or giving money to the poor. Jesus summarized the New Law in these two Gospel teachings:

- "Do to others whatever you would have them do to you" (Mt 7:12).
- "Love one another as I love you" (Jn 15:12).

The New Law is called the law of love because it operates out of the love infused in us by the Holy Spirit. It does not operate out of fear. The New Law helps us translate the love we receive into loving others. The New Law is also a law of grace because it gives us the supernatural power of grace to be able to follow the Law by faith and participation in the sacraments. Finally, the New Law is a law of freedom. It gives us freedom from the ritualistic practices of the Old Law. Rather than acting from rote, our choices to love can be made spontaneously and out of friendship with Christ.

Besides the teachings from the Sermon on the Mount, the evangelical counsels also spring from the New Law. These counsels—poverty, chastity, and obedience—are intended to remove anything from our lives that keeps us from loving God, others, and ourselves.

All Christians are called to follow the evangelical counsels, but according to each person's grace and vocation. Particularly, men and women in the **consecrated life** are dedicated to living by the evangelical counsels. They profess the counsels within a permanent state of life recognized by the Church, characterized as a life consecrated to God. Traditional ways the consecrated life is practiced in the Church include living in community with others (sisters or brothers), typically called the "religious life." Other styles of consecrated life include an eremitic lifestyle as a hermit, taking a vow as a consecrated virgin or widow, or participating in a society of apostolic life. In all of these models, the evangelical counsels are embraced.

Church Law

The Church is the living Body of Christ that also nurtures our growth in holiness. The Church gives us grace-filled moments in the sacraments. In the Liturgy of the Eucharist, we share in Christ's Paschal Mystery of his Passion, Death, Resurrection, and Ascension, and we do so in communion with those around us in faith. In the Church, we have the example of Mary and all the saints, who show the way for living a moral life.

The Church is not a family limited by time or space. The Church is a living family with leaders in the Magisterium who continually call us to the moral truth of Jesus, who is "the Way, the Truth, and the Life."

Like all families, the Church has certain rules for us to follow in order to guarantee our minimal growth

precepts of the Church
Rules Catholics follow to help them become good and moral people. They include attending Mass on Sundays and holy days of obligation, confessing sins at least once a year, receiving Communion at minimum during the Easter season, observing days of fasting and abstinence, and providing for the needs of the Church.

in becoming good and moral people. They are known as the **precepts of the Church** and must be obeyed by all Catholics. These precepts are:

1. "You shall attend Mass on Sundays and on holy days of obligation and rest from servile labor."

The "obligation" to attend Sunday Mass is rooted in the Law of the Lord and expressed in the Third Commandment. Participating at Mass helps us celebrate Christ's Resurrection. In addition, Sundays are to be days when we relax and unwind from the week, spend time with family, and avoid unnecessary work.

Like the Sunday obligation, we are to attend Mass on specially designated holy days. In the United States, these are the Feast of the Immaculate Conception (December 8), Christmas (December 25), the Solemnity of Mary (January 1), the Feast

Pope Benedict XVI delivering his Easter address

of the Ascension (when celebrated on a Thursday, forty days after Easter), the Assumption of Mary (August 15), and All Saints' Day (November 1).

2. "You shall confess your sins at least once a year."

The Sacrament of Penance ensures we will be properly prepared to receive the Eucharist. We must confess our sins any time we have sinned mortally. We can also use the sacrament to confess venial sins. Additionally, it is good to use this sacrament during the seasons of **Advent**, **Lent**, and **Easter**. The start of school is another good reminder to go to confession.

3. "You shall receive the Sacrament of the Eucharist at least during the Easter season."

This precept is a minimal obligation to receive Jesus in the Sacrament of Eucharist. However, we should receive Communion frequently whenever we are in the state of grace.

4. "You shall observe the days of fasting and abstinence established by the Church."

The Church has prescribed days, such as Ash Wednesday and Good Friday, when we are to fast and abstain from certain types of food. Fasting regulations require that on those days a person eat just one full meal and two smaller meals and not eat between meals. Abstinence laws require not eating meat. In addition, we should practice these habits at other times in imitation of Christ and at his instruction in the Beatitudes and the Sermon on the Mount.

5. "You shall help to provide for the needs of the Church."

Catholics have the duty to support the Church with gifts of their time and talents and with monetary gifts.

REVIEW

1. What is the purpose of law for living a moral life?
2. Define *moral law.*
3. What are three basic drives and needs to which natural law corresponds?
4. What did Jesus teach about the Old Law? What do Christians acknowledge about the Ten Commandments?
5. How did Jesus summarize the New Law?
6. What are some ways men and women in the consecrated life live the evangelical counsels?
7. Name the Church laws.

WRITE OR DISCUSS

- What are other human behaviors besides those listed that seem to have origins in the natural law?
- Share an insight about how the Ten Commandments have helped you in moral decision making.

LIVING A NEW LIFE IN CHRIST

Christians gauge their personal morality in reference to Jesus Christ, who is "the way and the truth and the life" (Jn 14:6). How do you and your actions measure up with Jesus and what he would do? That question should never be far from your heart as you go about making decisions—easy and difficult ones alike.

What did Jesus do when he walked the earth? In summary, Jesus did what pleased God, his Father. This meant that Jesus loved others, himself, and God. Included among the

"others" Jesus loved were his enemies. Among those "enemies" of Jesus were the Samaritan people despised by many of his fellow Jews and even those out to put him to death. His reasoning: It is easy to love those who love us in return. It is much more difficult to love those who offer us no love and, in fact, hate us. Yet this is what God the Father does, so we are to do the same in order to "be perfect, just as your heavenly Father is perfect" (Mt 5:48).

We cannot be "perfect" without God's help or grace. Grace is God's favor to us. It is the free and undeserved help God gives to us so we can respond to him and share in his friendship and eternal life. Grace is a participation in the life of God.

Different types of grace can assist us. ***Sanctifying grace*** is the habitual, permanent grace received in Baptism that enables us to live with God, act by his love, and inherit Heaven. It is distinguished from ***actual grace***, which refers to the ways God intervenes in our lives, either at the beginning of our conversion to Christ or as we work toward being more holy. There are also *sacramental graces*, which are received when we participate in the sacraments, and *special graces*, or **charisms**, which are both ordinary and extraordinary but whose common purpose is to serve the Church. Among the special graces are "graces of state," which are given to those who have responsibilities for life and ministries in the Church.

charisms
Special gifts the Holy Spirit bestows on individual Christians to help the Church grow.

Ultimately, we are **justified** and saved by grace, though grace is beyond our human experience and cannot be known except by our faith. St. Joan of Arc famously said when asked if she knew whether she were in a state of grace, "If I am not, may it please God to put me in it; if I am, may it please God to keep me there."[10]

Practically, "life in Christ" translates to making good choices and avoiding sinful behavior, as modeled by Jesus himself. This section explores factors that can help in making good choices. Two factors that help include careful conscience formation and the practice of virtues. This section also addresses the criteria for determining whether a moral choice is objectively good or evil.

Listening to Conscience

Deep within us, we have a drive or, as the documents of the Second Vatican Council described, a "most secret core and sanctuary" that helps us distinguish between good and evil. Known as ***conscience***, it allows us at the appropriate times to do good and avoid evil. Conscience also

> judges particular choices, approving those that are good and denouncing those that are evil. It bears witness to the authority of truth in reference to the supreme Good to which the human person is drawn, and it welcomes the commandments. (*CCC*, 1777)

When we listen to our conscience, we can hear God speaking to us. Our conscience enables us to take responsibility for the things we do or fail to do. While the gift of conscience allows us to know and do good, we do not have an ingrained program that automatically makes the right choice for us. This means we must continually form our conscience in keeping with the true good willed by God, our Creator. Christians primarily form their conscience through learning and living the life and the teachings of Jesus Christ and putting into practice the Christian virtues. More concretely, this means studying the Scriptures, praying, examining our conscience, listening to the witness and the advice of others, and being guided by the authoritative teaching of the Church.

Apologetics:
CATHOLIC FAQs

- If the Bible permits justice in terms of "an eye for an eye," then why is the Church opposed to capital punishment?
- Can rich people go to Heaven?
- Why does God allow death?

We must always follow our conscience, but we must also realize that our conscience can err if it is not informed. For example, a child raised by parents who routinely swear could not initially know that swearing is wrong. When the child grows in experience and begins to learn from others that swearing is offensive, he or she becomes more and more culpable for actions or inactions in this area.

Simply put, our conscience helps us distinguish between sin and virtue.

Practicing Virtues

Virtues are defined as a "habitual and firm disposition to do the good" (*CCC*, 1803). They counteract **vices**.

Virtues help a person not only perform good acts, but also to give his or her best. A virtuous person uses all his or her

cardinal virtues
The "hinge" virtues from which all other virtues come. They are prudence, justice, fortitude, and temperance.

bodily senses and spiritual powers to pursue the good and make good choices. As St. Gregory of Nyssa put it, "The goal of a virtuous life is to become like God." Putting virtues into practice is an effective way to avoid poor choices and sinfulness.

Virtues acquired by human effort are known as "moral" or "human" virtues. Four of these virtues form the hinge that connects all the others. These **cardinal virtues** are prudence, justice, fortitude, and temperance. The more you put these virtues into practice, the easier time you should have in doing what is right and good.

Prudence equates with common sense and wisdom. St. Thomas Aquinas called prudence "right reason in action." Prudence helps us discern good in every life circumstance and choose the right means to achieve it. Also, a prudent person seems to have a plan for his or her life and rarely deviates from it in any given situation. You may know many prudent people or be prudent yourself. Think of anyone planning for college and career. This person has a plan. He or she will not do anything to jeopardize the plan, whether by doing something illegal or something immoral.

Justice consists in a person's always giving his or her due to God or neighbor. Being just means respecting the rights of others. There are several distinctions of justice—*distributive* (protects common welfare), *legal* (governs what individuals owe society), and *social* (applies the Gospel to structures of society). All forms of justice have to do with relationships between people and with protecting the human rights of all. As you have grown up, you have witnessed what it means to be fair and unfair. You may have seen a classmate receive an award that should have been awarded to another person. You may have failed to make a team or missed a part in a play because of favoritism a coach or teacher showed another student. You may also have witnessed teachers going out of their way to make sure a student passes a course, even after the person has already failed several times. Remember that justice means giving each person his or her rightful due.

Fortitude is another word for courage. It enables a person to conquer fears, even the fear of death, for a just cause. The virtue of fortitude helps in situations that may not seem as clear-cut as life and death. A person with fortitude can resist the many challenges that accompany peer pressure.

Temperance moderates a person's attractions to pleasures and helps balance the way we use created goods. We can temper our desire for pleasures such as food, alcohol, drugs, and sex by practicing self-denial. As St. Paul's Letter to Titus explains, we ought "to live temperately, justly, and devoutly in this age" (Ti 2:12).

We acquire human virtues "by education, by deliberate acts and by a perseverance" that is "ever-renewed in repeated efforts" and "purified and elevated by divine grace" (*CCC*, 1810). In other words, together with God, we are responsible for practicing and perfecting these virtues.

The human virtues have their roots in the **theological virtues**, the virtues related directly to God. The theological virtues—faith, hope, and love (charity)—are the foundation of a Christian's moral life. These virtues are not gained by our efforts. They are infused into our souls by God to make us capable of choosing goodness over sin,

theological virtues
Three important virtues bestowed on us at Baptism that relate us to God: faith (belief in and personal knowledge of God), hope (trust in God's salvation and his bestowal of the graces needed to attain it), and charity (love of God and love of neighbor).

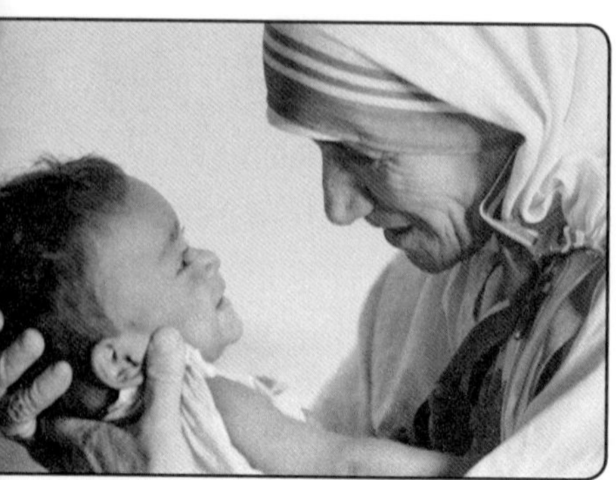
Blessed Mother Teresa of Calcutta

of choosing right from wrong, and of meriting eternal life. Above all, practicing the theological virtues embodies Christian love and raises our human efforts to love to the supernatural perfection of divine love. This type of love or charity is what binds us together as members of Christ's Mystical Body.

The gifts of the Holy Spirit sustain Christian moral life. In the Sacrament of Confirmation, the bishop extends his hands over the candidates and evokes the outpouring of the Holy Spirit in seven gifts: wisdom, understanding, counsel, fortitude, knowledge, piety, and fear of the Lord. These gifts complete and perfect the virtues of those who receive them.

The **fruits of the Holy Spirit** are the rewards for Christians who practice the virtues. The Tradition of the Church lists twelve fruits: charity, joy, peace, patience, kindness, goodness, generosity, gentleness, faithfulness, modesty, self-control, and chastity. The fruits are not only rewards for this world; they also serve "as the first fruits of eternal glory" (*CCC*, 1832).

Making Good Choices

As long as we have the gift of **free will** and are not bound by force to God, who is the ultimate good, it's possible that we can choose good over evil or evil over good. The gift of freedom makes us moral. Using the helps mentioned above can help us make good choices. But how do we determine what is good or evil? Freely

free will
The capacity to choose among alternatives. Free will is "the power, rooted in reason and will . . . to perform deliberate actions on one's own responsibility" (CCC, 1731). True freedom is at the service of what is good and true.

chosen acts can be evaluated as good or evil. The morality of human acts depends on:

- the object chosen
- the intention
- the circumstances of the action

These elements are explained further in the following sections.

The Moral Object

The moral object is the "what" of morality; it is what we do. There are good moral actions and evil actions. Some actions are objectively good; for example, providing food for a poor person in the neighborhood. The object of a human act is good when it promotes the well-being and the true good of others and when it conforms to objective norms of morality such as the Ten Commandments. Such actions lead us to God. Some actions are objectively bad—lying, cheating, stealing, and murder are examples.

Sometimes there may be a difference of opinion about what is good and what is bad. In this case, we are speaking of subjective truth ("truth as it appears to me") rather than objective truth ("truth as it is in reality"). Take this example:

> Jack, a sixteen-year-old, volunteered to help Sam, an eighth grader who was struggling with algebra. This is obviously a very caring act.
>
> However, what if Jack was tutoring the younger boy only so he could meet Sam's sister, whom he had a crush on?
>
> Worse yet, what if Jack tutored Sam so he could "case the house" with the idea that he might steal valuables?

This example points out that while certain acts are always wrong regardless of the intention or the circumstances, with other acts the rightness or the wrongness is determined by the intention and/or the circumstances. "A *morally good* act requires the goodness of the object, of the end, and of the circumstances together" (*CCC*, 1755).

The Intention

"The end does not justify the means." What this common saying refers to is that a good intention (such as helping a friend pass a final exam) does not make a behavior that is objectively wrong (such as cheating) good or just.

One action can have several intentions, some of them bad and some of them good. A bad intention can make an act evil that is of itself good.

For example, Matt, a high school junior, signed up to serve food to the homeless on Thanksgiving. Helping the homeless is obviously a good deed. But Matt signed up to help the homeless primarily so he could put this service event on his college applications. This intention, associated with vanity or pride, goes against what Jesus told us. He admonished all his followers to "not let your left hand know what your right is doing" (Mt 6:3) when we do good deeds. Besides that, Matt has occasionally displayed a poor attitude toward the homeless. Once, he even teased a homeless man while walking home from school with a friend.

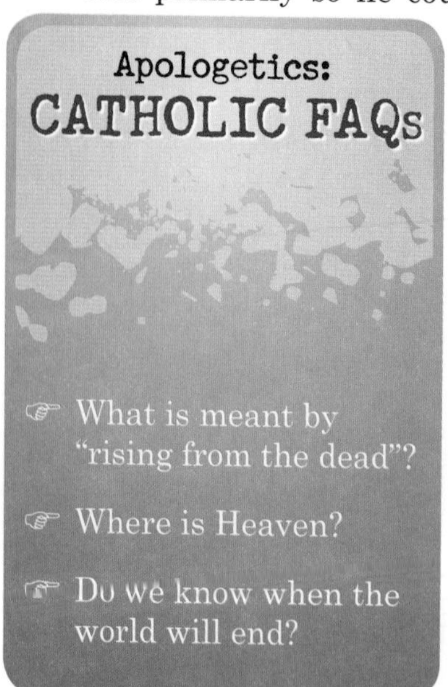

Apologetics:
CATHOLIC FAQs
What is meant by "rising from the dead"?
Where is Heaven?
Do we know when the world will end?

Determining the intention of a specific moral situation usually involves asking a question beginning with "why." *Why am I doing this? Why do I want to do this?* Asking why determines our motives for what we do—whether good or bad.

Circumstances

The circumstances of an action—the answers to questions beginning with *who, where, when,* and *how*—cannot make an action that is evil good or right. Rather, the circumstances contribute to the increasing or diminishing good or evil of a particular act.

For example, consider the case of a high school teen who stole bus fare from a fellow student:

- It doesn't matter if the victim of the theft was a sophomore or a freshman (the answer to the *who* question).
- It doesn't matter if the theft took place on the bus or off the bus (the answer to the *where* question).
- It doesn't matter if the money was stolen on the bus ride to school or on the bus ride home (the answer to the *when* question).
- It doesn't matter if the theft was done secretly or with the victim's knowledge (the answer to the *how* question).

None of these circumstances has any effect in making a morally wrong act, stealing, right.

How, then, can the circumstances increase or diminish the good or the evil of an action?

Returning to the example of stealing: physically injuring the victim adds to the serious nature of the evil act. In a similar case, stealing five dollars from a homeless man who needs the money for food is more serious than stealing five dollars from a

millionaire on his way to a Las Vegas gambling table. The evil in the first example is increased, in the second diminished.

Two additional helps must be mentioned for helping Christians determine and make good choices.

Prayer sustains Christian moral living. The *Catechism of the Catholic Church* defines *prayer* as "the living relationship of the children of God with their Father who is good beyond measure, with his Son Jesus Christ and with the Holy Spirit" (*CCC*, 2565). This definition of *prayer* focuses on the "living relationship" we must have with a God who loves us. This living relationship allows us to lead a moral life.

God tirelessly calls us to a mysterious encounter with him through prayer. Also, prayer teaches us to turn to God for help. Prayer teaches us that God's love is present all around us. We can find God's love in parents, friends, teachers, and priests who are willing to guide us; in the Scripture, which speaks of God's truth; and in the sacraments.

St. Paul's First Letter to the Thessalonians says we should "pray without ceasing" (1 Thes 5:17). We can always pray, anytime and anyplace. Prayer and living a Christian life are inseparable.

Participating in the sacraments is another help for a moral life. As mentioned, sacramental grace is a benefit of participation. The sacraments celebrate the mysteries of faith—the Incarnation, the love of Christ for us, the Paschal Mystery, and more. Receiving Jesus in the Eucharist is a tangible way to foster a moral life.

Living a Christian moral life means living like Jesus. Jesus looked upon his neighbors as "other selves." We are challenged to do the same. No rules or laws can force us to treat another with this type of respect. Only through cultivating love in our hearts—the love of and for Christ—can we look at each person as a brother or a sister, as another self.

St. Francis de Sales put Christian morality this way: "One of the most excellent intentions that we can possibly have in all our actions is to do them because our Lord did them."

REVIEW

1. Differentiate between different types of grace: sanctifying grace, actual grace, sacramental grace, and charisms.
2. How does our conscience help us make good choices?
3. Explain how the human virtues are connected with the theological virtues.
4. What does asking who, what, where, when, how, and why have to do with making a moral decision?

WRITE OR DISCUSS

- Which gift of the Holy Spirit would you most like to possess? Why?
- Create a choice between good or evil in which the object chosen, the intention, and the circumstances of the choice can help you make a good decision.
- In the situation you described above, how can prayer and participation in the sacraments also help with making a good decision?

WE BELIEVE IN EVERLASTING LIFE

When you are young, you don't wake up each day expecting it to be your last. But even at your age, you likely have an awareness of how fragile and tentative life on earth really is.

Twenty-three-year-old Julie Welch, a foreign language interpreter for the Social Security Administration, certainly did not expect to die when she went to work in downtown Oklahoma City on April 19, 1995. The bomb blast at the federal building killed Julie Welch and one hundred sixty-seven others.

Julie, a Marquette University graduate, went to daily Mass at Little Flower parish in a predominantly Hispanic area of Oklahoma City. "There's little kids there, some that can't speak much English, and a girl like Julie can talk to them and give them a ray of hope. We've lost that now," her father, Bud Welch, remembered just days after Julie's death.

In the years since, however, Julie's life has continued to cast a ray of hope through her father. Before the Oklahoma City bomber, Timothy McVeigh, was executed in 2001, Bud Welch began traveling around the world speaking out against the death penalty.

Julie Welch did not expect to die when she was only twenty-three. She had recently gotten engaged. A productive career and family life were ahead of her. Her life ended in an instant.

Thousands of teens are killed each year in accidents involving drinking and driving. Motor vehicle accidents are the number one cause of teen deaths in the United States. Other teens die from acts of crime and violence. Some die from rare illnesses or natural disasters. In March 2007, eight students were killed at Enterprise High School in Alabama when walls and the roof of their school collapsed during a tornado. Fr. James Dane of the local Catholic parish said, "I can't give you answers" for the tragedy. "I can give you promises from God's Word that he will be here for us and guide us."

The fact is that no matter what age we are, our lives on earth are uncertain. Speaking of the end of the world but also applicable to our own deaths, Jesus said, "But of that day and hour no one knows, neither the angels of heaven, nor the Son, but the Father alone" (Mt 24:36).

A reminder of your own mortality is a fitting way to end a course on knowing Jesus and the essentials of being Catholic. When we live each day aware it could possibly be our last, our focus on what is really important becomes much clearer. Awareness of death brings a sense of urgency to our lives. We have a clearer understanding of what will happen to us after we die; we know the meanings of the **particular judgment** and the Last Judgment. In the former, we receive individually at the time of our death a judgment made by God declaring whether we will go to Heaven, hell, or Purgatory. The Last Judgment will occur at the end of the world when the truth of each person's relationship with God will be laid bare in the presence of Christ, the King of the Universe.

Remaining aware of our mortality and these events that will occur after our death also reminds us we are given only a limited amount of time to bring our lives to fulfillment.

In our creeds, we state, "We believe in life everlasting." Isn't this what it's all about? Isn't this the reason for *why* you believe?

Let that statement sink in. We believe we will live forever. What could this mean in practical terms? For one, time and space will never control us. What else? Will we be reunited with our family members and friends who have died before us? Yes, we expect to. Will we never be burdened with sickness, disease, pain, and suffering again? True again.

Remember that the main message of the Gospel is that Jesus is risen! Because of Jesus Christ, Christian death has a positive meaning. Christ's Death was his final act of self-giving. With his Death, we are saved. In Baptism, we have already "died with Christ"; our physical death merely completes our incorporation into his act of redemption. In death, we are called back to God. With faith, a Christian can legitimately long for death. St. Teresa of Avila wrote, "I want to see God, and in order to see him, I must die." Or, as in the words of St. Thérèse of Lisieux, "I am not dying; I am entering life." Only through death can we pass into the fullness of God's Kingdom.

GETTING TO KNOW JESUS

Passions are strong feelings that lead us to act or not act on something that is either good or bad. The passions—such as sadness, pity, love, and even anger—are not good or bad in themselves. But how we act on those feelings can have good or bad implications.

As a man, Jesus experienced the same human passions we do. The Gospels tell how Jesus responded to his feelings and encouraged others to do so. Read each Gospel passage below. Identify the *feeling* described in the passage. Then determine how Jesus *responded* to the feeling or encouraged others to do so.

Matthew 5:21–26; 5:43–45; 20:29–34
Mark 10:13–16; 14:32–36
Luke 24:36–42
John 11:33–44; 15:11–13

When have you acted on your passions in a negative way?

When did an experience of your passions lead to a good choice?

Rate how strong your passion is—on a 1-to-10 scale—for following Jesus Christ.

PRAYER

The Road Ahead
My Lord God,
I have no idea where I am going.
I do not see the road ahead of me.

I cannot know for certain where it will end.
Nor do I really know myself,
and the fact that I think that I am following
your will does not mean that I am actually doing so.

But I believe that the desire to please you does in fact please you.
And I hope I have that desire in all that I am doing.
I hope that I will never do anything apart from that desire.
And I know that if I do this, you will lead me by the right road
though I may know nothing about it.

Therefore will I trust you always though I may seem to be lost
and in the shadow of death. I will not fear, for you are ever with me,
and you will never leave me to face my perils alone.
Amen.
—Thomas Merton

Appendix 1: Selected Topics and Resources

STUDYING SACRED SCRIPTURE

Sacred Scripture, the books of the Bible that contain God's Revelation, were composed by human authors inspired by the Holy Spirit. The Bible is composed of forty-six books of the Old Testament and twenty-seven books of the New Testament.

As the authors of the Bible were inspired by the Holy Spirit, the books of the Bible "must be acknowledged as teaching firmly, faithfully, and without error that truth God wanted put into the sacred writings for the sake of our salvation" (*Dei Verbum*, 11).

Yet, as God speaks in Scripture through human authors, it is necessary to apply tools of critical reading to our study of

Scripture. Among these tools are the following methods briefly introduced here:

- *Source criticism* tries to determine what source or sources the authors used to compose their works. For example, when Matthew wrote his Gospel, what did he have in front of him as he set out to perform his task? What did he take from the oral tradition? Did he use another Gospel to help him in his general outline? Note that in the synoptic Gospels (Matthew, Mark, and Luke), Matthew reproduces nearly 80 percent of Mark's verses. Luke reproduces nearly 65 percent of Mark's verses. This observation has led to an understanding that perhaps Mark's Gospel was the first Gospel written.
- *Historical criticism* attempts to discover what the author really wanted to say when he wrote a particular text. It looks at ancient languages, dating techniques, archaeology, and customs related to the historical context of a passage.
- *Form criticism* is concerned with recognizing the different forms of writing used in Scripture. There are, for example, parables, Psalms, pronouncement stories, miracle stories, and discourses, among several others.
- *Redaction criticism* focuses on the authors as editors, how and why they arranged their sources the way they did (*redact* means "to edit for publication"). Redaction criticism tries to discover the particular theological insight of the given author and how that influenced his arrangement of the material. For example, it is understood that Matthew

wrote for Jewish Christians while Luke wrote for Gentile Christians. Mark presented a Gospel focusing on Jesus as the Suffering Servant. John wrote for a wide spectrum of churches around the Roman Empire and presented a rich view of Jesus as the Word of God.

- *Textual criticism* compares the minor changes and mistakes the copyists made down through the centuries so that the translations of Scripture we have today are as accurate as possible.

Chapter and Verse

As mentioned, the Old Testament has forty-six books, and the New Testament has twenty-seven books. There are about 900,000 words in the Old Testament and 150,000 words in the New Testament. Matthew's Gospel is the longest book of the New Testament (approximately 18,000 words).

The books of neither the Old Testament nor the New Testament were originally divided with chapters and verses as found in Bibles today. However, the Hebrew Scripture portions of the Old Testament were divided into sections for use in synagogue worship prior to the origin of Christianity and the New Testament. The Hebrew Scriptures today do not have the same chapter and verse divisions as the Christian Old Testament. The New Testament ordering by chapter and verse was invented in the thirteenth century by Stephen Langton, a professor in Paris, who put these in the **Vulgate**. The chapter and numbering system familiar today was perfected by Parisian book printer Robert Stephanus and was commonly used with the printing of the entire Bible in Latin in 1555, more than one hundred years after the invention of the Gutenberg printing press.

How to Locate a Scripture Passage

Example: *2 Tm 3:16–17*

1. Determine the name of the book.

   The abbreviation "2 Tm" stands for the Second Letter of Paul to Timothy.

2. Determine whether the book is in the Old Testament or the New Testament.

   The Second Letter of Paul to Timothy is one of the New Testament letters.

3. Locate the chapter where the passage occurs.

   The first number before the colon—'3'—indicates the chapter. Chapters in the Bible are set off by the larger numbers that divide a book.

4. Locate the verses of the passage.

   The numbers after the colon indicate the verses of the passage. In this case, verses 16 and 17 of chapter 3.

5. Read the passage.

   For example: "All Scripture is inspired by God and is useful for teaching, for refutation, for correction, and for training in righteousness, so that one who belongs to God may be competent, equipped for every good work."

Books of the Bible with Abbreviations

Listed below are the categories and the books of the Old Testament:

THE OLD TESTAMENT

The Pentateuch

Genesis	Gn
Exodus	Ex
Leviticus	Lv
Numbers	Nm
Deuteronomy	Dt

The Historical Books

Joshua	Jos
Judges	Jgs
Ruth	Ru
1 Samuel	1 Sm
2 Samuel	2 Sm
1 Kings	1 Kgs
2 Kings	2 Kgs
1 Chronicles	1 Chr
2 Chronicles	2 Chr
Ezra	Ezr
Nehemiah	Neh
Tobit	Tb
Judith	Jdt
Esther	Est
1 Maccabees	1 Mc
2 Maccabees	2 Mc

The Wisdom Books

Job	Jb
Psalms	Ps(s)
Proverbs	Prv
Ecclesiastes	Eccl
Song of Songs	Sg
Wisdom	Wis
Sirach	Sir

The Prophetic Books

Isaiah	Is
Jeremiah	Jer
Lamentations	Lam
Baruch	Bar
Ezekiel	Ez
Daniel	Dn
Hosea	Hos
Joel	Jl
Amos	Am
Obadiah	Ob
Jonah	Jon
Micah	Mi
Nahum	Na
Habakkuk	Hb
Zephaniah	Zep
Haggai	Hg
Zechariah	Zec
Malachi	Mal

THE NEW TESTAMENT

The Gospels

Matthew	Mt
Mark	Mk
Luke	Lk
John	Jn

Acts of the Apostles	Acts

The New Testament Letters

Romans	Rom
1 Corinthians	1 Cor
2 Corinthians	2 Cor
Galatians	Gal
Ephesians	Eph
Philippians	Phil
Colossians	Col
1 Thessalonians	1 Thes
2 Thessalonians	2 Thes
1 Timothy	1 Tm
2 Timothy	2 Tm
Titus	Ti
Philemon	Phlm
Hebrews	Heb

The Catholic Letters

James	Jas
1 Peter	1 Pt
2 Peter	2 Pt
1 John	1 Jn
2 John	2 Jn
3 John	3 Jn
Jude	Jude

Revelation	Rv

HISTORY OF THE CATHOLIC CHURCH

The Church refers to three realities: Catholics who come together at liturgy; the local diocese, a fellowship of believers in Jesus Christ; and the universal community of believers throughout the world. The *Catechism of the Catholic Church* teaches:

> "The Church" is the People that God gathers in the whole world. She exists in local communities and is made real as a liturgical, above all a Eucharistic, assembly. She draws her life from the word and the Body of Christ and so herself becomes Christ's Body. (*CCC*, 752)

The word *catholic* means "universal." Today, the Catholic Church is present in every nation of the world. Whereas Christianity is the world's largest religion (with more than two billion members, about one-third of the world's population), Catholics are the largest group of Christians, numbering more than one billion, around 17 percent of the world's population and about 53 percent of the Christian population.

Catholics are distinguished as people who:

- believe in one, holy, catholic, and apostolic Church and all that she teaches through the Pope and the bishops, who are the successors to Peter and the Apostles
- accept all Seven Sacraments of the Catholic Church

- submit to the teaching authority of the Magisterium (the Pope and the bishops, who are in union with him) in matters of faith and morals

Prior to his Ascension, Jesus said: "I am with you always, until the end of the age" (Mt 28:20). Hence, the history of the Church can be traced from the time of Christ to the present.

Timeline of Key Events

ca. 6–4 BC	Jesus is born
ca. 30–33	Jesus' Death and Resurrection, Pentecost
ca. 50	Council of Jerusalem (Gentiles can be admitted to the Church)
ca. 64	Persecutions of Christians begin under Roman emperor Nero
ca. 64 or 67	Peter and Paul martyred in Rome
ca. 70	Temple destroyed
ca. 100	St. John the Evangelist dies; apostolic era ends
311	Emperor Constantine ends persecution of Christians
313	Edict of Milan
325	Council of Nicaea (Arian heresy refuted; Nicene Creed composed)
381	First Council of Constantinople (Nicene Creed expanded; divine nature of Holy Spirit defined)
410	Visigoths invade Rome
431	Council of Ephesus (refutes Nestorianism; states Mary is Mother of God)
432	St. Patrick begins missionary work in Ireland

451 Council of Chalcedon defends two natures of Christ
476 Roman Empire in West collapses
529 St. Benedict founds order of monks, the Benedictines
590 St. Gregory the Great becomes Pope
722 St. Boniface evangelizes Germanic people
800 Pope Leo III crowns Charlemagne Roman emperor
1054 Final schism between Eastern and Western churches, which remains today
1073 Pope St. Gregory VII begins reforms of the Church
1095 Pope Urban II calls First Crusade to free Holy Land from Muslims
1170 St. Thomas Becket murdered in Canterbury Cathedral
1209 St. Francis of Assisi founds Franciscan order
1215 St. Dominic founds Dominican order of preachers
1378 The Great Schism in the Church begins (lasts until 1417), with two or three men claiming to be Pope
1431 St. Joan of Arc executed
1517 Martin Luther posts ninety-five theses, beginning Protestant Reformation
1533 King Henry VIII excommunicated, leading to start of Anglican Church
1540 St. Ignatius of Loyola founds Society of Jesus (Jesuits) to assist in reform of the Church
1545 Council of Trent begins (lasts until 1563), advances Catholic Reformation

1642 Jesuits evangelizing Native Americans martyred (into 1649)
1769 First of twenty-one California missions founded (nine by Junípero Serra)
1789 John Carroll appointed first bishop of United States
1820 Beginning of swell of nine million Catholic immigrants to United States (into 1920s)
1869 First Vatican Council convenes (into 1870)
1891 Pope Leo XIII writes *Rerum Novarum* encyclical, first of the Church's body of social teaching doctrine
1903 Pontificate of St. Pius X begins (into 1914)
1917 Apparitions of Our Lady of Fatima
1962 Second Vatican Council convenes (into 1965)
1978 Pontificate of Pope John Paul II begins
1994 Vatican and state of Israel establish formal relations
2005 Joseph Ratzinger elected Pope Benedict XVI

LIVING AS A DISCIPLE OF JESUS CHRIST IN SOCIETY

The United States Conference of Catholic Bishops recently highlighted seven principles that are the foundation for the Church's social teaching. This social doctrine refers to the teaching of the Church on:

1. the life and the dignity of the human person
2. the call to family and community participation
3. rights and duties

4. the preferential option for the poor
5. the dignity of work and rights for workers
6. **solidarity**
7. **stewardship** (care for God's creation)

The first principle—the life and the dignity of the human person—is paramount to all the others. From human dignity all of the other principles flow. We have dignity because we are made in God's image and likeness. Human dignity means we have worth and value. Having human dignity is why all the other principles that follow are true. As the United States Catholic Bishops put it, "Every human being is created in the image of God and redeemed by Jesus Christ, and therefore is invaluable as a member of the human family" (*Sharing Catholic Social Teaching*).

Tracing the Church's social doctrine usually begins in the nineteenth century with Pope Leo XIII, even though the Church has shown respect for human dignity and preference for the poor in all generations. The reason this is so is that prior to the nineteenth century, there was little need for a social doctrine any more explicit than that found in the Gospels. It was enough to follow the traditional corporal (bodily) works of mercy and the spiritual works of mercy:

Corporal Works of Mercy

- Feed the hungry.
- Give drink to the thirsty.
- Clothe the naked.
- Visit the imprisoned.
- Shelter the homeless.

- Visit the sick.
- Bury the dead.

Spiritual Works of Mercy

- Counsel the doubtful.
- Instruct the ignorant.
- Admonish sinners.
- Comfort the afflicted.
- Forgive offenses.
- Bear wrongs patiently.
- Pray for the living and the dead.

With the Industrial Revolution in the eighteenth and nineteenth centuries, new challenges arose as the "Gospel encountered modern industrial society with its new structures for the production of consumer goods, its new concept of society, the state of authority, and its new forms of labor and ownership" (*CCC*, 2421). Pope Leo XIII and succeeding popes understood the Church's role in shaping justice and fairness in the new society. A need for systematic teachings that would help governments, families, and individuals apply the principles of the Gospel to changing social teachings was needed.

Since Pope Leo, "The development of the doctrine of the Church on economic and social matters attests the permanent value of the Church's teaching at the same time as it attests the true meaning of her Tradition, always living and active" (*CCC*, 2421).

An overview of key **social justice** doctrines from the nineteenth and twentieth centuries follows.

Overview of Key Social Justice Documents

1891 Leo XIII—*The Condition of Labor* (*Rerum Novarum*)

- seminal document that begins a century-plus of forward-looking social teaching
- criticizes the extremes of capitalism in which a few own all the wealth while the majority work under near-slavery conditions
- makes it clear that all people have basic human rights that flow from the natural law
- emphasizes the role of the state to pass laws to preserve the rights of workers, including the right to work and unionize, to a just wage, and to own private property

1931 Pius XI—*The Reconstruction of the Social Order* (*Quadragesimo Anno*)

- reaffirms *Rerum Novarum* on just wages and unions
- critiques unbridled capitalism and communism
- urges international economic cooperation
- introduces the idea of **subsidiarity,** which states that communities of higher order are not to interfere in the internal life of communities of lower order; rather, they should help coordinate the activities of the lower order to serve the common good

1961 John XXIII—*Christianity and Social Progress* (*Mater et Magistra*)

- criticizes disparities between rich nations and poor nations

- points to the ways the arms race has contributed to world poverty
- urges global interdependence
- encourages worker participation and collective bargaining for modern industrial workers

1963 John XXIII—*Peace on Earth* (*Pacem in Terris*)

- addressed to Catholics and all people of good will
- details basic human rights and corresponding responsibilities that flow from human dignity
- decries the arms race
- stresses the concept of the common good, which includes peace, that can be maintained only when personal rights and duties are maintained

1965 Vatican Council II—*The Church in the Modern World* (*Gaudium et Spes*)

- analyzes the modern world in light of human dignity
- states that the Church is not bound to any political party or social system but is nonetheless called to influence society in order to improve the world
- treats issues of the family, society, politics, economics, and world peace

1967 Paul VI—*The Development of Peoples* (*Populorum Progressio*)

- discusses the relationship between development and peace
- focuses on fair trade relationships to help underdeveloped nations; advocates a form of taxation of rich nations and international cooperation

1971 Paul VI—*A Call to Action* (*Octogesima Adveniens*)

- addresses the problems caused by modern urbanization
- condemns discrimination based on race, color, culture, gender, and religion
- encourages political action and involvement

1971 Synod of Bishops—*Justice in the World*

- defines justice as an essential ingredient of the Gospel and the Church's mission
- cites modern injustices, especially against the poor and powerless, for whom the Church should speak in a special way
- encourages the Church herself to be an exemplar of justice in the way she treats her own members

1981 John Paul II—*On Human Work* (*Laborem Exercens*)

- develops a strong spirituality of work as it supports unions and workers' rights
- emphasizes the importance of work as the tangible expression of human dignity and the key to making life more humane
- reaffirms family life
- emphasizes free will in choosing work; says workers should feel they are working for themselves
- criticizes both Marxism and capitalism

1986 U.S. Bishops—*Economic Justice for All*

- applies the Christian vision of economic life to the American economy
- issues a challenge to examine the inequalities in income, consumption, power, and privilege and their impact on the poor

1987 John Paul II—*On Social Concern* (*Sollicitudo Rei Socialis*)

- notes the obvious disparities in wealth between Northern and Southern hemispheres
- critiques the West as succumbing to materialism and **consumerism**
- points out the moral bankruptcy of the East that ignores basic human rights
- decries the arms race as an injustice to the poor
- calls for refocusing of resources and cooperation for international development
- highlights theme of preferential option for the poor

1991 John Paul II—*The One Hundredth Year* (*Centesimus Annus*)

- written in the wake of the collapse of communism and celebrates the centenary of *Rerum Novarum*
- examines strengths and weaknesses of various forms of capitalism
- reiterates themes of work, just wages, unemployment, profit, unions, atheism, family, and the like
- explains how the Church offers a vision of human dignity rooted in Jesus, who became one of us
- underscores special option for the poor while critiquing the abuses of consumerism as an excessive drain on the environment

1995 John Paul II—*The Gospel of Life* (*Evangelium Vitae*)

- defends the most fundamental right we have—the right to life—while covering the topics of abortion, euthanasia, assisted suicide, capital punishment, and other modern-day threats to human life

1998 U.S. Catholic Bishops—*Sharing Catholic Social Teaching: Challenges and Directions*

- stresses the importance of bringing together the two gifts of Catholic education and catechesis and Catholic social teaching in an effort to make Catholics more aware of the body of Catholic social teaching
- highlights several key themes at the heart of Catholic social teaching with the intent that they will serve as starting points for those interested in exploring Catholic social teaching more fully
- presents several options for schools, adult education programs, colleges, seminaries, and the like to further the catechesis of Catholic social teaching

1998 John Paul II—*Faith and Reason* (*Fides et Ratio*)

- treats how faith and reason should work hand in hand in searching for truth
- shows how the search for knowledge is a search for God and that Christians find the ultimate meaning in life in the Paschal Mystery of Christ
- warns against some modern philosophies that lead to nihilism, which denies ultimate truth, and states firmly that humans have the ability to find the truth

Many of the Church's documents on social teaching can be located at the following websites:

- www.vatican.va
- www.usccb.org/sdwp/foundationdocs.shtml

LIVING THE CALL OF JESUS CHRIST

Vocation means "calling." For Christians, the primary calling is a call to be a disciple of Christ. This call, given at Baptism, requires Christians to bring God's love to others and to share the Good News of redemption offered by Jesus Christ to all.

The perfection of love is holiness. We carry out this basic Christian call in the context of a particular state of life, which is also known as vocation. Taken in this context, a vocation is to the ordained, religious, or lay state of life. An ordained man may also be religious (a member of a religious community). A more specific vocation within the lay state of life is to marriage. Some lay people also have a specific vocation to the single life.

In years past, high school graduates were more likely to commit to one of the specific vocations such as marriage, priesthood, or religious life within a few years after high school or college graduation. Today, the average age for marriage in the United States is rising (approximately twenty-seven years for men, twenty-five years for women). It is also more typical for men in their thirties to be ordained. In any case, now is the appropriate time to consider how the specific vocations within your primary Christian vocation fit with your dreams and goals for life.

Vocation of Marriage

Marriage is a sacrament administered by the couple to one another. The priest or the deacon who officiates serves as a witness on behalf of the Church. The sacrament is based on the mutual consent of the man and the woman to give themselves to one another until death in order that they might make their relationship one of faithful and fruitful love.

Why might you want to marry eventually? People marry for many reasons. Some people marry because they are "in love," though they may not clearly understand what being in love means. Others marry to escape a situation at home or to get a "new start." Some marry because a pregnancy is involved.

The decision to enter into marriage should never be taken lightly. The intimate bond of marriage is intended to represent the same bond Jesus formed with his Church. It is an unbreakable bond; that is the reason the Church does not recognize divorce. It is a bond in which the couple is expected to bring forth new life and to raise children in the Christian Faith. The Church, "on the side of life," teaches that every act of sexual intercourse in marriage must remain open to the procreation of human life. Children are made in the "image of the invisible God" (Col 1:15), that is, in and for Christ. They find their fulfillment in Christ alone and are called to be Christ for the world.

Besides just thinking about what it would be *like* to be married, you can do several things right now to prepare for a future marriage. Marriage is based on respect and honor between spouses. You can practice these skills in the ways you treat friends of both sexes. Marriage also includes many opportunities for "give and take" and for truly listening to the needs and concerns of the other. For now, you may be the person who compromises more frequently in your current relationships as a way to practice for when you are married. Marriage demands faithful and unbroken commitment. You can practice this skill through your commitment to your own family and friends, to a job, and to your schoolwork. Finally, in marriage, the wife and

the husband are faithful to each other physically. You should keep this gift of chastity in your current state of life. Saving sex for marriage is the best gift you can give to your future spouse on your wedding night and beyond.

Vocation of Priesthood and Religious Life

The term *vocation* is traditionally used to describe callings to the ordained ministry of a priest or the religious life of a sister or a brother. Certainly neither priesthood nor religious life is typical in the sense that planning and training for these vocations take place in logical, sequential steps.

The ministerial priesthood is different from the common priesthood of the baptized in that it confers a sacred power for the service of the faithful. Ordained ministers—in three degrees of bishop, priest, and deacon—serve the Church by teaching, by leading worship, and by their governance.

The Sacrament of Holy Orders is conferred only on baptized men, following the example of Jesus and the early Church, who called only men to be Apostles and bishops. In the Roman Catholic Church, priests are men who live **celibate** lives and promise to remain celibate "for the sake of the kingdom of heaven" (see *CCC*, 1619). Ordination is conferred in silence through the laying on of hands by a bishop and the bishop's solemn prayer of consecration, followed by a Mass with concelebrating priests.

A man doesn't just become a priest; he is called by God to that vocation. The vocation of most priests began with a "nagging feeling"—often present from grade school on—that this is the life God wants for them. Other signs that a man is being called to priesthood may include:

- other people telling him he would make a good priest
- a desire to pray
- going to Mass more than usual and imagining himself as presider
- trying out ministries associated with priesthood (e.g., teaching, caring for the sick, counseling others)

The term *religious life* does not mean the same thing as the ordained priesthood. Religious life is one form of consecrated life. Religious are not a separate classification of people in the Church "in between" priests and lay people. In fact, religious can be from either state of life, ordained or lay. Religious can also be women or men. Women religious are called sisters, and men religious are called brothers. Some men religious are also priests. Religious live in communities usually founded by a charismatic leader to serve a specific purpose in the Church.

Religious take vows to live out the evangelical counsels of poverty, chastity, and obedience. Prior to their profession of vows, they live a period of religious formation that helps them and the community decide if they are right for each other.

As with marriage, your late teen and early adult years are a time to think about a possible call to priesthood or religious life. If you feel a call to serve Christ in a radical way, if you want to use your talents to serve others, and if you are capable of making a commitment, you may want to explore a vocation to priesthood or religious life.

Fr. Vincent Coppola, C.S.C., offered this suggestion for someone considering the priesthood or religious life:

> Act on faith—take the leap into the unknown. Go with what is in your heart. If your honest discernment leads you to conclude that this isn't the life for you, then you will be a better person for going through the discernment process. God's grace works in such mysterious ways, you may discover something you would have never dreamed of considering previously. Either way, it is a "win-win" situation.

Until God calls you to a vocation of marriage, priesthood, or religious life, you fall naturally into the single state of life. For some people, however, the single life is not a transitional state; rather, it is a permanent vocation, though one not marked by a Church rite. Examples of people who are called to a single life vocation are adult children who care for their invalid parents and lay people who are called to be missionaries in either their own country or another country. People with a homosexual orientation who try to live the Church's call to chastity also take up the vocation to the single life in many cases.

ECUMENICAL AND INTERFAITH ISSUES

Ecumenical efforts among Christians to encourage the unity Christ bestowed on his Church from the beginning are a "gift of Christ and a call of the Holy Spirit" (*CCC*, 820) and are accompanied by efforts detailed on pages 169–171.

The Second Vatican Council was truly an Ecumenical Council. Not only were bishops, theologians, and other Catholics present, but the council invited many religious leaders from other Christian denominations and non-Christian representatives to participate. The milestone document *Nostra Aetate* (*In Our Time*) called for a mutual understanding between Catholics and people of all faiths, exhorting Catholics:

> through dialogue and collaboration with the followers of other religions carried out with prudence and love and in witness to the Christian faith and life, they recognize, preserve and promote the good things, spiritual and moral, as well as the socio-cultural values found among these men.

Pope John Paul II wrote a response to *Nostra Aetate* while addressing the question "Why so many religions?" in his book *Crossing the Threshold of Hope*. Pope John Paul II wrote that all religions demonstrate "the unity of humankind with regard to the eternal and ultimate destiny of man." As with the council document, he encouraged Catholics to study and explore various ways we are related to those who have not yet received the Gospel. Worthy of brief consideration is the Church's relationship with the Jewish People, Muslims, and those who practice other non-Christian religions.

The Church's Relationship with the Jewish People

Judaism is held in special honor because the Jewish People were "the first to hear the Word of God" (*Roman Missal*, Good Friday Liturgy). The Jews received the first, or original, covenant with God.

Catholicism and Judaism have much in common. Both are monotheistic religions. Both share Abraham as a patriarch. Catholics share in and affirm the covenants God made with the

Jews, including acceptance of God's Revelation on Mount Sinai to Moses, then to the Jewish People, and then to all humankind (*CCC,* 72). We accept the Ten Commandments as a minimum guide for moral living (*CCC,* 1980).

The most noted difference between Catholics and Jews is in the person of Jesus. Jews do not accept the divinity of Jesus. Jews still expect a messiah or a messianic age to come.

Catholics and Jews have had a history together both rich and troubled. Christians, including Catholics, often perpetuated anti-Semitism. There are other examples of Catholics and Jews coming to each others' aid. For example, when the first Crusaders plundered Jewish communities in the Rhineland, there are stories of when Jews went to the bishop of the region for help. They not only received help, but sometimes the bishop was killed for helping the Jews.

The Second Vatican Council document *Nostra Aetate* set a course for improving the relationship between Catholics and Jews. Jews were and remain God's Chosen People. God never severed the covenant made on Mount Sinai. There is no collective guilt of Jews for the Death of Jesus (*CCC,* 597). The *Catechism* also teaches that for the future, Catholics and Jews "tend towards similar goals"—each anticipating the coming (or return) of the Messiah (see *CCC*, 840).

The Church's Relationship with Muslims

The Second Vatican Council also mentioned the Church's high regard for Muslims and spoke of similarities in faith:

> They worship God, who is one, living and subsistent, merciful and almighty, the Creator of heaven and earth, who has also spoken to humanity.

> They endeavor to submit themselves without reserve to the hidden decrees of God, just as Abraham submitted himself to God's plan, to whose faith Muslims eagerly link their own. Although not acknowledging him as God, they venerate Jesus as a prophet; his virgin Mother they also honor, and even at times devoutly invoke. Further, they await the day of judgment and the reward of God following the resurrection of the dead. For this reason they highly esteem an upright life and worship of God, especially by way of prayer, almsdeeds and fasting. (3)

Islam—the official name for the religion (its adherents are called Muslims)—is one of the fastest-growing religions in the world. After the death of its founder, Muhammad, Islam spread rapidly throughout the Middle East and North Africa and into southern Europe (especially the Iberian Peninsula) and India. During the Middle Ages, Islam was very influential in the creation of Western civilization, especially in the areas of science, philosophy, and medicine.

Effective dialogue between Catholics and Muslims begins at the starting point of common beliefs. The nature of one God, the heritage of peoples formed from Abraham, and the sharing of positive and peaceful human values are the best place to start. Another important area is the common struggle both religions have with modern "isms" such as secularism, materialism, and **racism**. Family life is central to both Catholics and Muslims. Preserving religious values and practices while avoiding these creeping outside pressures and strategies to do so are worthy goals of discussion. Issues such as systemic prejudice, poverty, and the care of the environment also form common concerns. As the Second Vatican Council asserted, "There must be a sincere effort on both sides to achieve mutual understanding" (*Nostra aetate,* 2).

The Church's Relationship with Other Non-Christians

Catholics also share a bond with other non-Christian religions, including Eastern religions such as Hinduism and Buddhism. Primarily this is the common origin we all share in the "origin and end of the human race" (*CCC*, 842). The Church rejects nothing that is holy in these religions.

For example, in Hinduism "people explore the divine mystery and express it both in the limitless riches of myth and the accurately defined insights of philosophy" (*Nostra aetate*, 2). Buddhism, too, encourages people to see truth, liberation, and illumination both through their own efforts and with divine help.

Salvation within the Catholic Church

The Church does recognize in these and other religions the limits and errors of non-Christian beliefs. She continues to offer non-Christians the fullness of truth in Jesus Christ in the "bark" of salvation that is in the Catholic Church.

In ways known only to God himself, he can lead those who, through no fault of their own, are ignorant of the Gospel to faith in Jesus Christ and to life in the Church, for "all salvation comes from Christ the Head through the Church which is his Body" (*CCC*, 846).

Appendix 2: Traditional Creeds, Devotions, Novenas, and Prayers

CREEDS

Apostles' Creed

I believe in God, the Father almighty,
Creator of heaven and earth.
I believe in Jesus Christ, his only Son, our Lord.
He was conceived by the power of the Holy Spirit,
and born of the Virgin Mary.
He suffered under Pontius Pilate,
was crucified, died, and was buried.
He descended into hell.
On the third day he rose again.
He ascended into heaven,

and is seated at the right hand of the Father.
He will come again to judge the living and the dead.
I believe in the Holy Spirit,
the holy catholic Church,
the communion of saints,
the forgiveness of sins,
the resurrection of the body,
and the life everlasting. Amen.

Nicene Creed

We believe in one God,
the Father, the Almighty,
maker of heaven and earth,
of all that is seen and unseen.
We believe in one Lord, Jesus Christ,
the only Son of God,
eternally begotten of the Father,
God from God, Light from Light,
true God from true God,
begotten, not made, one in Being with the Father.
Through him all things were made.
For us men and for our salvation
he came down from heaven:
by the power of the Holy Spirit
he was born of the Virgin Mary, and became man.
For our sake he was crucified under Pontius Pilate;
he suffered, died, and was buried.
On the third day he rose again in fulfillment of the Scriptures;
he ascended into heaven and is seated at the right hand of the Father.

He will come again in glory to judge the living and the dead,
and his kingdom will have no end.
We believe in the Holy Spirit, the Lord, the giver of life,
who proceeds from the Father and the Son.
With the Father and the Son he is worshiped and glorified.
He has spoken through the Prophets.
We believe in one holy catholic and apostolic Church.
We acknowledge one baptism for the forgiveness of sins.
We look for the resurrection of the dead,
and the life of the world to come. Amen.

DEVOTIONS

The Rosary

Joyful Mysteries

1. The Annunciation
2. The Visitation
3. The Nativity
4. The Presentation in the Temple
5. The Finding of Jesus in the Temple

Mysteries of Light

1. Jesus' Baptism in the Jordan River
2. Jesus' Self-manifestation at the Wedding of Cana
3. The Proclamation of the Kingdom of God and Jesus' Call to Conversion
4. The Transfiguration
5. The Institution of the Eucharist at the Last Supper

Sorrowful Mysteries

1. The Agony in the Garden
2. The Scourging at the Pillar
3. The Crowning with Thorns
4. The Carrying of the Cross
5. The Crucifixion

Glorious Mysteries

1. The Resurrection
2. The Ascension
3. The Descent of the Holy Spirit
4. The Assumption of Mary
5. The Crowning of Mary as the Queen of Heaven and Earth

How to Pray the Rosary

Opening

1. Begin on the crucifix and pray the Apostles' Creed.
2. On the first bead, pray the Our Father.
3. On the next three beads, pray the Hail Mary. (Some people meditate on the virtues of faith, hope, and charity on these beads.)
4. On the fifth bead, pray the Glory Be.

The Body

Each decade (set of ten beads) is organized as follows:

1. On the larger bead that comes before each set of ten, announce the mystery to be prayed (see above) and pray one Our Father.
2. On each of the ten smaller beads, pray one Hail Mary while meditating on the mystery.
3. Pray one Glory Be at the end of the decade. (There is no bead for the Glory Be.)

Conclusion

Pray the following prayer at the end of the rosary:

Hail, Holy Queen (see pages 323–324).

Stations of the Cross

The Stations of the Cross are individual pictures or symbols hung on the interior walls of most Catholic churches depicting fourteen steps along Jesus' way to the cross. Praying the stations means meditating on each of the following scenes:

1. Jesus is condemned to death.
2. Jesus takes up his cross.
3. Jesus falls the first time.
4. Jesus meets his Mother.
5. Simon of Cyrene helps Jesus carry his cross.
6. Veronica wipes the face of Jesus.
7. Jesus falls the second time.
8. Jesus consoles the women of Jerusalem.
9. Jesus falls the third time.
10. Jesus is stripped of his garments.
11. Jesus is nailed to the cross.
12. Jesus dies on the cross.
13. Jesus is taken down from the cross.
14. Jesus is laid in the tomb.

Some churches also include a fifteenth station, the Resurrection of the Lord.

NOVENAS

A novena consists of the recitation of certain prayers over nine days. The symbolism of nine days refers to the time Mary and the Apostles spent in prayer between Jesus' Ascension into Heaven and Pentecost.

Many novenas are dedicated to Mary or a saint with the faith and the hope that she or he will intercede for the one making the novena. Novenas to St. Jude, St. Anthony, Our Lady of Perpetual Help, and Our Lady of Lourdes remain popular in the Church today.

The Divine Praises

These praises are traditionally recited after the Benediction of the Blessed Sacrament.

Blessed be God.
Blessed be his holy name.
Blessed be Jesus Christ, true God and true man.
Blessed be the name of Jesus.
Blessed be his most Sacred Heart.
Blessed be his most Precious Blood.
Blessed be Jesus in the most holy sacrament of the altar.
Blessed be the Holy Spirit, the **Paraclete**.
Blessed be the great Mother of God, Mary most holy.
Blessed be her holy and Immaculate Conception.
Blessed be her glorious Assumption.
Blessed be the name of Mary, Virgin and Mother.
Blessed be Saint Joseph, her most chaste spouse.
Blessed be God in his angels and his saints.

PRAYERS

Some common Catholic prayers are listed below. The Latin translation for three of the prayers is included. Latin is the official language of the Church. There are several occasions when you may pray in Latin, for example, at a World Youth Day when you are with young people who speak different languages.

Sign of the Cross

In the name of the Father,
and of the Son,
and of the Holy Spirit. Amen.

In nómine Patris,
et Filii,
et Spíritus Sancti.
Amen.

Our Father

Our Father
who art in heaven,
hallowed be thy name.
Thy kingdom come;
thy will be done on earth as it is in heaven.
Give us this day our daily bread
and forgive us our trespasses
as we forgive those who trespass against us.
And lead us not into temptation,
but deliver us from evil.
Amen.

Pater Noster qui es in caelis:
sanctificétur Nomen Tuum;
advéniat Regnum Tuum;
fiat volúntas Tua,
sicut in caelo, et in terra.

Panem nostrum
cotidiánum da nobis hódie;
et dimítte nobis débita nostra,
sicut et nos
dimíttimus debitóribus nostris;
Et ne nos inducas in tentatiónem,
sed libera nos a Malo.
Amen.

Glory Be

Glory be to the Father
and to the Son
and to the Holy Spirit,
as it was in the beginning,
is now,
and ever shall be,
world without end. Amen.

Glória Patri
et Filio
et Spiritui Sancto.
Sicut erat in princípio,
et nunc et semper,
et in sae'cula saeculórum.
Amen.

Hail Mary

Hail Mary, full of grace,
the Lord is with thee.
Blessed art thou among women
and blessed is the fruit of thy womb, Jesus.
Holy Mary, Mother of God,

pray for us sinners now
and at the hour of our death. Amen.

Ave, María, grátia plena,
Dóminus tecum.
Benedicta tu in muliéribus,
et benedíctus fructus ventris
tui, Iesus.
Sancta María, Mater Dei,
ora pro nobis peccatoribus
nunc et in hora mortis nostrae.
Amen.

Memorare

Remember, O most gracious Virgin Mary,
that never was it known
that anyone who fled to your protection,
implored your help,
or sought your intercession was left unaided.
Inspired by this confidence,
I fly unto you,
O virgin of virgins, my Mother,
To you I come, before you I stand,
sinful and sorrowful.
O Mother of the Word incarnate,
despise not my petitions,
but in your mercy hear and answer me. Amen.

Hail, Holy Queen

Hail, holy Queen, Mother of Mercy,
our life, our sweetness and our hope!
To you do we cry,

poor banished children of Eve;
to you do we send up our sighs,
mourning and weeping in this valley of tears.
Turn then, O most gracious advocate,
your eyes of mercy toward us,
and after this exile,
show us the blessed fruit of your womb, Jesus.
O clement, O loving, O sweet Virgin Mary.
V. Pray for us, O holy mother of God.
R. that we may be made worthy of the promises of Christ. Amen.

The Angelus

V. The angel spoke God's message to Mary.
R. And she conceived by the Holy Spirit.
Hail Mary . . .
V. Behold the handmaid of the Lord.
R. May it be done unto me according to your word.
Hail Mary . . .
V. And the Word was made flesh.
R. And dwelled among us.
Hail Mary . . .
V. Pray for us, O holy mother of God.
R. That we may be made worthy of the promises of Christ.
Let us pray: We beseech you, O Lord, to pour out your grace into our hearts. By the message of an angel we have learned of the Incarnation of Christ, your Son; lead us by his Passion and cross, to the glory of the resurrection. Through the same Christ our Lord. Amen.

Regina Caeli

Queen of heaven, rejoice, alleluia.
The Son you merited to bear, alleluia,
has risen as he said, alleluia.
Pray to God for us, alleluia.
V. Rejoice and be glad, O Virgin Mary, alleluia.
R. For the Lord has truly risen, alleluia.
Let us pray.
God of life, you have given joy to the world by the resurrection of your Son, our Lord Jesus Christ. Through the prayers of his mother, the Virgin Mary, bring us to the happiness of eternal life. We ask this through Christ our Lord. Amen.

Grace at Meals

Before Meals
Bless us, O Lord,
and these your gifts,
which we are about to receive from your bounty,
through Christ our Lord. Amen.

After Meals
We give you thanks, almighty God,
for these and all the gifts
which we have received
from your goodness
through Christ our Lord. Amen.

Guardian Angel Prayer

Angel of God, my guardian dear,
to whom God's love commits me here,
ever this day be at my side,
to light and guard, to rule and guide. Amen.

Prayer for the Faithful Departed

V. Eternal rest grant unto them, O Lord.
R. And let perpetual light shine upon them.
V. May their souls and the souls of all faithful departed, through the mercy of God, rest in peace.
R. Amen.

Morning Offering

O Jesus, through the immaculate heart of Mary, I offer you my prayers, works, joys, and sufferings of this day in union with the holy sacrifice of the Mass throughout the world. I offer them for all the intentions of your Sacred Heart: the salvation of souls, reparation for sin, the reunion of all Christians. I offer them for the intentions of our bishops and all members of the apostleship of prayer and in particular for those recommended by your Holy Father this month. Amen.

Act of Faith

O God,
I firmly believe all the truths that you have revealed
and that you teach us through your Church,
for you are truth itself
and can neither deceive nor be deceived.
Amen.

Act of Hope

O God,
I hope with complete trust that you will give me,
through the merits of Jesus Christ, all necessary grace
in this world

and everlasting life in the world to come,
for this is what you have promised
and you always keep your promises.
Amen.

Act of Love

O my God, I love you above all things, with my whole heart and soul, because you are all good and worthy of all my love. I love my neighbor as myself for the love of you. I forgive all who have injured me, and I ask pardon of all whom I have injured. Amen.

Act of Contrition

O my God, I am heartily sorry for having offended Thee, and I detest all my sins because of thy just punishments, but most of all because they offend Thee, my God, who art all good and deserving of all my love. I firmly resolve with the help of Thy grace to sin no more and to avoid the near occasion of sin. Amen.

Glossary of Selected Terms

A

Abba—An Aramaic term of endearment meaning "Daddy." Jesus used this word to teach that God is a loving Father.

Abortion—The direct and deliberate ending of a pregnancy by killing the unborn child. Direct abortion, willed either as a means or an end, gravely contradicts the moral law.

Absolution—The prayer by which a priest, by the power given to the Church by Jesus Christ, pardons a repentant sinner in the Sacrament of Penance.

Actual grace—God's special help to turn us from sin or to help us act more like Christ.

Adoration—Prayer that acknowledges that God is God—Creator, Savior, Sanctifier, Lord, and Master of all creation, the source of all blessings and worthy of our total love and devotion.

Adultery—Infidelity in marriage whereby a married person has sexual intercourse with someone who is not the person's spouse.

Advent—In the liturgical year, the four-week season that prepares for the coming of our Savior on Christmas.

Agnosticism—The opinion that no one knows for sure whether God exists.

Amen—A Hebrew word for "truly" or "it is so," thus signifying agreement with what has been said. New Testament and liturgical prayers, creeds, and other Christian prayers end with "Amen" to show belief in what has just been said.

Anointing of the Sick—A Sacrament of Healing administered by a priest to a baptized person in which the Lord extends his loving, healing touch through the Church to those who are elderly, facing surgery, seriously ill, or dying.

Anti-Semitism—Unfounded prejudice against the Jewish People.

Apostasy—The denial of Christ and the repudiation of the Christian Faith by a baptized Christian.

Apostles—Those sent to be Christ's ambassadors to continue his work. In the widest sense, the term refers to all of Christ's disciples whose mission is to preach his Gospel in word and deed. Originally, it referred to the Twelve whom Jesus chose to help him in his earthly ministry. The successors of the Twelve Apostles are the bishops.

Ascension—Jesus' passage from humanity into divine glory in God's heavenly domain forty days after his Resurrection. It is from this domain that Jesus will come again.

Assumption—The Church dogma that teaches that the Blessed Mother, because of her unique role in her Son's Resurrection, was taken directly to Heaven when her earthly life was over. The Feast of the Assumption on August 15 is a holy day of obligation.

Atheism—Denial of the existence of God.

B

Baptism—The first Sacrament of Initiation. It is "the basis of the whole Christian life, the gateway to life in the Spirit, and the door which gives access to the other sacraments" (*CCC*, 1213).

Beatitudes—Beatitude means "supreme happiness." The eight Beatitudes preached by Jesus in the Sermon on the Mount respond to our natural desire for happiness.

Benediction—A prayer in which the Blessed Sacrament is used to offer blessings to the people.

Bishops—Successors to the Apostles who govern the local Church in given dioceses and the worldwide Church in union with the Pope and the college of bishops. A bishop receives the fullness of the Sacrament of Holy Orders.

Blasphemy—Any thought, word, or act that expresses hatred or contempt for God, Christ, the Church, saints, or holy things.

Blessing—A prayer that invokes God's care on some person, place, thing, or undertaking.

C

Calumny—Slander, that is, lies told about another person to harm his or her reputation and lead others to make false judgments about the person.

Canon—The official list of inspired books of the Bible. Catholics list forty-six Old Testament books and twenty-seven New Testament books in the canon.

Canonization—A process that recognizes the particular example of a Christian who has led a good and holy life and died a death faithful to Jesus and that declares the person to be a saint.

Capital Sins—Sins that are the root of other sins and vices. There are seven capital sins: pride, covetousness, envy, anger, gluttony, lust, and sloth.

Cardinal Virtues—The "hinge" virtues from which all other virtues come. They are prudence, justice, fortitude, and temperance.

Catechesis—A process of "education in the faith" for young people and adults with the goal of making them disciples of Jesus Christ.

Catechism of the Catholic Church—A compendium of Catholic doctrine on faith and morals published in 1992 that serves Catholics as "a sure norm for teaching the faith" and "an authentic reference text."

Catechumenate—A process of formation and instruction for an unbaptized person to prepare to receive all the Sacraments of Christian Initiation.

Catholic—From a Greek word meaning "universal" or "general." The Catholic Church is the Christian community that is one, holy, apostolic, and catholic—that is, open to all people everywhere at all times—and that preaches the fullness of God's Revelation in Jesus Christ.

Celibate—The state of being unmarried that priests and other religious choose in order to dedicate their lives totally to Jesus Christ and God's People.

Charisms—Special gifts the Holy Spirit bestows on individual Christians to help the Church grow.

Chastity—The moral virtue that enables people to integrate their sexuality into their stations in life.

Chosen People—The descendants of Israel (also called Jacob). God chose the Israelites to be his People. In this covenant, the Israelites also promised to worship YHWH.

Christ—The Greek term for "Messiah." It means "the anointed one."

Church—The Body of Christ, that is, the community of God's People who profess faith in the Risen Lord Jesus and love and serve others under the guidance of the Holy Spirit. The Pope and his bishops guide the Roman Catholic Church.

Common Good—The sum of social conditions that allow people, either as a group or as individuals, to reach their fulfillment more fully and more easily.

Common Priesthood—The priesthood of all the baptized in which we share in Christ's work of salvation.

Communion of Saints—The unity in Christ of all those he has redeemed—the Church on earth, in Heaven, and in Purgatory.

Concupiscence—An inclination to commit sin. It can be found in human desires and appetites as a result of Original Sin.

Confirmation—A Sacrament of Initiation, it is sometimes known as "the Sacrament of the Holy Spirit." It completes Baptism, seals the recipient with the Holy Spirit, and confers the seven gifts of the Holy Spirit.

Conscience—A person's most secret core and sanctuary that helps the person determine between good and evil.

Consecrated Life—A life dedicated to living by the evangelical counsels of poverty, chastity, and obedience. Besides religious life, other styles of consecrated life include an eremitic lifestyle as a hermit, taking a vow as a consecrated virgin or widow, or participating in a secular institute of consecrated life or a society of apostolic life.

Consumerism—The uncontrolled buying and selling of goods and services, most of which are unneeded.

Contemplation—Wordless prayer whereby a person's mind and heart rest in God's goodness and majesty.

Contrition—Heartfelt sorrow and aversion for sins committed along with the intention of sinning no more. Contrition is the most important act of penitents, necessary for receiving the Sacrament of Penance.

Covenant—The open-ended contract of love between God and human beings. Jesus' Death and Resurrection sealed God's New Covenant of love for all time. *Testament* translates to *covenant.*

D

Day of Atonement—Called *Yom Kippur*, the Day of Atonement is the holiest day of the year for Jews. It is a day when Jews ask forgiveness for both communal and personal sins.

Despair—Giving up hope in God's saving graces, his forgiveness of sins, and his promise of salvation.

Detraction—Without a legitimate reason, disclosing a person's faults to someone who did not know about them, thus causing unjust harm to that person's reputation.

Diaconate—The third degree in the hierarchy of Holy Orders. The diaconate is not a degree of the ministerial priesthood. Deacons are ordained ministers who assist bishops and priests in the celebration of the liturgy, distribute Communion, witness and bless marriages, proclaim and preach the Gospel, celebrate funerals, and perform various ministries of Christian charity, all under the authority of their bishop.

Diocese—The Church in a particular local area. It is united to its local leader, the bishop.

Disciple—A follower of Jesus Christ. The word comes from a Latin word that means "learner."

Divine Office—The official daily prayer of the Church; also known as the Liturgy of the Hours. The prayer offers prayers, Scripture, and reflections at regular intervals throughout the day.

Dogma—A central truth of Revelation that Catholics are obliged to believe.

Domestic Church—A name for the family, the Church in miniature.

E

Easter—In the liturgical year, the feast and the season that commemorate Christ's Resurrection from the dead.

Economic Trinity—See **Salvific Trinity**.

Ecumenical Council—A worldwide, official assembly of the bishops under the direction of the Pope. There have been twenty-one Ecumenical Councils, the most recent being the Second Vatican Council (1962–1965).

Ecumenism—The movement, inspired and led by the Holy Spirit, that seeks the union of all Christian religions and eventually the unity of all peoples throughout the world.

Encyclical—A letter written by the Pope about some important issue and circulated through the entire Church.

Epiphany—The feast that celebrates the mystery of Christ's manifestation as the Savior of the world.

Episcopate—The degree of Holy Orders received by bishops. The episcopate represents the fullness of the Sacrament.

Essential rite—That portion of the liturgical celebration of a sacrament that is strictly necessary for the sacrament to be valid.

Eucharist—The source and summit of Christian life, the Eucharist is one of the Sacraments of Initiation. The word *Eucharist* comes from a Greek word that means "thankful." The Eucharist commemorates the Last Supper, at which Jesus gave his Body and Blood in the form of bread and wine, and the Lord's sacrificial Death on the cross.

Euthanasia—"Any action or omission which of itself and by intention causes death, with the purpose of eliminating all suffering" (*The Gospel of Life*, No. 65). This is distinguished from palliative care that alleviates a person's suffering as the inevitable death nears. Euthanasia is a serious violation of the Fifth Commandment, a crime against life, and an attack on humanity.

Evangelical Counsels—Vows of personal poverty, chastity understood as lifelong celibacy, and obedience to the demands of the community being joined that those entering the consecrated life profess.

Evangelization—To bring the Good News of Jesus Christ to others.

Excommunicated—The condition of a baptized person's no longer being "in communion" with the Church. Some excommunications are automatic, including those involving the sins of apostasy, heresy, or schism.

Exegesis—A Greek word meaning "to lead." It is the study or the explanation of a biblical book or passage.

F

Faith—One of the theological virtues. Faith is an acknowledgment of and an allegiance to God.

Free Will—The capacity to choose among alternatives. Free will is "the power, rooted in reason and will . . . to perform deliberate actions on one's own responsibility" (*CCC*, 1731). True freedom is at the service of what is good and true.

Fruits of the Holy Spirit—Perfections that result from living in union with the Holy Spirit.

G

Gentiles—A term that means "non-Jews."

Gifts of the Holy Spirit—An outpouring of God's gifts to help us live the Christian life. The traditional seven gifts of the Holy Spirit are wisdom, understanding, knowledge, counsel (right judgment), fortitude (courage), piety (reverence), and fear of the Lord (wonder and awe).

Gospel—A term meaning "Good News." The term refers to 1) Jesus' own preaching, 2) the preaching about Jesus the Savior, and 3) the four Scripture-inspired versions of the Good News—the Gospels of Matthew, Mark, Luke, and John.

H

Heaven—Our final communion with the Blessed Trinity, Mary, the angels, and all the saints.

Hell—Eternal separation from God that results from a person's dying after freely and deliberately acting against God's will (that is, not repenting of mortal sin).

Heresy—An obstinate denial after Baptism to believe a truth that must be believed with divine and Catholic faith, or an obstinate doubt about such truth.

Hierarchy—The official, sacred leadership in the Church, made up of the Church's ordained ministers—bishops, priests, and deacons. The symbol of unity and authority in the Church is the Pope, the Bishop of Rome, who is the successor of St. Peter.

Holy Orders—The sacrament of apostolic ministry at the Service of Communion whereby Christ, through the Church, ordains men through the laying on of hands. It includes three degrees: episcopate, presbyterate, and diaconate. Those who exercise these orders are bishops, priests, and deacons.

Holy Trinity—The central mystery of the Christian faith. It teaches that there are three Persons in one God: Father, Son, and Holy Spirit.

I

Icons—Traditional religious images or paintings that are especially popular among many Eastern Christians.

Idolatry—Worshiping something or someone other than the true God.

Immaculate Conception—The belief that Mary was conceived without Original Sin. The Feast of the Immaculate Conception is on December 8.

Immanent Trinity—Means "existing completely within." When we explore the immanent Trinity, we ask, How does God exist in God?

Incarnation—The dogma that God's eternal Son assumed a human nature and became man in Jesus Christ to save us from our sins. The term literally means "taking on human flesh."

Infallibility—A gift of the Spirit whereby the Pope and the bishops are preserved from error when proclaiming a doctrine related to Christian faith or morals.

Intercession—A prayer of petition for the sake of others.

J

Justified—Describes a person who through the Holy Spirit's grace has been cleansed from sin through faith in Jesus Christ and Baptism and made right with God. Justification not only frees us from sin, but sanctifies us in the depth of our being.

K

Kerygma—The essential message of our faith that Jesus Christ is Lord and is risen.

Kingdom of God—The reign of God proclaimed by Jesus and begun in his life, Death, and Resurrection. It refers to the process of God's reconciling and renewing all things through his Son and his will being done on earth as it is in Heaven.

L

Laity—All the members of the Church who have been initiated into the Church through Baptism and are not ordained (the clergy) or in consecrated life. The laity participates in Jesus' prophetic, priestly, and kingly ministries.

Last (Final) Judgment—Jesus Christ's judgment of the living and the dead on the last day when he comes to fully establish God's Kingdom.

Lectio Divina—Literally, "divine reading." This is a prayerful way to read the Bible or any other sacred writings.

Lent—In the liturgical year, the season of intentional prayer, fasting, and alms giving in preparation of Christ's Resurrection and our redemption at Easter.

The season begins on Ash Wednesday and continues to Holy Thursday, a period of forty weekdays and six Sundays.

Liturgy—The official public worship of the Church. The sacraments and the Divine Office constitute the Church's liturgy. Mass is the most important liturgical celebration.

M

Magisterium—The official teaching office of the Church. The Lord bestowed the right and the power to teach in his name to Peter and the other Apostles and their successors. The Magisterium is the bishops in communion with the successor of Peter, the Bishop of Rome (Pope).

Marks of the Church—The four essential signs or characteristics of Christ's Church that mark her as his true Church. The Church is one, holy, catholic, and apostolic.

Matrimony—A Sacrament at the Service of Communion in which Christ binds a man and a woman into a permanent covenant of love and life and bestows his graces on them to help them live as a community and as a loving family, if he blesses them with children.

Ministerial Priesthood—The priesthood of bishops and priests that confers on them a sacred power for the service of the faithful.

Modesty—The virtue of temperance that applies to how a person speaks, dresses, and conducts himself or herself. Related to the virtue of purity, modesty protects the intimate center of a person by refusing to unveil what should remain hidden.

Monotheism—Describes religions that believe there is only one God. Christianity, Judaism, and Islam are the three great monotheistic world religions.

Morality—Putting your faith and religion into practice through making good decisions in word and action.

Mortal Sin—A serious violation of God's law of love that results in the loss of God's life (sanctifying grace) in the soul of the sinner. To commit mortal sin, there must be grave matter, full knowledge of the evil done, and full consent of will.

Mystagogia—A period of intense prayer in which neophytes can gradually assume their role in the Church.

Mystery—A reality filled with God's invisible presence. This term applies to the Blessed Trinity's plan of salvation in Jesus Christ; the Church, which is his Body; and the sacraments.

N

Natural Law—God's plan for human living that is written in the very way he created things. Binding on all people at all times, it is the light of understanding that God puts in us so we can discover what is good and what is evil.

Neophytes—Those newly received into the Church through the Sacraments of Initiation at the Easter Vigil.

O

Oath—A statement or a promise that calls on God to be witness to it.

Omnipotence—An attribute of God that he is everywhere, unlimited, and all-powerful.

Original Holiness and Original Justice—The state of man and woman before sin. "From their friendship with God flowed the happiness of their existence in paradise" (*CCC*, 384).

Original Sin—The fallen state of human nature into which all generations of people are born. Christ Jesus came to save us from Original Sin.

P

Pantheism—The belief, in opposition to Christian doctrine, that God and nature are one and the same.

Parables—Favorite teaching devices of Jesus in which he told a short story with a striking, memorable comparison that taught a religious message, usually about some aspect of God's Kingdom.

Paraclete—Another name for the Holy Spirit. It means "advocate, defender, or consoler."

Particular Judgment—An individual's judgment immediately after death, when Christ will rule on one's eternal destiny to be spent in Heaven (after purification in Purgatory, if needed) or in hell.

Paschal Mystery—The saving love of God most fully revealed in the life and especially the Passion, Death, Resurrection, and glorious Ascension of his Son, Jesus Christ.

Passions—Our emotional responses to the good or the evil we encounter.

Patriarchs—Male rulers, elders, or leaders. The patriarchs of faith of Israel are Abraham, Isaac, and Jacob.

Penance—The Sacrament of Healing, also known as Reconciliation or confession, through which Christ extends his forgiveness to sinners, bringing about reconciliation with God and the Church. Its essential elements consist of the acts of the penitent (contrition, confession of sins, and satisfaction) and the prayer of absolution of the priest.

Pentecost—The day when the Holy Spirit descended on the Apostles and gave them the power to preach with conviction the message that Jesus is risen and is Lord of the universe.

Perjury—False witness under oath.

Polytheism—The belief, in opposition to Christian doctrine, that there are many gods.

Praise—A form of prayer whereby we acknowledge God and his goodness and glorify him for who he is.

Prayer—Conversation with God; lifting of one's mind and heart to God or requesting good things from him; joining one's thoughts and love to God in adoration and blessing, petition, intercession, thanksgiving, and praise.

Precepts of the Church—Rules Catholics follow to help them become good and moral people. They include attending Mass on Sundays and holy days of obligation, confessing sins at least once a year, receiving Communion at minimum during the Easter season, observing days of fasting and abstinence, and providing for the needs of the Church.

Presbyterate—Priests or members of the order of priesthood who are coworkers with the bishops and are servants to God's People, especially in celebrating the Eucharist.

Protestant—A baptized Christian who does not accept all the teachings of the Catholic Church. Protestant communities first came into existence during the Reformation in the sixteenth century.

Protoevangelium—A term that means "the first gospel," which is found in Genesis 3:15, when God revealed he would send a Savior to redeem the world from its sins.

Providence—God's leading and guiding us to our final end, salvation and union with him.

Purgatory—The state of purification that takes place after death for those who need to be made clean and holy before meeting the all-holy God in Heaven.

R

Racism—One of the most hateful forms of prejudice; the belief that one race is superior to another.

Reconciliation—Another term for the Sacrament of Penance, in which Christ extends his forgiveness to sinners through the absolution conferred by a priest.

Redemption—A word that literally means "ransom." Jesus' Death is the ransom that defeated the powers of evil.

Religion—The relationship between God and humans that results in a body of beliefs and a set of practices: creed, cult, and code. Religion expresses itself in worship and service to God and by extension to all people and all creation.

Religious Life—The vocation of men or women who take vows to live out the evangelical counsels of poverty, chastity, and obedience.

Resurrection—Jesus' rising from the dead three days after he was buried in a tomb. Belief in the Resurrection is central to our Christian faith.

Revelation—The way God communicates knowledge of himself to humankind, a self-communication realized by his actions and words over time, most fully by his sending us his divine Son, Jesus Christ.

S

Sacrament—An outward (visible) sign of an invisible grace; an "efficacious" symbol that brings about the spiritual reality to which it points. This term applies to Christ Jesus, the great sign of God's love for us; to the Church, his continuing presence in the world; and to the Seven Sacraments.

Sacred Scripture—The inspired Word of God; the written record of God's Revelation.

Sacred Tradition—The living transmission of the Church's Gospel message found in the Church's teaching, life, and worship. It is faithfully preserved, handed on, and interpreted by the Church's Magisterium.

Saints—"Holy ones" of God who live in union with God through the grace of Jesus Christ and the power of the Holy Spirit and whom God rewards with eternal life in Heaven.

Salvation—The extension of God's forgiveness, grace, and healing to the world through Jesus Christ in the Holy Spirit.

Salvific (or Economic) Trinity—The active and inseparable work of the Triune God—Father, Son, and Holy Spirit—in salvation history.

Sanctifying Grace—The grace, or gift of God's friendship, that heals fallen human nature and gives us a share in the divine life of the Blessed Trinity. A habitual, supernatural gift, it makes us perfect, holy, and Christ-like (*CCC*, 1999).

Schism—A major break in Church unity. The Great Schism occurred between the churches of the West (centered in Rome) and the East (centered in Constantinople). The Roman Church had added "and the Son" to the article of the Nicene Creed referring to the Holy Spirit ("he proceeds from the Father and the Son") without seeking approval from a Church-wide council of bishops.

Second Coming—The final judgment of all humanity when Christ returns to earth. It is also known by its Greek name, *Parousia*, which means "arrival."

Sin—An offense against God through a violation of truth, reason, and conscience.

Social Justice—The Church's teaching on the way the Gospel and Tradition apply in our society. Social justice doctrine includes basic life and death rights. It also involves rights of everyday living such as the rights of workers to a fair wage, the rights of people to food and shelter, the rights of people not to be discriminated against on the basis of race, and the rights of all people to worship God.

Society—Any community of human beings that unites them in a common purpose.

Solidarity—A Christian virtue of charity and friendship whereby members of the human family share material and spiritual goods.

Sorcery—Attempts to tame occult powers in order to use them to gain a supernatural power over others.

Soul—The innermost or spiritual part of a person. The soul is eternal.

Stewardship—The proper use of the gifts God has given us, in particular the care for creation that will allow the earth and its resources to flourish and be long lasting.

Subsidiarity—The principle of Catholic social doctrine that says no community of higher order (such as a national or state government) should do what can be done equally well or better by a community of lower order (such as a family or a local community).

T

Ten Commandments—A source of Christian morality. God revealed them to Moses. The first three Commandments have to do with love for God. The last seven refer to love for neighbor.

Theological Virtues—Three important virtues bestowed on us at Baptism that relate us to God: *faith* (belief in and personal knowledge of God), *hope* (trust in God's salvation and his bestowal of the graces needed to attain it), and *charity* (love of God and love of neighbor).

Transfiguration—An occasion when Jesus revealed his divine glory before Peter, James, and John on a high mountain, where his face "shone like the sun and his clothes became white as light" (Mt 17:2).

Transubstantiation—What happens at the consecration of the bread and wine at Mass, when their entire substance is turned into the substance of the Body and Blood of Christ, even though the appearances of bread and wine remain. The Eucharistic presence of Christ begins at the moment of consecration and endures as long as the Eucharistic species subsist.

V

Venial Sin—A sin that weakens and wounds our relationship with God but does not destroy divine life in our souls.

Viaticum—Holy Communion received by dying persons to help them pass over to God in the afterlife.

Vices—Bad habits linked to capital sins (pride, covetousness, envy, anger, gluttony, lust, and sloth).

Virgin Birth—A Church dogma that teaches that Jesus was conceived through the Virgin Mary by the power of the Holy Spirit without the cooperation of a human father.

Virtues—Good habits that help us live a moral life.

Vulgate—The name, meaning "common speech," for St. Jerome's translation of the entire Bible into Latin in the fourth century.

W

Works of Mercy—Charitable actions that remind us how to come to the aid of a neighbor and his or her bodily and spiritual necessities.

Y

YHWH—The sacred Hebrew name for God. It means "I Am Who Am," "I Am," or "I Am Who I Am."

Notes

1

St. Augustine, *Confessions* 1, 1, 1: PL 32, 659-661 quoted from *CCC*, 30.

2

Suestonius, *Claudius* 25.4

3

Pliny to Trajan, *Letters* 10.96-97.

Adapted from "Luke 19" from the *Faith Difference* by Kieran Sawyer, SSND (Notre Dame: Ave Maria Press, ©2001)

5

Ambigua: PG 91, 1156C; cf. Gen. 5 quoted in *CCC*, 398.

6

Cf. P. Hansen, *Vita mirabilis* (Louvain, 1668).

7

The story of Caitlin Riley is paraphrased from an article titled “Bald and Beautiful: How Cailin’s Faith Helps Her Deal with Alopecia” quoted in http://faithmag.com/issues/sep06.html , September, 2006.

8

Center for Applied Research in the Apostolate, Georgetown University, Fall 2002

9

St. Augustine, *De moribus eccl.* 1, 3, 4: PL 32, 1312

Acts of the trial of St. Joan of Arc.

Index

SUBJECT INDEX

A

D

H

N

P

SCRIPTURE INDEX

CATECHISM OF THE CATHOLIC CHURCH INDEX

PHOTOGRAPHY CREDITS

Agnus Images 56, 220, 221

Janet McKenzie 58 © "Jesus of the People" copyright 1999 Janet McKenzie, www.janetmckenzie.com

Wittman Photography 201, 209, 220

Tom Generra Photography 139

Notre Dame archives 112

Trinity Stores 10 © JESUS, LOUIS GLANZMAN, 2003, Courtesy of Trinity Stores, www.trinitystores.com, 1-800-699-4482, 58 © CHRIST OF MARYKNOLL, BR. ROBERT LENTZ, OFM, 2002, Courtesy of Trinity Stores, www.trinitystores.com, 1-800-699-4482

Veer 23 © Craig Martinez

SuperStock 32 © SuperStock, Inc., 44 © Christie's Images, 46 © Digital Vision Ltd., 46 © Image Source, 53 © Brand X, 57 © SuperStock, Inc., 79 © SuperStock, Inc., 86 © Bridgeman Art Library, London, 91 © Anatoly Sapronenkov, 105 © SuperStock, Inc., 111 © Hanan Isachar, 111 © age fotostock, 119 © Anatoly Sapronenkov, 124 © SuperStock, Inc., 127 © SuperStock, Inc., 128 © SuperStock, Inc., 129 © SuperStock, Inc., 135 © SuperStock, Inc., 156 © Age Fotostock, 157 © Age Fotostock, 157 © Pixtal, 157 © SuperStock, Inc., 166 © Hemis.fr, 166 © Age Fotostock, 166 © Ingram Publishing, 173 © Bridgeman Art Library, London, 178 © Christie's Images, 189 © Richard Cummins, 196 © SuperStock, Inc., 213 © Age Fotostock, 221 © Hemis.fr, 257 © Greer & Associates, Inc., 273 © Greg Martin

Corbis 40 © Dave Bartruff, 47 © Smart Creatives, 47 © Stephanie Maze, 73 © Penny Tweedie, 73 © David Katzenstein, 75 © Bettmann, 110 © Charles & Josette Lenars, 132 © Bernd Kohlhas/zefa, 144 © Bettmann, 159 © Reuters, 193 © P Deliss/Godong, 205 © Krzysztof Œwiderski/PAP, 221 © Goupy Didier/Corbis Sygma, 221 © Shawn Thew/epa, 224 © Keith Dannemiller, 225 © P Deliss/Godong, 232 © Pascal Deloche /Godong, 235 © Roy McMahon, 246 © Steve Schapiro, 250 © Richard T. Nowitz, 262 © P Deliss/Godong, 270 © Ettore Ferrari /epa, 278 © Nik Wheeler/Sygma